THREE VICTORIAN WOMEN WHO CHANGED THEIR WORLD

THREE VICTORIAN WOMEN WHO CHANGED THEIR WORLD

Josephine Butler, Octavia Hill, Florence Nightingale

Nancy Boyd

New York/Oxford
Oxford University Press
1982

First published in Great Britain in 1982
by The Macmillan Press Ltd

First published in the United States in 1982
by Oxford University Press, Inc.

Copyright ©1982 Nancy Boyd Sokoloff

ISBN 0 — 19 — 520271 — 6

Printed in Hong Kong

For these Friends

Ilyana Y. Adams

John and Marjean Bailey

Susan Herter

Sylvia Stallings Lowe

Ethel Landon Penzel

Leroy and Rita Rouner

Arthur and Helen Siegrist

Contents

OCTAVIA HILL

FLORENCE NIGHTINGALE

Preface

Contemporary feminists search the past for models of liberated women and for the emergence of themes that, because they have only been partially realized, remain of critical interest: the assertion of the feminine as a psychological principle of importance; the right of women to legal, economic, educational, and professional parity. Currently, historians reflect the values of our society in the push for reform of what we read as abuses, and in their haste to fill the gaps left by the selective vision of an earlier scholarship trace the direct lines of ancestry of contemporary concerns. Such single-mindedness brings a welcome vitality to scholarship. In the focusing of vision, however, important figures whose position is not central tend to be ignored. Social historians chronicle the changes in the position of women and the politics of the suffragist movement, and biographers gave us revisionist studies of Mary Wollestonecraft and the literary women, but scant attention has been given England's three great nineteenth-century pioneers of social reform — Josephine Butler, Octavia Hill, and Florence Nightingale.

There was a time when their stock was high. In his gallery of portraits of people who 'made the century', George Frederick Watts placed the fragile, haunted face of Josephine Butler, the only woman in his solemn conclave of notables. Octavia Hill, described by David Owen as one of the 'classic monuments of Victorian philanthropy',[1] was commended by Sir Reginald Rowe in 1906. 'I doubt if in the field of human service there has ever been any other woman who has sown seeds from which so much has grown and is still growing.'[2] The *Dictionary of National Biography* devoted five pages to Florence Nightingale; her inclusion in that delightful compendium of popular history, *1066 and All That*, as 'the Lady with the Deadly Lampshade' is perhaps a greater tribute to her fame. In 1954 O. R. McGregor, noting the neglect of many other outstanding women in social policy, attributed it to their having worked 'within the giant shadow' cast by Josephine Butler and Florence Nightingale.

These reputations are based on a record of solid accomplishments. Josephine Butler against all political odds raised opposition to the state regulation of prostitution and defeated the Contagious Diseases Acts; she drew attention to the poverty that gave rise to prostitution and became the leader of an international alliance that fought for the civil rights of women. Octavia Hill, noting the overcrowding and high rents that threatened family life, provided housing for thousands and created a new profession for men and women, that of the social worker. As a founder of the National Trust and a great conservationist, she helped keep England's countryside and its heritage for the British people. Florence Nightingale not only established a precedent-shattering training school for nurses; her pioneering work in the use of statistical analysis played an important role in the reform of medical practice and public health.

If these women, eulogized by historians, have been recently neglected, one must look for the reason not in their accomplishments but in their attitudes toward the feminist issues of their day and in their link with a world-view, Christianity, that is rooted in the past. To some of the questions that were of compelling interest to other women, these leaders remained ambivalent. Florence Nightingale said that she wished to make a better life for women yet she also said that she was 'brutally indifferent' to the rights of her own sex. She signed the petition for women's suffrage reluctantly, and she gave little encouragement to women who wished to become doctors. Octavia Hill opposed the extension of the suffrage, she extolled the 'home-making' virtues of women as their primary function. Even Josephine Butler, who did so much for the advancement of women, was in some ways conservative. She, too, placed a high value on women's traditional role as home-maker, wife and mother. While she believed in votes for women, she was distressed by the suffragists' methods.

The issue of women's rights placed these leaders in a dilemma. As Christians they affirmed the rights of the powerless; they also, however, placed self-giving and service to others above the striving for power. As women, they found it difficult to press for their own self-advantage. In addition, as educated, upper-class women of exceptional abilities, they were not always aware of the limitations that constrained other women. Florence Nightingale was honest in admitting her self-centredness, her difficulty in understanding and sympathizing with other women and their needs. When she could bring a Prime Minister and a clutch of Members of Parliament to her door with a hastily written note, why did she need the vote? Why, she asked, when the world called for nurses and her school sought qualified candidates, should women demand to be doctors? Josephine Butler believed that women should be given a university education and the right to vote. But to a woman who spoke four languages, translated Chaucer, and won for her cause the support of Members of Parliament, Abolitionists in the United States, leading French statesmen, and the Pope — the right of a woman to education and the vote must have seemed so obvious as to be taken for granted. Octavia Hill, teacher, college administrator, member of the Poor Law Board and the Ecclesiastical Commission had, like the others, moved far beyond the issues of basic rights. All had achieved a degree of self-fulfilment that enabled them to understand feminism not as a separatist movement but as an essential element of humanism.

These three moved confidently into the world because they had a clear purpose and an awareness of their own gifts and energies. Florence Nightingale spoke of the responsibility given to each person to 'work out God's ideal' for her own nature.

> To work at one or more objects interesting in the view of God, important in God's purposes for man, to work with one or more between whom there is a mutual attraction and who are mutually interested in these objects, not only for each other's sakes, but from their own natures and for God's sake and man's sake, this only is human happiness. Who has it?[3]

'This ... happiness ... who has it?' Not many men, fewer women. But what for most remained a disembodied hope was the certainty that guided and supported the lives of these three. The freedom to develop one's abilities, to seek a position and an activity in the world in keeping with one's gifts and temperament, available in theory to men, these women had acquired for themselves. Each had paid a price: Florence Nightingale experienced debilitating inner conflicts, many of which must have arisen from the tensions of being a woman playing a man's role in a man's world. Josephine Butler, a woman speaking in defence of women, encountered male hostility. The frustrations and exhaus-exhaustion of Octavia Hill, on the other hand, were intrinsic to the nature of her work. If one of the goals of the feminist bill of rights is the 'equal right to suffer equally' they had achieved it.

How were these particular women able to achieve a degree of self-fulfilment that a hundred years later still remains for many a distant ideal? In an era when men depicted women as fragile, dependent and unreliable, charming but not profound, bright but not intelligent, and put them on a pedestal in order not to have to deal with them face to face, they found freedom. In defiance of a view that isolated and limited women, they stepped down from the pedestal and put their talents to work in the world.

Born with outstanding gifts of mind and temperament, they were encouraged to develop these talents by a Christianity that presented them with the ideal of a 'liberated' humanity: a society in which the estrangement between rich and poor, male and female, had been healed by a God of justice and compassion. To their work as social reformers they brought, not only practical energies, but the single-mindedness of the visionary: their task was the building of the New Jerusalem. In the light of this cosmic vision they found the courage to transcend the cultural expectations of time and place; in conveying this vision to others, they found an authentic life for themselves.

Although their views sometimes diverged from the tenets of orthodoxy, all had their origin in Christianity. Josephine Butler was an Anglican of a Low-Church, evangelical bent. Octavia Hill, a Unitarian by tradition, adopted the social concerns of the Christian Socialists and the sacramental theology of one of its leaders, Frederick Denison Maurice. Florence Nightingale developed ideas on the nature of God that anticipate some of the 'process' and 'death-of-God' theologians of the twentieth century and combined these with a taste for empiricism and an attraction to the mystical theology of the Early Church.

These theological views appear in their writings. Josephine Butler wrote biographies of two religious figures, St Catherine of Siena and Jean Frederick Oberlin, and many pamphlets and political speeches which can, and should, be read as sermons. In her letters Octavia Hill confronts her friends and relatives with her reflections on theology, the comfort and hope imparted by her faith. Florence Nightingale obsessively worked and reworked her ideas, correcting and editing through sleepless nights ideas she had developed ten or twenty years earlier. This 'stuff' — a three-volume treatise, *Suggestions for Thought,* she hoped might one day lead to a revival of faith. Yet none of these women claimed to be a theologian. Josephine Butler and Octavia Hill felt that their views were hardly original and not important to anyone except themselves. Florence Nightingale, though, affirming the general direction of her argument, admitted that in the course of her 800 pages she had got a bit muddled.

They were interested in religious thought because they believed that right thought would lead to right action. They did not wish to solve the philosophical questions that had puzzled humanity from the beginning; they wished to live a life that was in constant touch with the faith it professed.

The purpose of this study then is not to present these women as theologians but as social activists whose lives and vocations were shaped and directed by their theology. What was their vision of society? As Christians how did they understand the relations between men and women? What did Florence Nightingale mean when she said that nursing is a 'calling'? Are there theological reasons behind Octavia Hill's dislike of almsgiving? What aspects of Josephine Butler's faith led her to choose the prostitute as the focus of her concern? Although the study will include the material of spiritual biography, its purpose is wider: to work out the relation between the development of the inner and the outer self, between contemplation and action, vision and programme.

It is only fair to state some assumptions. The first is that a world view, the attempt to make sense out of the discontinuity and chaos of experience, can and does shape action. Robert Coles, in analysing Erik Erikson's thought, speaks of ideology as a 'working unity', an 'unconscious tendency' to create a sense of identity by drawing together facts and ideas, observation and reflection. Josephine Butler, Octavia Hill, and Florence Nightingale were sustained by such a 'working unity'. Like Erikson's Gandhi, they were the *homines religiosi* of their age.

They are not necessarily trained to minister, to preach the tenets of a particular religion. They are men who become living bridges to an eventual clarity of existence, or at least to a sense of consolation which makes it possible to produce, create, and serve without debilitating despair.[4]

Erikson's approach is useful, not only because his definition of ideology takes it out of the realm of the purely intellectual, but because his emphasis upon faith as a process of integration precludes any simplistic one-to-one relationship of cause and effect. He does not claim, nor would I, that an emphasis on religious experience as a determining force denies the reality of the psychological. Were Florence Nightingale's obsessive energies the product of inner conflicts or a response to a call to become a 'saviour' of mankind? Octavia Hill spent much of her working life helping the homeless create homes for themselves. Did she feel compelled to do this because, having been deprived at an early age of the security of her own home life, she felt the need to recreate that unity for others? Or did she extend home life to the poor because she believed that the family was the chief means of conveying the love of God? Did Josephine Butler choose to work with prostitutes because she believed that it was God's will that she help those whom society had rejected? Or did she choose her path because, devastated by the death of her only daughter, she sought the company of those unhappier than herself and the relief of plunging into a totally demanding activity?

These three women believed in 'both ... and' answers. They felt both that their faith had been shaped by their experience as unique human beings and that their psychological development had been informed by a faith that relied on prayer, the practice of the presence of God. They regarded the split between 'sacred' and 'secular', 'spiritual' and 'psychological', 'thought' and 'action' as artificial constructs, fabricated by man's fractured vision.

Admittedly, the acceptance of a 'both ... and' answer as a method of organization poses problems. The relation of evidence to a thesis is at best ambiguous. What constitutes 'proof' in one field may in another be considered inconsequential or irrelevant. David Hume hears the crack of billard balls; he sees them fall into the pocket. Unlike the physicist, however, he does not conclude that there is a 'necessary connection'. The student of Quatrocento iconography, noting an arrow and a dead man, identifies his saint. Tom Stoppard, observing the scene, construes it as mathematical paradox: Zeno was the archer, Sebastian died of fright. Professor W. L. Burn, writing on 'selective Victorianism', reminds us that a nimble-witted researcher can find valid evidence for practically any thesis. Led by the author, 'cause' and 'effect' enter into collusion, supporting each other in a mutual rejection of the incompatible. The author further buttresses his argument with parallel — indeed, often interchangeable — book-ends, deceptively marked 'introduction' and 'conclusion'.

The clash of opposing theses, each supported by an equally impressive mustering of evidence, creates confusion. Hardly less troublesome, however, is the gathering of evidence to support a single thesis. Having broken down a complex event into separate causes — economic, social, intellectual — the historian is hardpressed to put them back together again; he can only guess at their interrelation. Unlike a detective who searches for a single agent, he knows that the victims of history have many murderers. In the clash of knives it is impossible to tell who struck the fatal blow.

The 'both . . . and' answer, while partially thwarting the brain's lust for analysis, fulfils the heart's need for truth. My aim is simple: to examine the connective tissue that binds the religious views of these three women to their social actions. My method, depending more on description than analysis, is equally simple. On the basis of their writings I will examine their theology. I will then search out their social policies and actions for evidence of these views. Finally, I will present these three, not only as individual lives responsive to inner forces, but as women who were shaped by their surroundings and who in turn gave 'a colour to their age'.

Acknowledgements

In listing the names of those who have enabled me to write this book, I am reminded of many happy hours spent in the company of interesting books and people: the staff of the Manuscript Department of the British Library; the staff of the Dartmouth College Library; M. R. Perkin, Curator of Special Collections, University of Liverpool; E. V. Quinn, Librarian of Balliol College, Oxford. I am especially grateful to David Doughan, Assistant Librarian, and the staff of the Fawcett Society for their interest and enthusiasm.

To these friends who read various drafts of the manuscript I am indebted: Sally and Louis Cornell, Sylvia Stallings Lowe, Sony Lipton, Robert Siegel, Leroy Rouner, and Mildred Wilsey. I would also like to thank Cynthia Read, a perceptive critic and sensitive editor.

My children at home, Kate and Andrew, encouraged me on a course that often ran counter to their immediate interests and cheerfully put up with the preoccupation and erratic house-keeping of a scholar mother. From further afield my daughter Julia alternated the adulation of the fan with the discrimination of the critic. I am grateful for both.

Introduction
An Age in Need of Heroism:
Great Britain, 1860

During the decade that opened in 1860, Josephine Butler, Octavia Hill, and Florence Nightingale became prominent figures whose policies and activities shaped national life. By 1860 Florence Nightingale had initiated essential reforms of Army medicine, had laid the foundations for a new profession for women — nursing — and was about to tackle the problems of a huge subcontinent halfway around the world — India. With the purchase of houses in Paradise Place in 1865, Octavia Hill began her long battle to help the poor. The passage of the Contagious Diseases Act of 1869 was the start of Josephine Butler's Crusade. Such was their response to their analysis of the needs of Great Britain, an analysis made in the light of the ideal society presented by their Christian faith.

While these three took the measure of Britain's social imperfections, other citizens searched the horizon for signs and portents, not of morality, but of stability. Exhausted by the rumours and alarums of Chartism and the 'hungry forties', they eagerly sought reassurance. Was not the relative calm of the 1850s an indication that Britain had recovered her footing? She had brought great energies to the universal problems of providing a people with a decent life (food, housing, a secure and salubrious environment) and a world-view that would enable them to affirm its pleasures and accept its vicissitudes with a sense of dignity and self-worth. The dislocations of the 1840s were perhaps but a temporary aberration in the history of a country that had long congratulated itself on providing both livelihood and a bracing creed.

It was too early, however, for complacency. It was possible that the social peace of the 1850s represented not a genuine synthesis

1

of warring interests but a temporary respite from conflict. No-one could deny that the circumstances under which Britain's problems were to be resolved were changing rapidly. While the British citizen in 1860 looked out across a calm and prosperous land, under his feet he felt the tremor and heard the rumblings of vast subterranean forces.

Although the Army remained quietly at home, the news from abroad was disturbing. The press reported the invasion of Italy by the colourful revolutionary Garibaldi and the increasingly aggressive behaviour of Napoleon III, who had added Savoy to his conquests. In response the English formed a Volunteer Brigade; the Queen stood in review and in 1860 fired the first shot at the opening meeting of the National Rifle Association. In the United States tension was building between North and South. In 1859 John Brown seized the arsenal at Harpers Ferry. Esteemed by the Abolitionists as a martyr for their cause, he was tried for treason and executed in Virginia. The break-up of the Democratic Party over the slavery issue virtually assured the election of Abraham Lincoln, regarded by the South as a 'wild man from nowhere' who would encourage slave insurrections.

While there was little in this news that threatened the security of Britain, the reports of foreign conflicts and rumours of war came as unpleasant reminders of the near past. The Crimean War had demonstrated that the bravery of the British soldier was second to none; it had also raised distressing questions about the management of the Army, the competence of its leaders, and the wisdom of the policies that had committed it to battle. The Poet Laureate had eulogized the bravery of the cavalry man but was his heroic verse not also testimony to the stupidity of the officers who had sent him to an unnecessary death? In 1853 people of every political persuasion from Tory to Manchester Radical had clamoured for war; only John Bright and the Quakers held out. Now hardly anyone could remember the causes of the war, let alone give a coherent account of what it had achieved. Only five years after the peace was signed, *The Times*, in an article that would be often quoted by twentieth-century historians, wrote: 'Never was so great an effort made for so worthless an object. It is with no small reluctance that we admit a gigantic effort and an infinite sacrifice to have been made in vain.'[1]

More recent events within the Empire were similarly disquieting. Government dispatches had glossed over the deep-seated problems exposed by the Indian Mutiny of 1857, making much of the bravery of the British soldier and the courage and endurance of the unfortunate prisoners in the Residency at Lucknow. But could politics that led to the massacre of hundreds of men, women, and children, and the deaths of thousands of soldiers, both British and Indian, be said to have been successful? The men of Whitehall pompously declared that they had 'taught the natives a lesson', but what lessons had they themselves learned? Nor were the problems of the relation between Britain and a subject people being kept at arm's length; Ireland, as always, was making trouble. Judging from the history of the past 400 years, the inhabitants of this small island would continue indefinitely to harass their English rulers, deflecting energies and talents that should have been applied to the resolution of pressing domestic concerns. Indeed Ireland had become part of England's domestic problem. Irish refugees from poverty aggravated by English policy during the 1840s, poured into London, asking for food and lodging, creating confusion and overcrowding that made it almost impossible for them to get either.

Memories of this recent past forced the British leaders to look more closely at the roots of their imperial and foreign policy — their reasons for expanding British power, their relations to a subject people. Because of their ambition the walls of English parish churches were crowded with delicately veined marble tablets, listing the names of young Englishmen who had died as the result of wounds, tropical disease — or as Florence Nightingale would point out — simple stupidity, in places with strange, unpronounceable names — Oudh, Meerut, Cawnpore. Were those deaths necessary to the well-being of the British people? Did the prosperity of the business interests that had been built on those deaths provide the necessities of life for the worker as well as luxuries for the banker? How should one view the native, who along with the soldier and the capitalist, was a key element in a successful imperial policy? Was he a benighted though fully human creature who could be brought by Britain into the fulness of the gospel of Christianity, representative government, and sanitary reform? Or was he merely a necessary factor in the shrewd calculations of the East India Company? Was the Mother Hubbard of the South Sea Islands the symbol of Christianity's belief that man is a soul and the possessor of a body that needs to be clothed; or was it rather witness to the increasingly insatiable productivity — and demands — of the mills of Lancashire, Cheshire, Derbyshire, and the West Riding?

It had been a good year at home. In an era in which most people felt that no news was the best news, many took satisfaction in small accomplishments. There had been another strike, but the Builders Association had failed in achieving its objective of the nine-hour day and had gone peacefully back to work. Taking greater responsibility for the health of its people, the government had passed the Food Adulteration Act. As an indication of the growing interest in art — and the declining power of the Sabbatarian Evangelicals — the Museums were now kept open on Sunday. Industrialists happily read of the development of armourplate by John Brown, an invention that would revolution-ize the ship- and the bridge-building industries; the armchair explorer eagerly followed the reports of Speke's discovery of the source of the Nile.

The most important events of the year, however, appeared not in *The Times* headlines but in the publishers' lists for 1859—61. The literary-minded bought George Meredith, *The Ordeal of Richard Feverel*; Charles Dickens, *Great Expectations*; George Eliot, *Adam Bede* and *Mill on the Floss*; Wilkie Collins, *The Woman in White*; Alfred Lord Tennyson, *Idylls of the King*; and Edward Fitzgerald, *The Rubaiyat of Omar Khayyam*. The practical-minded read Samuel Smiles, *Self-Help* and Isabella Beeton, *Book of Household Management*; those with a taste for political and economic theory, John Stuart Mill, *On Liberty*, and John Ruskin, *Unto This Last*. The reader who wished to keep abreast of the new theological and scientific thought turned to an anthology of Anglican treatises, *Essays and Reviews*; Henry Loungueville Mansel, *The Limits of Religious Thought*; and Charles Darwin, *On the Origin of Species*.

With these books as a means of interpreting the present and foreseeing the future, the reader could find both grounds for hope and reasons for pessimism.

John Stuart Mill's *On Liberty* was one of the more heartening selections. An eloquent defence of free speech, it is very much a product of mid-century harmony, its message conveyed not only in its argument but in its assumptions. Britain's stability, built on the strength of its middle class, makes freedom of speech possi-ble. In this view recent events, including the changes of government (in 1859 the Liberals under Palmerston had come to power) could be understood not as signs of instability but of a balance of interests in which all parties had accepted certain facts as basic: the need to curb the ills created by the Industrial Revolution and to move towards a more representative form of government through extending the franchise. Mill is confident that the clash of opinions will lead to a common acknowledgement of what is true.

As mankind improves, the number of doctrines which are no longer doubted or disputed will be constantly on the increase and the well-being of mankind may almost be measured by the number and gravity of the truths which have reached the point of being uncontested.[2]

Faith in the benign effects of knowledge, articulated by Mill, was given a fuller expression by the Positivists. There cannot have been many who actually read Harriet Martineau's two-volume translation of Comte's treatise, *Positive Philosophy*, which appeared in 1853, but its theme was widely disseminated through the reviews and the discussion it evoked. To some it seemed a timely reassertion of the old Utilitarian premises, which had come from Jeremy Bentham and John Stuart Mill's father, James Mill. 'The greatest happiness of the greatest number' would be ensured in Comte's new world when the myths of religion and the irrelevancies of metaphysics had been replaced by the facts of science and the new 'religion of humanity'. It gave the imprimatur of modernity to the old Whig belief in progress — factory reform, Food Adulteration Acts, and Brown's armourplate were seen as the heralds of a bright future in which science would lead mankind towards new horizons of health, prosperity, and well-being.

While Comte made a link with the perfectible future, Samuel Smiles' individualism was indebted to the past. To the 20,000 aspirants to middle-class prosperity who bought his book in 1860, the aptly named Smiles brought happy tidings. In a homely style liberally laced with long quotations from wealthy businessmen and prominent divines and statesmen, he asserted that prosperity brings social, as well as economic, benefits; furthermore, provided that it has been preceded by the small amount of suffering implicit in the title 'self-help', prosperity is good for the soul. Smiles grows rhapsodic in his description of that social and moral paragon, the gentleman. The gentleman embodies the highest virtues: honesty, energy, kindness, perseverance, patience, courage, tact, cheerfulness. That his cheerfulness arises, not from character, but from the satisfaction of surveying the steadily increasing total in his bank account, Smiles will not admit. The society of gentlemen is open to all, poor as well as rich. While his message is directed to the middle class, the poor will also benefit from it.

> Simple industry and thrift will go far towards making any person of ordinary working family comparatively independent in his means . . . . If he takes care of the pennies — putting some weekly into a benefit society or an insurance fund, others into a savings bank and confiding the rest to his wife to be carefully laid out, with a view to the comfortable maintenance and education of his family, he will soon find that his attention to small matters will obediently repay him, in increasing the means, growing comfort at home, and a mind comparatively free from fears as to the future.[3]

Viewed through Smiles' rosy glasses, the mid-century looked very promising. New fertilizers, new techniques that could be used in the large holdings made possible by the Enclosures Acts, the use of the railroad as a means of transporting food to distant parts of the island, had brought wealth to the farmer and more plentiful, and less expensive, food to the people. The alliance between technical invention and financial initiative swelled the figures of production of coal, iron, ships, cotton, and wool. Across 50,000 miles of silver track ran steam engines, bursting with a sense of self-importance, linking one island city of prosperity with another. The places where they came to rest, disgorging their cargo of bankers, traders, and shop-keepers, had been designed as monuments to capital and technology. The beauty of the railroad station — the miraculous blending of the strength of steel and the fragility of glass — was all the more remarkable when one contrasted it to the filthy slums that it had replaced. Science, however, did not limit itself to the production of goods. Scientists proposed to deal directly with the ills that affect the human body. Lister and Pasteur worked on research that would lead in the 1870s to the acceptance of the germ theory of disease; the development of the anaesthetic properties of chloroform brought relief to those undergoing surgery and to women in childbirth.

There were, however, several books on the publishers' lists that did not make for pleasant bedtime reading. In constrast to Mill, Smiles, and Comte, the messages of John Ruskin and Charles Darwin were deeply troubling.

The security of many mid-Victorians had been built on two cardinal assumptions — one social and economic, the other theological: the capitalism that had provided them with a comfortable livelihood would bring a better life to men and women of all classes; the value of this earthly life is assured by a Heavenly Father, a benevolent Creator — God whose immutable ways are laid out in the authoritative words of scripture. Ruskin struck at one principle, Charles Darwin by implication struck at the other.

The development of science and capital, the economic progress of the middle class and its opportunities for all, which brought such pleasure to Samuel Smiles, appear in a sombre vision to John Ruskin. In a series of articles for *Cornhill Magazine* he takes his text 'Unto this last' from the parable of the workers in Matthew 20. As a Christian he raises the obvious objection to the enthronement of 'mammon service' and laissez-faire capitalism. He reminds the reader that the privileges of the rich are paid for by the deprivations of the poor. 'Consider whether, even supposing it guiltless, luxury would be desired by any of us, if we saw clearly at our sides the suffering which accompanies it.'4

This was not the first time that capitalism had come under attack. Engels' *The Condition of the Working Class in England* had appeared in 1844; Marx's and Engels' *Communist Manifesto* in 1847. British intellectuals had sketched some alternatives to capitalism, alternatives that seemed to Marx and Engels merely eccentric, totally incapable of dealing with the realities. David Owen set up small utopian communities that in their dissolution proved to be, not proof of the superior strength of communism, but witness to the ineradicable force of individualism. Equally irrelevant to the Marxists appeared the efforts of the Christian Socialists with their professions of brotherly love, their faith in the cooperation between the classes, and their organization of small workshops based on a sharing of profits.

For Ruskin and other critics of capitalism the peace and relative affluence of the 1850s were signs that the social disease

was merely in remission. The docility of labour was deceptive.
The builders had gone back to work — but only after management had agreed to allow them to associate with other labour
groups. If the working man's demand for the vote had been less
insistent in the 1850s than in the 1840s, it was perhaps because he
had come to realise that the franchise was only one step in a
larger programme. He was not interested in whether the picture
galleries were open on Sundays, or even on weekdays. He was
only moderately interested in prison and Poor Law reform. He
wanted power. This he would achieve, not through his individual
vote, but through cooperation with other labourers in the trade
union.

Recent events were Janus-faced; every positive carried with it
a negative: every solution gave birth to new problems. The
technology that had constructed the glass and steel palace for the
railroad passenger had built nothing for the thousands of people
whom it had displaced and who now wandered through the
streets, cramming into tiny rooms at night or sleeping under
bridges. The development of industry had brought along with
prosperity attendant ills. Carlyle fulminated against the ugliness of England; the countryside was disappearing. Long before
Ruskin, Wordsworth had railed at a people who had lost their
souls to Mammon, 'getting and spending' in the market place.
The noise of machinery drowned out the meadow lark and the
nightingale. The trees around the cities drooped from the smoke
of soft coal. The medical progress that was bringing the relief of
suffering would also lower the death rate, adding to the number
of mouths to feed.

By the middle of the century it had become clear that Malthus,
while underestimating the ability of England to feed itself, had
been correct in predicting enormous increases in population. In
1780 the population of England and Wales was 7½ million; by
1871 it would be 26 million. More disruptive than the numerical
increase was the shift from the country to the city. While larger
holdings had made for more efficient food production, they had
forced the small farmer off the land, sending him to the city
where he had no means of gaining a livelihood and no place to
live. Early in the eighteenth century 87 per cent of the population lived in the country; by 1851 half the population lived in
towns and cities. By 1871 the population of London was increasing
at the rate of 80,000 people a year. The government urged

emigration for the working man, but this policy had its negative aspects. Those who left for the open spaces and grazing fields of Australia, Canada, and New Zealand were the able-bodied and male; those who remained were the old, the infirm, the female. To their numbers were added the destitute and needy from other lands: the Irishman and the European Jew. In the exchange of population Britain was losing the strong and acquiring the weak.

Poverty and suffering are of course perennial. In view of the late-Victorian obsession with these problems, it is easy to forget that throughout European history people have suffered from cholera, typhoid, plague, death in childbirth, starvation, murder. For the first time in England's history, however, these facts were revealed in a detailed and systematic way. Throughout the dreadfully severe winter of 1860 the depth and breadth of human misery were detailed in the pages of the daily newspaper. Gustave Doré, William Stead, and the pages of the *Pall Mall Gazette* chronicled the lives of the poor, confirming the grim impressions of Disraeli (*Sybil*, 1845), Charles Kingsley, and Dickens. The census of 1851 provided abundant material for researchers; the National Association for the Promotion of Social Science, founded in 1857, provided field workers. Mayhew's *London Labour and the London Poor* (1851) added details and gave poignant biographical sketches of hundreds of destitute men and women. By 1860 the verdict had not yet been handed down, but the evidence was not encouraging.

Carlyle, Ruskin, and the Christian Socialists agreed that the greatest evil of capitalism, however, was not the economic hardship it had inflicted upon the worker, but its destructive effect on his family, his life, and his sense of self-worth. They contrasted modern society to an idealized picture of Britain's agrarian past. In the Middle Ages a man carried his occupation with him, often it was embedded in his name — Miller, Weaver, Goldsmith, Carpenter. He handed down both trade and name to his sons. Training in his craft offered not only the means of livelihood but the companionship of men with similar occupations and backgrounds. But in the move from country to city he had lost the comfortable landmarks of parish church and pub, the game of bowls on the green, Boxing Day visits to nearby cousins, fishing expeditions with his children — that sense of continuity with the past which had steadied his forebears. Work had become specialized. Industry required technical skills that were necessary in a particular industry but could not be transported. Men off the land became 'casual labour', the last to be hired, the first to be laid off. The labourer in search of work would move his family and their few belongings from one set of rooms to another. At a higher level of employment the separation between professional and amateur had become fixed. The body of knowledge was growing at such a rate that the education required to become a doctor, a lawyer, or an architect was long, difficult, and expensive. This education was closed to women.

That women were denied education and jobs was of course nothing new. Still, many felt that the Industrial Revolution had been particularly hard on women. Feminists looked back to the Middle Ages as an era in which women of all classes had played an active role. Since men spent long periods, often years, at war or on a pilgrimage, some women found themselves in charge of a fief the size of a small county. Their responsibilities touched every aspect of the lives of their vassals — farming, cooking, the making of clothes, nursing, and the settling of legal problems. In fulfilling these responsibilities they were helped by other women. Now, however, most of these tasks that women had once done voluntarily had been taken over by paid professionals who were invariably men. Doctors replaced the midwife, chefs took over the cooking, and weaving, crafts and the making of clothes were taken out of the home and placed in the factory. Women were left with a steadily contracting sphere of responsibility.

Lower-class women employed as 'hands' in a factory found the work monotonous and exhausting. Their chances for promotion were limited by a system that placed men in the upper levels as overseers. Some women felt that the measures passed by Parliament to protect them from the exploitation and harshness of the work — the prohibition against women working in the mines, for example — were but another form of discrimination, closing yet another opportunity to them. By the middle of the century the lack of work had become a critical problem. Over the centuries marriage had been offered to women as the only legitimate occupation. But now the men were leaving; the women stayed. New Zealand, Australia, Canada called for trappers, miners, farmers, cattlemen; they did not want the unattached female. The 'surplus women'[5] were left in England with three professions open to them — two legitimate but sadly limited in their

pleasures and opportunities, that of the domestic servant ,
the governess; the other unmentionable — that of the prostitu
    The presence of a large population of potential servants maɑ
it possible for middle-class women to aspire to upper-class
values. Just as Samuel Smiles had welcomed middle-class men
who wished to emulate the style of their betters, so Isabella
Beeton opened the doors of upper-class gentility to the 60,000
women who bought the *Book of Household Management* in the
first year of its publication. She offered specific practical
training and she reassured women on the importance of their
domestic responsibilities.

As with the Commander of an Army, or with the leader of any
enterprise, so is it with the mistress of a house. Her spirit will
be seen through the whole establishment and just in propor-
tion as she performs her duties intelligently and thoroughly,
so will her domestics follow in her path.[6]

While describing the daily rounds of the mistress, Mrs Beeton
relies heavily on domestic virtues that had their origin in
Christianity. Earlier proponents of the sanctity of the hearth and
the necessity for diligence, punctuality, thrift, and hospitality,
had built their case on religion. Sarah Ellis and Hannah More
had stressed family prayers and the spiritual bond between
servants and mistresses. Mrs Beeton, however, ignores religion.
    She knew, perhaps, that there was no consensus among her
readers. Religion was no longer a universal support and
consolation. Charles Darwin, in *On the Origin of Species*, bringing
new evidence to bear upon a recent thesis, suggested that
evolution through natural selection was the key to the diversity
of the plant and animal kingdom. Geologists had already cast
doubts on the history of creation as recorded in the Old Testament. Along with Darwin they rejected as mythological the
comfortable picture of perfectly paired animals, the ancestors of
the docile creatures admired and petted in the Regents Park
Zoo, marching with matched step into the Ark. They claimed
that nature was a chaotic battleground where ungainly creatures
skirmished over a terrain composed of decayed orchids, turtle
shells, butterfly wings, and mis-shapen bones. This principle of
evolution with its messy and wasteful method Darwin also
applied to man. Rejecting the classic profile given to Adam by

Michelangelo, Masaccio, and the humanists, he recast early man in the image of his own rather simian humanity. Man was not the subject of a special divine creation: he was merely an animal among animals.

Those who turned to the Anglican *Essays and Reviews* for a spirited rebuttal did not find it. The majority of Churchmen — Anglican, Roman Catholic and Dissenter — had stood their ground, refusing even to consider the arguments of science and rationalism and invoking the wrath of God upon a nation of unbelievers. Liberal Anglicans, however, many themselves scientists — Adam Sedgwick, William Buckland, Charles Kingsley — accommodated their faith to the new evidence of science. Their spokesmen, the authors of the six essays, pointed out that there was little new or revolutionary in contemporary biblical criticism; as early as 1823 German scholars had claimed that the Old Testament had been written by many people, each with his own particular blend of fallibility and divine inspiration. The authors of *Essays and Reviews* affirmed that the Bible contains a variety of subject-matter — poetry, philosophy, and history — and that religious truths express themselves through parable and myth, as well as through historical events. The truths of scripture are not tied to the historicity of every jot and tittle of scriptural evidence but grow out of a view of revelation that affirms the universality of truth: all truth comes from God; therefore, there can be no conflict between theologian, geologist, and historian. Christianity, they concluded, has nothing to fear from biblical criticism.

To the ordinary churchgoer (and the not-so-ordinary — Ruskin was among many highly intelligent Christians whose faith was demolished by the attacks on the Bible) this explanation was of little comfort. The places around him in the parish church had already been left empty by those who had found they could no longer take literally the lessons read from the lectern. A plain man, he wanted to hear plain speaking. He could not trouble his mind with truths of myth and 'progressive' theology. He did not want to hear that the Bible is an 'expression of devout reason' (H. B. Wilson); he wanted to know that it was true.

He might have been momentarily cheered by Bishop Wilberforce's stated opinion that the writers could not 'with moral honesty maintain their posts as clergymen of the established church'[7] and by the proceedings against two of the essayists, Rowland Williams and H. B. Wilson. The charges against these divines, however, were dismissed by the judicial committee of the privy council in 1864. The two men were issued minimal warnings and the Church continued in what seemed to the conservative churchgoer to be an almost perverse course of self-destruction. A cutting attack on the literal truth of scripture was mounted, not by a scientist but by a Bishop of the Anglican Church. John Colenso, the Bishop of Natal and a mathematician, said that Noah had not been a competent carpenter; the Ark, had it been built according to the sacred specifications given in Genesis, would not have floated. He continued in the course of his statistical musings by laboriously analysing the whole of the Pentateuch, listing a catalogue of errors and inconsistencies that added up to over 800 pages.

Confronted by the scientists, the liberals admitted the fallibility of scripture as science and history. But when confronted by the ethicists who pointed out that Jehovah was an arbitrary and unmerciful God, who condoned behaviour that would not have been acceptable in any Christian society, let alone one with the high standards of Victorian morality, biblical literalists insisted upon retaining every detail of the smitings of the wrathful Jehovah — the murder of innocent, if misguided, priests of Baal, the killing of young children by Elisha and his bears.

Henry Longueville Mansell's *The Limits of Religious Thought* attempted to resolve these questions by placing them in the sweeping context of epistemology. Students flocked to hear the popular Oxford lecturer, thinking that if anyone could restore philosophical respectability to Christianity, he would be the man. But they came away exhausted by arguments which had perhaps left open the door to faith but had provided no vision of what might fill the empty frame. Mansell's thesis was that the knowledge of God is impossible; the categories which shape human values by their very nature eliminate knowledge of the supernatural; therefore, we cannot judge God's actions by human standards. To many this sounded as if he were saying, not that God is above contempt, but that he is beneath contempt; it put them right back with Elisha and the bears.

The intellectual and ethical problems posed by the rationalist attack on the Bible were only one aspect of the loss of faith. The social and political facts were as important. The Anglican Church struggled — sometimes not very hard — against an identification with conservatism that had been built into the social fabric and even the architecture of England. What was now a parish church had been originally constructed in the Middle Ages by the lord as an adjunct and private chapel to the manor house. Discouraged by their failure to win over the working classes, the most rapidly growing group in Britain, Anglican leaders preoccupied themselves with internal problems — clergy deployment, sinecures, multiple livings, and methods of tithing and distributing alms that were no longer suited to a society where people, many of them unchurched, were on the move. They struggled with their ambivalent relationship with a state that gave them support as an institution but was by and large not in harmony with their goals. They were infuriated by the Members of Parliament who eagerly exercised their prerogative to vote on church matters, though they never attended church services and did not subscribe to its beliefs.

To this disheartening picture the Dissenters added a moral tone; the growth of the Roman Church added colour but created further instability. The keen concern for social problems shown by Chapel, the Quakers, and the Unitarians was a powerful force in Victorian England. Along with the low-church wing of the Anglican Church, the Non-conformists were responsible for the evangelical morality and social concern that gave its flavour to the century. They produced theologians of stature, James Martineau and Joseph Priestley; they are remembered for their preachers, Edward Irving, Charles Haddon Spurgeon, and tract writers who presented a strong and simple faith that appealed to the working man. The recognition of the Roman Catholic Church in 1852 righted an old wrong; however, the installation of Wiseman as Archbishop of Westminster and his elevation to the College of Cardinals, and the presence in England of believers, many of them Irish and European, who owed their primary allegiance to a 'foreign' leader, inevitably evoked the old fear of 'popery'. More significantly and at a time when the Church of England could least afford it, in attracting some of the best Anglican minds — John Henry Newman, Henry Edward Manning, Richard Hurrell Froude — the Roman presence further weakened the Anglican Church. The High Church movement had started with the recovery of spiritual commitment as its goal; Keble's verses, *The Christian Year* had proved popular among Christians of all sects. Yet it had helped create an atmosphere in which incense, vestments, and the presence or absence of candles on the altar were matters of grave import, a factionalism in which its adherents were judged not by the depth of their faith but by their susceptibility to Roman influence.

Taken altogether, it was not an easy time for Christianity. While most of the great military hymns of the 1860s and 1870s were Anglican, Christians of all sects joined their voices in Samuel Sebastian Wesley's hymn of 1864:

> Though with a scornful wonder
> Men see her sore opprest,
> By schism rent asunder
> By heresies, distrest,
> Yet saints their watch are keeping
> Their cry goes up, 'How Long?'

*   *   *

In 1860 Josephine Butler was 32. For reasons of health, the Butlers had moved in 1857 from Oxford to the milder climate of Cheltenham, an agreeable Gloucestershire watering-place. Its elegant terraces and squares, its Pump Room, and the multi-coloured gardens of Pittvillege Park had received the royal nod of approval when George III paid a visit to Cheltenham in 1788.

Enjoying the companionship of her attentive husband George, and the affection of four energetic and healthy children, Josephine busied herself with the household, with hours of practice at the piano that her father had bought her at the Great Exhibition of 1851, and with walks in the rolling countryside. Aristocratic in bearing, beautiful, and elegantly dressed, Josephine looked the part of Coventry Patmore's 'Angel in the House'.

Appearances, however, are deceptive. Josephine Butler was a radical Christian, committed by birth, temperament, and training to the estabishment of a just society. Already men — some of them Britain's leading intellectuals — had learned to quail before her steady gaze. The Oxford years had not been entirely happy. To their surprise the Butlers found themselves aliens in a community that by birth and education they had expected to claim as their own. As a woman in a male society, Josephine had felt particularly isolated. Oxford had scorned her Christian profession, rebuked her interest in higher education for women, and ignored a single-heartedness that heard the claims of truth, not only in the theorems of Euclid and the Alexandrines of Pope, but in the cry for help of the prostitute.

In many ways Cheltenham proved more congenial. The Butlers made friends with William Charles Macready, the actor, and with Dorothea Beale, the head of the Cheltenham Ladies College. With their student boarders they discussed education; George wished to add geography, science, and art history to the classical curriculum. To her neighbours Josephine read aloud letters from her sister in Naples, relating the newest events in the progress of Garibaldi, knowing that she was reaching a sympathetic audience.

On the question of the Civil War in the United States, however, the Butlers found themselves a minority. The leaders of Cheltenham society were retired officers of the Indian service who considered the blacks an inferior race. They aligned themselves with the aristocratic and cultivated Southerners, claiming that the scenes in *Uncle Tom's Cabin* had been greatly exaggerated and that slavery was a respectable, and even beneficent, institution. To the Butlers this was intolerable. Josephine, brought up to believe that every human being — rich and poor, male and female, white and black — is a Child of God, reared on stories of suffering and loss from the pages of Clarkson's *History of the Slave Trade*, could not remain silent. Once again the Butlers found themselves isolated.

> Feeling ran very high, public opinion among the upper and educated classes, led by *The Times*, was almost universally in favour of the Southern Party. Anyone with a contrary opinion . . . was regarded as a person of unsound judgment, if not of low and vulgar prejudices. . . . We were impelled to give up visiting, finding ourselves out of sympathy with the persons we met daily, among whom we were scarcely welcome and by whom we were looked askance, as audacious dissenters from the verdict of the august authority, Society.[8]

The bracing against hostility and the mustering of energies to swim against the tide, were disciplines that she would come to depend on during the course of a long and tumultuous life.

* * *

The year 1860 was the tenth anniversary of Octavia Hill's move to London. In 1850 she had arrived with her mother and four sisters to take up work offered to the family by the Christian Socialists. She had run a toymaking cooperative whose purpose was to provide a living for its child-workers and their families. In 1857 the Hill family resigned from the cooperative to protest the dismissal of the controversial theologian F. D. Maurice. Assuming the price for theological conviction and loyalty to a friend, the Hill women sought work elsewhere.

In 1860 Octavia was living with her sister Emily in rooms at 103 Milton Street. Early in the morning she rose to attend the daily service at the Chapel at Lincoln's Inn where Maurice was the preacher. After morning prayer she travelled to the Dulwich Gallery where she copied Turners and worked on drawings that John Ruskin had commissioned for his next edition of *Modern Painters*. She then proceeded to the Working Woman's College where, as secretary, she handled the financial transactions, the book-keeping, and took over the teaching responsibilities of absent faculty members. In addition to these duties she attended classes in mathematics at Queen's College, gave drawing lessons, and kept up her friendships with the children of the toymaking establishment. In April she read the *Idylls of the King* and reported that she had seen Holman Hunt's picture 'The Scape-goat', adding that it had 'cast no light on the subject'. In the spring she went twice to Spitalfields where she visited the silk weavers, descendants of the Huguenots, who had recently been put out of work by foreign competition.

She worried about her country, about the divisions and bitterness between classes. She shared her feeling with Ruskin:

> We spoke about the wickedness of rich and poor people . . . . I spoke about the frightful want of feeling in all classes but added that I thought rich people were now waking up to a sense of their duties. 'Yes', he said, 'I'm glad that you and I have probably a good deal of life still to come. I think we may live to see some great changes in society.'[9]

These discussions about the future of England had an immediate and intensely personal meaning for the 22-year-old woman who was seeking professional direction. What role could she play in the 'great changes'? Should she give her life to art or to people? Could she do both?

*   *   *

The sitting room at 30 Old Burlington Street, the 'little War Office', had become very crowded; five yellow-striped cats prowled about, knocking over vases of flowers as they circumvented piles of Blue Books, architects' renderings of hospital plans, and brown paper bundles marked 'Indian Reports'. From her sofa Florence Nightingale observed the exchange between the cats and an infant visitor. 'It put out its hand with a kind of gracious dignity and caressed them, as if they were presenting Addresses, and they responded in a humble, grateful way, quite cowed by infant majesty.'[10]

It was a rare moment of frivolity; generally the letters that came and went concerned matters of life and death: a letter to the Home Secretary asking that in the census questions for Britain he include inquiries on health and disease; a letter to the Prince Consort urging him as a member of the Board of Governors of St Thomas's to erect a new hospital building; letters to John Farr planning the summer meeting of the International Statistical Congress and promoting the Model Forms that would standardize the record-keeping in hospitals; a letter expressing concern about the Spitalfields weavers and suggesting that they might be transplanted to Manchester where they could find work. With satisfaction she received the reports on the sale of *Notes on Nursing* and agreed to write a second edition on 'Minding Baby'. She carefully scrutinized the responses to the advertisement that had appeared in *The Times* in May for candidates for the newly formed training school for nurses. She thanked Sir George Trevelyan for his account of the Madras Hospital, which had been built according to Nightingale specifications. This correspondence dealt with principles of preventive medicine that, when followed, would change the course of mankind.

Her greatest satisfaction of the year, however, lay not in her own accomplishments but in the appointment of Sidney Herbert to the position of Secretary of War. Now at last her work would be done; hardly a day passed without a visit or a letter from the Secretary. He would write, 'Here is a dispute which is Hebrew to me; would you look it over with Sutherland?' 'Can Miss Nightingale give me the names of some Governors for our new General Hospitals?' The building of sanitary hospitals and barracks, the establishment of an Army medical school, the reorganization of the keeping of records, provisions for recreation for soldiers — these she would bring about with Sidney

Herbert's position as her access to power, his strength as her right arm. Then perhaps the voices of the 'murdered' men in the Crimea who cried out to her during the long night watch — cried out, not for revenge but that others might be spared their deaths from neglect — would be stilled.

Then perhaps she could turn her full attention to India. 'I would work, oh how gladly, but I want direction how to work. I would suffer how willingly, but for a purpose', she had written.

> How penetrated must those have been who first, genuinely, had the conception, who felt, who thought, whose imaginations helped them to conceive, that the Divine Verity manifests itself in the human, partakes itself, becomes one with the human, descends into the hell of sin and suffering with the human . . . . To do it 'to the glory of God' must be to fulfil the Lord's purpose. That purpose is man's increase in truth, increase in right being.

She had been called to be a 'saviour'. As a 'saviour' she would work by 'calling ordinary people to be saviours'. She called all of her correspondents to be saviours — to accept the burdens placed on them by history, to throw off the stultifying weight of centuries of ignorance and inefficiency — to create a new future for mankind. 'Was there ever an age in so much need of heroism?' she wrote to her father.[11]

Josephine Butler

1 A Touch of Genius

1   Milfield and Dilston, 1828—52: Childhood and Adolescence

The day of the week on which Josephine Grey was born at Milfield, Northumberland, is unrecorded. But whatever the accident of the calendar she was in every respect a Sunday's child. Endowed by nature with beauty, intelligence, and vigour, she was equally blessed in her nurture. Her loving parents Hannah Annett Grey and John Grey were members of a prominent Border family of wealth and position, enlightened leaders and landlords whose liberal principles were based on Evangelical piety.

The only account we have of Josephine's childhood is the one she gives us in the biography of her father. The *Memoir of John Grey of Dilston*, with its vivid descriptions of family life, contains many autobiographical incidents. It is also autobiographical, however, in a less obvious way: in most of her comments about her father's character and temperament Josephine could have been describing herself. Josephine was not a fanciful biographer; in fact, father and daughter were much alike. Her life, though it took a radical turn, was an extension of the direction given by her parents.

During long years of conflict and political activity which took her far from the tranquil setting of her childhood, Josephine remained close to her family. It is significant that her recollections of her parents were set down, not in the uneventful repose of old age, but during the climax of her struggles. It is as if in the heat of battle and as an antidote to the psychological isolation that notoriety and violent hostility had brought her, she needed to touch base with the forces that had sent her on her way. As she worked through the tumult of ideas that went into her highly emotional pamphlets and books on prostitution, she pondered the meaning of her heritage and upbringing.

To her parents, and to her father in particular, she attributed her faith in a loving and merciful God, her dislike of narrowness and sectarianism, her fierce egalitarianism, and her belief in social activism as the hall-mark of piety. A spirituality based on prayer and expressed primarily in the context of the family complete the picture of the Evangelical in religion and the Liberal in politics.

Hannah and John Grey, both Anglican, were proud of their ecumenically minded forebears. Hannah came from a family of Huguenot silk-weavers who had known fierce religious persecution. Driven from France by the revocation of the Edict of Nantes, they found refuge in England. She remembered that when she was a child John Wesley, 'a man with white silvery hair and a benevolent countenance', had visited them, placing his hands upon the head of the little girl and blessing her. Hannah attended school among the Moravians of Fulneck and returned to a family which opened 'its hospitable doors to every one in the form of a religious teacher, of whatever sect, who happened to pass that way'.[1] John Grey's background was equally non-sectarian. His mother, a widow left with the upbringing of two girls and a boy, encouraged them to be independent and to think for themselves. John's sisters recalled her displeasure when they had taken to heart the opinion of a 'talkative lady' who criticized the Presbyterian Church and told them that the only way to heaven was in the Anglican Church.[2]

While the Greys mistrusted the distinctive formulations that set one denomination against another, there was nothing tentative in their profession of faith. They held emphatically to the classical Christian understanding of a God who is actively involved in human affairs. God is a loving Creator and Father who supports the weak, comforts the oppressed, and destroys the tyrant. Grey scorned those 'modern philosophers' (presumably the Utilitarians) who believe that

> man can perfect his own present existence, and drive away by the aid of science, sickness, disease, poverty, crime and every existing evil from the land. Yet he urged people 'to avail themselves, of the aids which God has placed at our disposal, powers, known or hidden, in the natural world, for the diminution of evil and pain'.[3]

While John Grey had little faith in the perfectability of man — this side of the Kingdom of God — he felt strongly that all men and women are equal in the sight of God. There are no spiritual distinctions between male and female, rich and poor, gentleman and farmer, educated and uneducated. Thus he did not think it strange that he should address the Royal Agricultural Society at Newcastle — accustomed to technical accounts of trade relations, the diseases of Highland cattle and the properties of various kinds of manure — on the beauties of poetry, reciting from memory Virgil, Shakespeare, and Milton.[4] The agricultural force, he reminded his listeners, were men and women first, and labourers second. 'They have still higher claims upon us, minds to cultivate and souls to save.'[5] Brought up in the company of gifted and energetic women, he especially admired his older sister Margaretta who held distinctly radical notions on the equality of women. (She had once dressed as a boy in order to gain admission to the visitor's gallery at the House of Commons.) His mother, reading to him from Clarkson's *History of the Slave Trade*, had passed on to him her hatred of injustice and her belief in the equal humanity of slave and free, man and woman.

With some pride and considerable political knowledge Josephine lists her father's political accomplishments: he circulated the petition for the abolition of the slave trade and pressed for the extension of the franchise; he kept up a steady correspondence with his cousin, Earl Grey, the sponsor of the Reform Bill, suggesting political manoeuvres and reporting on his own efforts to convert the North country. Josephine was too young to remember the passage of the Bill in the summer of 1832, but her description of the dramatic events that preceded it indicate that it was celebrated as a personal victory in the Grey household and that the bonfires and festivities became part of the collective family memory.

Josephine offers no full-scale portrait of her mother, no companion-piece to the *Memoir of John Grey*. Yet her remarks are warmly appreciative.

> We owed much to our dear mother, who was firm in requiring from us that whatever we did should be thoroughly done and that in taking up any study we should aim at becoming as perfect as we could in it without external aid. This was a moral discipline which perhaps compensated in value for the lack of a great store of knowledge. She would assemble us daily for the reading aloud of some solid book, and by a kind of examination

following the reading assured us that we had mastered the subject. She urged us to aim at excellence.[6]

Family prayers and lessons were supplemented by attendance at the local church where Josephine listened to 'an honest man in the pulpit who taught us loyally all that he probably himself knew about God'.[7] Occasionally she walked with her sister Hattie to the Methodist chapel that John Grey had built for his tenants. Years later in the Tyrol she was reminded of those services.

The old women going to church on Sunday carried in their hands a prayerbook, a pocket-handkerchief tightly folded, and a bunch of southern-wood (old man), mint, and marigold, just as we used to do when we were children and went to the Methodist meeting-house in Milfield with our nurse Nancy.[8]

Nancy was a follower of Edward Irving, an evangelical Methodist who proclaimed the advent of a new Pentecost, a new pouring out of the spirit.

I recollect she used to get us up very early, at dawn on Sunday mornings, and we used to start off for Dartmoor, in a cart with straw in it and a sack to sit on and we used to sit and hear the words and 'prophecyings' of some of those gifted men.

A friend and follower of John Wesley brought real Christianity to the 'barren wilderness' of the Border country.

My parents received him, and there followed such a wonderful revival, all among those sweet Cheviot Hills that the whole air seemed to be filled with the sound of prayer and praise, 'weeping and supplication' and joyful singing. It was like heaven on earth.[9]

Among the gentry the Greys were not alone in being touched by Methodist enthusiasm. Josephine describes the conversion of a neighbour.

One day out hunting, a lightning flash of conviction smote him, and, like Paul of Tarsus, he fell, or threw himself from his horse, and there, on his knees, on the hunting field, he prayed aloud to the awe and astonishment of his companions.[10]

In 1833 John Grey was appointed overseer to the Greenwich Hospital Estates. For the next forty years the management of these vast estates — comprising some seventy-six farms and 34,356 acres — would be his immediate responsibility. He moved his large family — nine children — to Dilston to be nearer the centre of the Estates.

His children had already learnt that book-learning is only a part of a larger experience. Their lessons in British history had been brought to life by pieces of rusty armour carried back from their walks to Flodden Field. Now they accompanied their father on horseback, making the rounds of the tenants and learning first-hand about rural poverty. They measured these observations against Edwin Chadwick's account of the sanitary conditions in cities. Agricultural reform, taxation, and the rights of tenants they put in the perspective of readings in constitutional law and the history of slavery. At the hunt balls at Alnwick Castle, Josephine and Hattie absorbed practical lessons in party politics.

> They are stately affairs and, in fact, political gatherings. I recollect my father and old Lord Grey, Lord Howick, and Lord Durham, all standing in a group in the very middle of the ballroom floor, regardless of the dancers all around them, deep in some liberal intrigue. Then the Duke and Duchess would arrive with the Taubervilles who were Conservatives, and the liberal group would break up. I used to dance with Lord Tauberville, though my father did not quite like me dancing with a Tory. Hattie and I were great belles in our showy book-muslin frocks, and natural flowers wreathed on our heads and waists.[11]

Along with political and intellectual training, the children were instructed in drawing, music, and in sports. Josephine was an ardent horsewoman, riding to hounds with her brother George. Her grandson, indeed, suggests that much of her courage and physical energy — the disciplined ferocity with which she confronted political hurdles — were inherited characteristics, developed on the hunting field.[12] A visitor from Scotland commented on Josephine's unusual nerve and ability. When told she was a Grey, he added, 'Ah, well, the girl cannot help it. It's in the blood.'

The wide horizons of this education were further expanded by the numerous guests who came through the open door of the Grey household: friends of Mazzini, American Quaker Abolitionists, agricultural experts from the Continent. Josephine summarizes her childhood movingly:

> Our home at Dilston was a very beautiful one. Its romantic historical associations, the wild informal beauty all round its doors, the bright large family circle, and the kind and hospitable character of its master and mistress, made it an attractive place to many friends, and guests. Among our pleasantest visitors there were Swedes, Russians, and French, who came to England on missions of agricultural or other inquiry, and who sometimes spent weeks with us. It was a house the door of which stood wide open, as if to welcome all comers, through the livelong summer day. (All the days seemed like summer days when looking back.)[13]

The 'summer days' of childhood were followed by the inevitable turmoil of adolescence. Despite the beauty of her surroundings and the harmony of family life, Josephine was troubled. . . . How could she love a God who permitted suffering and sin? This

> travail of soul began with me when I was only seventeen! In the virtuous and beautiful country home of my father, that is. There were extensive pathless woods near the house. So great was the burden on my soul about the inequalities, injustices and cruelties in the world that I used to run away into these woods where no one followed me; and kneeling on the ground, I used to shriek to God to come and deliver! This is awfully true; my sisters thought I was a little mad. Perhaps I was.
>
> For one long year of darkness the trouble of heart and brain urged me to lay all this at the door of the God, whose names I had learned was love. I dreaded Him — I fled from Him — until grace was given me to arise and wrest, as Jacob did, with the mysterious Presence, who must either slay or pronounce deliverance. And then the great questioning again went up from the earth to heaven, 'God, Who art Thou? Where art

Thou? Why is it thus with the creatures of Thy hand?' I fought the battle alone, in the deep recesses of the beautiful woods and pine forests.[14]

Was her despair the result of a trauma? Or part of the normal development of an intense and sensitive person, the extension of an awareness that had always been part of her education? How deep-seated was it?

A recent biographer, Glen Petrie, has suggested that Josephine's spiritual distress was the result of a single experience. While riding her pony Apple Grey, she emerged from the black recesses of the 'pathless woods' of Dipton and suddenly came across the body of a man hanging from a tree. Later she was told that the man was a valet of a neighbouring squire who had been dismissed for having fathered an illegitimate child. The shock of this ugly scene and its social implications must have been severe, but it is unlikely that it was a single cause.

Though particularly dramatic, it was not Josephine's first experience with death. Her brother John had been lost at sea. Her family was drawn together in its grief and Josephine records her mother's attempt to find peace.

Through the mercy of God some healing balm is ever derived not entirely from an abstract principle, but from those very sorrows themselves more immediately, as the antidote to the viper's sting sometimes lies in the plant among our feet from whence the venomous beast attacked us. In the sick-room of some dear one, close, dark, dull, and cheerless as it seems, I have often found real, even abounding joy, in the thought that I was God's prisoner, and sorrow and uneasiness and fear were often, strange as it may seem, lost in a positive sustaining pleasure.[15]

Josephine was also aware that her father's faith had developed from his boyhood response to death. During a period in which both he and his mother had been critically ill, he found comfort in prayer and in reading the Bible. Josephine records this event as the turning point in his life — his conversion from the tepid and ambivalent belief of the nominal Christian to the fervour of the true evangelical.

The reality of suffering, furthermore, was part of the education deliberately given her by her family. Blessed with the protection of material prosperity, set in the bright family circle, she had always been sensitive to the contrast between her own secure life and the fragile existence of others. She knew that her father's tenants lived with the constant knowledge that famine or disease might engulf them at any moment. Her reading was largely a history of death and oppression. Her imagination, like that of her father before her, was kindled by the accounts of the 'hideous wrongs' inflicted on Negro men and women — the separation of families, physical punishment and brutality, the murder of children. From her own account we would judge that the acknowledgement of evil had long been part of her life.

> It was my lot from my earliest years to be haunted by the problems which more or less present themselves to every thoughtful mind. Year after year this haunting became more tyrannous. The world appeared to me to be out of joint. A strange intuition was given to me whereby I saw as in a vision, before I had seen any of them with my bodily eyes, some of the saddest miseries practiced by man on man, by man on woman.[16]

There is evidence, however, that this 'vision' may not have been as traumatic as she subsequently remembered. One cannot help but notice that there is a marked contrast between the account of her youth given in the *Memoir* of her father and the account given some forty years later to her grandchildren. The emphasis in the *Memoir* is on the 'summer days': the acknowledgement of evil provides only a faint penumbra that delineates the highlights of an exuberant and happy life. In the *Portrait* the balance is reversed; the dark shadows have come forward casting the negative print. Josephine was then in failing health, living in solitude and inactivity. It seems likely that some of the pessimism, even the despair, of old age coloured her memories of the past. (Her other writings of the period are marked by a similar melancholia.) As an old woman, looking back on an adult life spent in confronting the powers of darkness, it is not surprising that she felt that there had never been a time when she had not heard 'the cries of lost spirits, the wail of the murdered innocents'.

2 Oxford, Cheltenham, Liverpool, 1852–69: Marriage and Maturity

In 1850 Josephine was a strikingly beautiful girl, blessed with an ardent temperament, trained intelligence, and the unconscious self-confidence that accompanies a heritage of privilege and social responsibility. In that year she met George Butler, son of the headmaster of Harrow. In many ways he was not unlike her father — an excellent athlete and an ardent fisherman,[17] a classicist and teacher, a liberal who actively aligned himself with the cause of the poor and oppressed, a convinced Christian. In addition he was ordained an Anglican priest. There is every evidence that the marriage (1852) between these exceptional people was an extra-ordinarily happy one, based on an intimacy and interdependence that served to strengthen and confirm the individuality of each.

One would have thought, given the security of her marriage and the scope that it afforded her, that Josephine would have followed the rewarding pattern established by her mother and the Grey women — a life devoted to the upbringing and education of gifted and attractive children, a life in which her natural role as wife and hostess would be an outlet for her social and political gifts. Josephine had not been brought up to believe that women should concern themselves only with domestic affairs; she had been raised by parents who valued their daughters as people, not merely as pawns on the marriage market. Furthermore, she had married a man whose love for her was expressed in the context of an egalitarianism that included the highest regard for the abilities of women. The Butler household, like the Greys', would be one in which the salon would be a political arena and an intellectual force, its doors open to the outside world. Why did she need to seek wider horizons?

Yet seventeen years later this well-bred woman of position who had found exceptional personal happiness in the institutions of marriage and motherhood chose to leave the security of her home and to embark on a course that led to social ostracism, violence, and the horror that comes from contact with a particularly vicious evil.

At Oxford the door between the salon and the outside world had been closed. She had lost the position of leadership that as a Grey had been hers in Northumbria. In a community dominated by distinguished intellectuals she was merely the wife of an untried, if promising, young scholar. A woman in a society led by male opinion, she found her views ignored.

As a result of her own experience of male hostility and rejection, she became more sensitive to the problems of other women. It occurred to her that the terrible civil injustices that had been so apparent in her study of the slave question in the United States had a counterpart, less dramatic but no less real, in the relations between men and women in Great Britain. The double standard that she was experiencing at the relatively painless level of social intercourse was a reality that cut deeply into the lives of innumerable women.

A young woman was in Newgate for the murder of her child. The father, a member of the Oxford community, had abandoned her and 'fallen back, with no accusing conscience, on his easy social life, and possibly his academic honours'.[18] With characteristic directness Josephine went to the woman and spoke to her of 'the God who saw the injustice done, and cares for her'. When her sentence had expired she came to live with the Butlers, the first of many 'fallen' women whom the Butlers sought out and took into their home.

One 'fallen' woman whom the Butlers were unable to help was an acrobat with a travelling circus which came to town. She told them of her hopes of abandoning her work, 'the most innocent part of which was probably her acrobatic performances', to serve the God of her newly found faith. She attended churches and chapels secretly, fled from the circus but was recaptured. Again Josephine expresses pity for the sufferer and condemns the acquiescence of educated male society.

It was a Sunday evening in hot summer weather. I had been sitting for some time at my open window to breathe more freely the sultry air, and it seemed to me that I heard a wailing cry somewhere among the trees in the twilight which was deepening into night. It was a woman's cry — a woman aspiring to heaven and dragged back to hell — and my heart was pierced with pain. I longed to leap from the window, and flee with her to some place of refuge. It passed. I cannot explain the nature of the impression, which remains with me to this day; but beyond that twilight, and even in the midst of that pitiful cry, there seemed to dawn a ray of light and to sound a note not wholly of despair. The light was far off, yet coming near; and the slight summer breeze in those tall trees had in them a whisper of the future. But when the day dawned it seemed to show me again more plainly than ever the great wall of prejudice, built up on a foundation of lies, which surrounded a whole world of sorrows, griefs, injustices, and crimes which must not be spoken of — no, not even in whispers — and which it seemed to me then that no human power could ever reach or remedy. And I met again the highly-educated, masculine world in our evening gatherings, more than ever resolved to hold my peace — to speak little with men, but much with God. No doubt the experience of those years influenced in some degree my maturer judgement of what is called '*educated* public opinion'.[19]

The chief charge which she brought against this 'educated public opinion' was that it refused to deal with most of the pressing human problems of the day. One might discuss the merits of different translations of Thucydides, but the double standard of sexual morality must not be questioned. If a woman became pregnant, she — not her seducer — was held to be at fault.

A book [*Ruth*] was published at the time by Mrs. Gaskell and was much discussed. This led to expressions of judgment which seemed to me false — fatally false. A moral sin in a woman was spoken of as immensely worse than in a man; there was no comparison to be found between them. A pure woman, it was reiterated should be absolutely ignorant of a certain class of ills in the world, albeit those evils bore with murderous cruelty on other women. One young man seriously declared that he would not allow his own mother to read such a book as that under discussion — a book which seemed to me to have a very wholesome tendency though dealing with a painful subject. Silence was thought to be the great duty of all on such subjects. On one occasion, when I was distressed by a bitter case of wrong inflicted on a very young girl, I ventured to speak to one of the wisest men — so esteemed — in the University in the hope that he would suggest some means not of helping her, but of bringing to a sense of his crime the man who had wronged her. The Sage, speaking kindly however, sternly advocated silence and inaction. It could only do harm to open up in any way such a question as this; it was dangerous to arouse a sleeping lion. I left him in some amazement and discouragement, and for a long time there echoed in my heart the terrible prophetic words of the painter-poet Blake — and indelicate as he may have been judged then — whose prophecy has only been averted by a great and painful awakening:

> The harlot's curse, from street to street
> Shall weave old England's winding sheet.[20]

Josephine struggled against the peculiar blend of stubbornness on some issues and scepticism on others. Those dons who might have been expected to share the Butlers' enlightened views were crippled by the intellectual detachment that had been part of their academic training and their need to find support in the scholarly community.

> What struck me more than all was the surprising want of courage in expressing, even if it were felt, any opinion differing from that of the celibate mass around. Original thinkers there were at Oxford who prepared, in the retirement of their studies, works which afterwards influenced not only the Universities, but the world. But in social intercourse caution and timidity prevailed. The need to keep every intellectual possibility open (except of course certain moral questions) became almost a mental disease. If on a splendid summer morning one remarked, 'It is a fine day,' the man addressed would hesitate to endorse the fact, — not lest his doing so should entail consequences, but simply from the habit of holding everything in suspense, the unhappy philosopher sometimes not being sure that he himself existed.[21]

This scepticism applied most particularly of course to theological matters. For the first time Josephine had to deal with people who questioned all of the religious assumptions that were so dear to her. She was taken aback when an acquaintance, smiling with pity and mild contempt, said to her, 'But you surely can't imagine that we regard as of any authority the ground upon which you base your belief.' The Greys, although enthusiastic supporters of free thought and the right of individuals to develop their own beliefs, had rarely had to deal with the scepticism that might follow from it. George and Josephine learned that the profession of Christian faith which they had taken for granted was a minority view that must be upheld in an indifferent and sometimes hostile world.

In 1857 the Butlers moved to Cheltenham. Josephine's ill health is usually given as the reason behind their decision to abandon Oxford. All of her life she suffered episodes of 'weakness' of the lungs; the dampness of the Thames valley brought on a series of bronchial attacks. One cannot help but wonder whether the uncongeniality of the moral, as well as the political, climate played a part in the decision to move; whether, indeed, Josephine's ill health had been exacerbated, or even brought on, by the tensions. Not only were the Butlers' general views rejected; George had been disappointed in his hope of introducing art and geography into the Oxford curriculum and he had failed to be elected to the Chair of Latin.[22]

In Cheltenham the Butlers found a more congenial atmosphere. Avoiding the colony of retired Army and Foreign Service officers, they made friends among the intellectuals. George became Vice-Principal of Cheltenham College and with Josephine attacked the question of education for women in general, and specifically at Cheltenham Ladies' College. The Butlers had time to enjoy the pleasures of their growing family: they had three sons, George, Stanley, and Charles, and just after the move to Cheltenham Josephine gave birth to a daughter, Eva. George and Josephine spent the winters reading modern Italian literature, discussing the American Civil War with students and planning for the summer holiday in Britain where they walked and fished, recording the countryside in finely articulated sketches and watercolours. (Although these trips became less frequent under the pressures of growing political involvement, they always remained a great source of pleasure.)

In 1863 tragedy struck. Its impact was so profoundly shattering that Josephine and George never entirely recovered. One evening when they returned from a drive the four children rushed to the upstairs landing to greet them. Eva, tripping, fell over the banister onto the floor below, to lie at her parents' feet. A few hours later she died.

This agonizing loss left an ineradicable impression. The contrast between good and evil that had played so large a role in Josephine's imagination, now became horrifyingly real. Passionate, strong-willed, generous and affectionate, the child had resembled her mother. 'Her life was one flowing stream of

mirth and fun and abounding love.' The contrast between the
life-affirming child and the corpse destroyed in one cruel blow
all of Josephine's attempts to hold good and evil together under
a benevolent God.

> Never can I lose that memory, — the fall, the sudden cry, and
> then the silence It was pitiful to see her, helpless in her father's
> arms, her little drooping head resting on his shoulder and her
> beautiful golden hair, all stained with blood, falling over his
> arm! Would to God that I had died that death for her.[23]

Each parent was upheld by the need to console the other, by the
demands of the remaining children and, finally, by a renewal of
faith.

It was, however, painful to remain at Cheltenham. They were
oppressed by their memories and troubled by Josephine's
intermittent illhealth, and it was a relief when in 1865 an
interesting offer came from Liverpool College. The post of
Headmaster to the College was not as academically distinguished
as the prestigious Chair of Latin at Oxford which George Butler
had hoped for and failed to receive, but it was work that was
particularly suited to his gifts. His liberal sympathies were fully
enlisted by a school that offered a public school education to
mercantile families, easing the transition into the upper middle
class. The college was unique in extending an invitation to
Jewish families. George had the pleasure of planning a
curriculum enlarged to include Old Testament and Hebrew
studies and, in a great seaport and shipping community, there
was finally a place for his beloved study of geography. Nor was
the traditional curriculum slighted; during George's years of
tenure, Liverpool College sent a series of able classical scholars
to Oxford and Cambridge.

Josephine, however, found no peace of mind. The pain of her
memories was not eased by playing her piano or working with
her paint-box. In the grimy outskirts of a large seaport the
healing pleasures of riding and walking in a beautiful countryside
were impossible. She felt a desparate need to be of use.

> I became possessed with an irresistible desire to go forth, and
> find some pain keener than my own — to meet with people
> more unhappy than myself (for I knew there were thousands

of such). I did not exaggerate my own trial; I only knew that my heart ached night and day, and that the only solace possible would seem to be to find other hearts which ached night and day; and with more reason than mine. I had no clear idea beyond that, no plan for helping others; my sole wish was to plunge into the heart of some human misery and to say (as I now knew I could) to afflicted people, 'I understand, I, too, have suffered'.[24]

Shunning the charitable societies and an aristocratic tradition that permitted a Lady Bountiful to bestow some small acts of kindness on the 'worthy' poor, Josephine sought out the forgotten and the derelict, the outcasts of society. She found them among the pauper women housed in the dark and prison-like caverns of Brownlow Hill Workhouse. Work of the most degrading kind was considered to be good for the character, and the inmates were given the task of picking oakum. Some were prisoners, some were vagrants who worked in return for a night's lodging and a piece of bread.

I went down to the oakum sheds and begged admission. I was taken into an immense, gloomy vault, filled with women and girls — more than two hundred, probably, at that time. I sat on the floor among them and picked oakum. They laughed at me, and told me my fingers were of no use for that work, which was true. But while we laughed we became friends.

Josephine's fervently evangelical faith seized this opportunity for missionary work and she suggested that they learn a few verses from the Bible. She describes her next visit.

I recollect a tall, dark, handsome girl standing up in our midst, among the damp refuse and lumps of tarred rope, and repeating without a mistake and in a not unmusical voice, clear and ringing, that wonderful fourteenth chapter of St. John's Gospel: — the words of Jesus all through, ending with 'Peace I leave with you, My peace I give unto you. Let not your heart be troubled, neither let it be afraid.' She had selected it herself; and they listened in perfect silence, this audience — wretched, draggled, ignorant, criminal, some; and wild and defiant, others. The tall, dark-haired girl had prepared the way for me; and I said, 'Now let us all kneel, and cry to that same Jesus who spoke those words,' and down on their knees they fell, every one of them, reverently, on that damp stone floor, some saying the words after me, others moaning and weeping. It was a strange sound, that united wail — continuous, pitiful, strong — like a great sigh or murmur of vague desire and hope, issuing from the heart of despair, piercing the gloom and murky atmosphere of that vaulted room, and reaching to the heart of God.[25]

Not content with comforting the victims of poverty, Josephine began to investigate its causes. She found, as would be expected in a great port like Liverpool, that in order to postpone the transition from poverty to destitution many poor women became prostitutes. This expedient solution, however, merely hastened their downward slide. When they became infected with venereal disease, they were turned out to die. With the exception of a few small refuges, there was nowhere they could go. Marion, young and vulnerable, desperately ill with what proved to be venereal disease, was one such woman. Josephine invited her into her own home. Braving the wrath of their respectable neighbours in Sefton Park, George met the carriage at the door, and offering their guest his arm, escorted her to her room. She lived with them until she died the following year. When she was buried Josephine had her coffin filled with white camellias, symbol of purity.

It soon became clear that the Butlers could not house the numbers of desperate, destitute women who found their way to the door. Josephine enlisted the support of her recently widowed sister Fanny, and secured a house nearby, financing the venture through a pointed appeal to 'wealthy and fashionable young men'.[26] The Home of Rest became a refuge, not only for the sick and dying, but also for those who were healthy but had no prospect of employment.

Though the Butlers' chief satisfaction came from the individuals whom they were able to help and the lasting friendships they formed, they were keenly aware of the need to deal with the social conditions by which these women had been victimized. Josephine had long been resentful of the society that deplored idleness and viewed poverty as a social crime and yet at the same time put paid work out of reach of all respectable women. In a bitter response to a man who had said that no occupations ought to be opened to women she wrote:

> I see now that you reject the ethics of Christianity altogether. Please reconsider about marriage. Two and a half million women working for bread. They would marry, but there are many more women than men in the country. According to your theory you have two and a half million women for whom there is starvation or prostitution.[27]

As an alternative to the oakum shed, she persuaded the Committee of the Workhouse to start a hostel which would provide different work. Sewing was first offered; later the girls were helped to start a small envelope factory.

These small efforts were, she believed, merely stop-gap; women would not find decent employment until they had been properly educated. Josephine's wide understanding of social issues, her keen interest in scholarship, her appreciation of the need for a practical, as well as an intellectual, education, and her social position as the wife of a distinguished educator — all made her an ideal leader of the movement for higher education for women. For a time it seemed likely that this cause would fully enlist her energies. Emily Davies and her London Committee had asked Cambridge University to permit women to take the University examinations. In 1868 a petition signed by 800 women was drawn up with this request. Josephine was chosen to present the petition and spent several weeks speaking with undergraduates and with sympathetic older men: F. D. Maurice, the founder of Queen's College for Women; Henry Sidgwick; and Frederick Myers. Her conviction that the advancement of women depended upon education that provided training for work led her to initiate correspondence with educational leaders in Europe and the United States and to collect and edit an important group of essays entitled *Woman's Work and Woman's Culture*, which appeared in 1869.

These activities were rudely interrupted. In 1869 when the Butlers returned from their annual holiday, Josephine was met by a telegram from her friend Elizabeth Wolstenholme[28] urging her to lead the campaign against the Contagious Diseases Act of 1866. Josephine hesitated. It was, she well knew, a battle against formidable odds, pitting the poor and female against the rich and male. Victorian society would not look kindly on a wife who, with every possibility of domestic happiness, left the sanctuary of her home and the security of marriage to an Anglican priest to go to the aid of women of the gutter. She would be exposed to a double evil: the viciousness of the life of the street and the equally dehumanizing anger of a male middle class that would turn on anyone who questioned its privileges and assumptions. The cause would consume all her energies and bring down scorn, hatred, and possibly even violence upon her family. It would certainly affect and might even ruin her husband's career. She shrank from accepting a burden that would inflict suffering not only on herself but on those who were close to her. For weeks she was tormented by indecision.

> I could not bear the thought of making my dear companion a sharer of the pain; yet I saw that we must needs be united in this as in everything else. I had tried to arrange to suffer alone but I could not *act* alone, if God should indeed call me to action. It seemed to me cruel to have to tell him of the call, and to say to him that I must try and stand in the breach. My heart was shaken by the foreshadowing of what I knew he would suffer. I went to him one evening when he was alone, all the household having retired to rest.[29]

George's response was simple and direct: 'Go and the Lord go with you.' And he did not merely offer the comfort and support of a loving husband at home; he went into the streets and the lecture halls on behalf of his wife's crusade.

3   *National Association for the Repeal of the Contagious Diseases Acts, 1869—1906: Commitment and Action*

The social implications of the Contagious Diseases Act of 1864 had not been perceived at once when, quietly introduced by the military as a means of checking the rise of venereal disease in the services, it made prostitutes liable to state inspection. On any pretext a policeman could detain a woman and require that she present herself before the Justice of the Peace. If the Justice decided that she was a prostitute, he would order the woman to submit to an examination — a procedure which the Abolitionists referred to as 'instrumental rape'. No definition of the word prostitute was given; the word of a single policeman, a member of a special police force which was not part of the regular British system of justice, sufficed to bring a woman to court; no corroborative witness was needed.

If the examination proved her to be diseased, she was detained in a special hospital until she was cured, though for not more than three months. If she refused the examination or ran away from the hospital, she was liable to imprisonment. This Act applied to eleven garrison towns: in 1866 and 1868 other Contagious Diseases Acts were passed extending the geographical scope of the provisions. Aldershot, Canterbury, Chatham, Colchester, Dover, Gravesend, Maidstone, Plymouth, Devonport, Portsmouth, Sheerness, Shorncliffe, Southampton, Winchester, Windsor, Woolwich; in Ireland, Cork, Queenstown, and the Curraugh were the affected areas. It was the Regulationists' hope that these provisions would one day be applied to the whole of England. This goal is reflected in the title of the organization: what was in 1866 called the British Branch of the Continental Association for the Control of Prostitution by Governmental Regulation, in 1868 became the Association for Promoting the Extension of the Contagious Diseases Act of 1866 to the Civil Population of the United Kingdom.

The Acts' supporters included most of the upper- and middle-class males whose view of society and sexuality was in some degree dependent upon the perpetuation of the institution of prostitution. It also included, surprisingly, many liberals who might have been expected to object to the suspension of civil rights and to the dangers of creating a corrupt and brutal police force with extra-legal powers. But while some liberals undoubtedly were uneasy about the social aspects of the Acts, they supported them as medical necessities. Venereal disease was spreading at an alarming rate. Dr Graham Balfour, in looking at the statistics in 1859, calculated that one man out of four was afflicted.[30] If it was a matter of choosing between the health of the Armed Services, the dedicated and heroic men who had made Britain the strongest country in Europe, and the civil rights of prostitutes, the choice was clear. Furthermore, venereal disease affected the unborn as well as the living; all measures to stamp it out must be enacted. The whole of the medical profession, including the few women doctors, supported the Act and the

Lancet waged an emotional campaign on its behalf. The Heads of the colleges at Oxford endorsed it. Liberal clergymen like F. D. Maurice and A. P. Stanley regarded it — at first, as a necessary evil.

In short, in her crusade against the Acts, Miss Wolstenholme would have all of powerful Britain against her. It would be a struggle against fearfully unequal odds: rich against poor, men against women. Little wonder that she felt the need of a saint, a person of superhuman strength to lead the campaign. She realized that the leader must be a woman, and a woman of special imagination, one who could identify with the wrongs which the Acts imposed on other women. She must be a married woman whose respectability could not be questioned. (While the Victorians did not use our psychological terms, 'sublimation' and 'repression', they were aware of the concepts. The motives of a single woman would immediately have been suspect.) Furthermore, she must be a member of the upper class, a lady who could deal with her opponents not as a supplicant but as an equal. Josephine Butler was uniquely qualified. In addition to being married and a 'lady', she was an extremely effective public speaker and a woman of tremendous energy and persuasive powers.

While Josephine and Miss Wolstenholme knew that they could ultimately succeed only through making converts among the rich and powerful, they began by appealing to their natural constituency — the poor. As head of the Ladies National Association for Abolition, Josephine published a manifesto in the *Daily News* which enumerated the objections to the Acts. Among these were the violation of civil rights of women, the condoning of vice, and the double standard. Florence Nightingale signed. So did many leading Quakers, including Mary Carpenter, Mary Priestman, and John Bright's sister, Ursula. Harriet Martineau, who had earlier written several articles questioning the Act, gave her full support. As the pace quickened, Josephine travelled from town to town speaking of the evils of regulation.

Though she was inspired by the vision of a unified society, Josephine was not above using society's divisions for her political ends. She pointed out that while all men, rich and poor, would gain from regulation, only the daughters of the poor would be required to pay the price. She was persuasive. The farmer, who was too near the poverty line to totally ignore the dangerous attractiveness of the city, and already willing to see the police as instruments of a repressive aristocracy, became alarmed. He pictured his innocent daughter walking home from prayer meeting with a basket of eggs over her arm being accosted by the dreaded police — or by a supplier for a brothel in Harley Street — and disappearing, perhaps for ever. (With the sensational suicide of Mrs Percy in 1875, who killed herself as the result of the humiliation of police detention, and by the later revelations of the scope of the white-slave trade in Britain and on the Continent he was to learn that his fantasy had its counterpart in reality.) At the urging of the Abolitionists, he came to see prostitution as the exploitation of the poor by the rich — the Industrial Revolution's sinister modern equivalent of the medieval *droit de seigneur*. So convincing were the Abolitionists' arguments, so widespread their activities (Josephine Butler travelled over 2700 miles in one year, addressing ninety-nine meetings and four conferences)[31] that they began to succeed. In a by-election in Colchester in 1870 they won their first election, defeating the regulationist Sir Henry Storks.

In addition to fanning the ardour of the poor, who had the most to gain by repeal — Josephine knew that she must also enlist support from the liberal rich who had traditionally and at the highest levels of government spoken on behalf of the weak and the poor. She must speak to her own class. Encouraged by the support of the Baptist minister, Charles Birrell, who had drawn her attention to the Brownlow Hill Workhouse, she and her husband had already appealed to the churches, especially to the Anglican clergy. F. D. Maurice and other churchmen began to be alarmed by the Acts' legal implications. By 1871 her political support had made her a powerful figure, whose views could no longer be ignored; the Royal Commission on the Contagious Diseases Acts asked her to testify. Her statement included evidence on the Acts' brutalizing effects and, more generally, on the evils of the money-making aspects of prostitution. Fearlessly she confronted her upper-class listeners.

I have seen girls bought and sold just as young girls were, at the time of the slave trade. Are you not aware that there are young gentlemen among the higher classes who will pay? When a young gentleman sends to a professional brothel for a girl, he pays for her — is that not paying? . . . I will set a floodlight on your doings — I mean the immorality which exists among gentlemen of the upper class. [She concludes that] the Acts are abhorred by the country as a tyranny of the upper classes against the lower classes, as an injustice practised by men on women, and as an insult to the moral sense of the people — an iniquity which is abhorred by Christian England.[32]

Her theological tone seems to have further stiffened the opposition of the majority of Lords on the Commission, but her point about child prostitution was taken up. The Bruce Bill, introduced in 1872, would have repealed the Acts, raised the age of consent from 12 to 14, and levied punishment against those who obtained women of any age by false pretences. It did not, however, abolish the principle of regulation; in fact by introducing a new law which would do away with the special police and give the same extraordinary powers of detainment to the police all over the country, it widened the net. When Josephine was asked to accept the Bill on the grounds that half a loaf is better than none, she replied, 'Not when it is poisoned.' The Abolitionists were divided, some supporting, others opposing, the Bill; in the end Josephine's views carried. The Bill, which suited no one, was withdrawn by Gladstone.

The confusion over the Bruce Bill and the disappointment at not winning more votes in the election of 1872, particularly among the newly enfranchised, was countered by the accomplishment of having made a new and powerful convert. As a consequence of the defeat of Gladstone, James B. Stansfeld was released from his duties as a Cabinet member and President of the Poor Law Board. He joined the National Association, thereby incurring the anger of *The Times*. 'It is to be sincerely regretted that a statesman of Mr. Stansfeld's eminence should identify himself with such an hysterical crusade, in which it is impossible to take part without herding with prurient and cynical fanatics.'[33] The regard in which he was held as a highly placed public servant and his knowledge of the practical workings of Parliament made him an invaluable leader. It was he who led the Crusade to its final victory and repeal of the Second Contagious Diseases Act in 1883.[34]

In the beginning Josephine had tried to confine the use of her energies to combating the state regulation of prostitution. After she had handed over her leadership to Stansfeld, she turned her attention to the traffic in prostitutes between Britain and the Continent. In 1874, armed with letters from the Society of Friends and from Lord Derby, the Tory Foreign Secretary, she proceeded on a grand tour of continental cities — their police, their brothels, and their lock hospitals. She visited all of the major cities that maintained the decrees inherited from the Code Napoleon, but she went first to the capital of vice — Paris.

Writing to her husband, Josephine gives a lengthy and unforgettable account of her meeting with C. R. Lecour, the chief of the dreaded Agents des Moeurs of Paris. The confrontation between the small, slight Englishwoman, immaculate in her dark silks, and the police officer whom another source describes as having 'the pedantry of ignorance and the pride of office'[35] has something of the dramatic flavour of the meeting between Scarpia and Tosca in Puccini's opera. It is uniquely revealing, both of Josephine's force — her honesty and directness, her fearlessness — and of the deviousness and tenacity of the male psychology which she faced. She begins by describing her approach to his office.

I spent a part of yesterday at the Prefecture of the Morals' Police; it was an exceedingly painful visit to me. I was struck by the grandeur of the externals of the Prefect's office, and the evidence of the political and social power wielded by this man Lecour. The office is one of those handsome blocks on the banks of the Seine. It has great gateways, within which guards are pacing up and down. It has a broad stone staircase. I reached the top of this and the Prefect's outer door, over which in large gold letters, were printed the words: *Arrestations, Service des Moeurs*. I was out of breath and an old guard stared at me as I gazed at those words — 'service of morals'. I knew it all before, but here the fact came upon me, with peculiar and painful vividness, that man had made woman his degraded slave by a decree which is heralded in letters of gold, and by a tyranny of procedure which, if it were applied to men, would soon set Paris in flames, and not merely a few of its buildings. That 'Service des Moeurs' seemed a most impudent proclamation of the father of lies; it so clearly and palpably means the 'Service de Debauche'.

After having been deliberately kept waiting for half an hour she was finally shown into Lecour's office.

Lecour appears to me — and I tried to judge without prejudice — very shallow, vain, talkative; his arguments are of the weakest; he has a certain dramatic cleverness, and acts all he says with face, arms and legs. His countenance is to me very repulsive, although his face, which is in the barber's block style, might be called handsome as to hair, eyes, eyelashes, etc. He has a fixed smile — that of a hypocrite. He is simply a shallow actor, an acrobat, a clever stage-manager. Intoxicated with the sense of power, chattering and gesticulating like an ape, at the head of an office which is as powerful as that of the Roman Prefects of the City in the time of Rome's corruption. And such is the man who stands in the position of holding in his hand, so to speak, the keys of heaven and hell, the power of life and death, for the women of Paris!

Josephine sets the tone.

I stood up before him, declining to sit. I told him who I was and why I had come to Paris. He said he knew very well who I was. His manner became rather excited and uneasy. I continued all the time to look steadily — but not rudely — at him, to see if there was any sincerity in him. He became more and more talkative, as if to drown me with words; in fact, I could hardly get a word spoken. Therefore I just put a distinct question or two in the few pauses allowed, as if desirous of information, and then he started off volubly with his answers. This was useful to me, for he surely said much more than was prudent. I asked him the latest statistical results. I asked if vice and disease were diminished or increased the last five years in Paris. He answered promptly. 'Oh! increased, they go always increasing, continually increasing.' Then I tried to hold him to a point. And got him to tell me the causes of this increase. He attributed it solely to two things, which I think will surprise you, i.e. the temporary ascendancy of the Commune and the increasing coquetry of women. I could not restrain an expression of contempt at this last remark, which he seemed to think quite a satisfactory and exhaustive answer. I then made an onslaught and said (looking up at a speck of blue sky which I saw through the window, and holding on to it, as it were) that I — we — consider the whole system which he represents an absurdity; that men are immoral and liable to the physical

scourge of vice as well as women, while the system only attacks
women; and that any theory of health, based on injustice and a
supposed necessity for vice, must end in not only ridiculous
and total failure, but an increased confusion and vice. He
listened impatiently, still with his fixed smile. I purposely
avoided speaking of morality or religion, and tried to nail him
to the logical view of necessary failure through injustice and
one-sidedness of application.

Lecour returns to his theme: the immorality of women.

I interrupted rather abruptly by reminding him that, in this
crime — prostitution — which he was denouncing, there were
two parties implicated. I asked him if he had been so long at
the Prefecture without it occurring to him that the men for
whose health he labours — and for whom he enslaves women
— are guilty, and perhaps a little irony in my tone roused him
and he became very excited. He left his retreat and came out
into the room and paced up and down. Then he acted, in the
most disagreeable manner, an imaginary scene between a poor
woman — a temptress — and a young man. He seemed to
think that I was an ignoramus and that this would convert me.
He described in the old hackneyed, sentimental manner, with
which we are familiar, an 'honourable young man', dining out
and partaking 'un peu genereusement' of wine; a girl meets
him, marks his unsteady gait — then he even acted how she
would place her arm in his and tempt him. There was no
comparison, he said, between the two; the man was simply
careless; the woman was a deliberate, determined corrupter.
'With what motive?' I asked, 'tell me, is it not often the case that
the woman is poor, for I know that in Paris work is scarcely to
be found just now; or else she is a slave in one of your
permitted houses, and is sent out by her employers on what is
their, other than her, business?' He smilingly denied that and
said, 'Oh, no, no, it is not poverty, it is simply coquetry.' Then
he said in a pompous and would-be impressive manner,
'Madam, remember this: that women constantly injure honest
men, but no man ever injures an honest woman.' Then he
stood as one who has cast down a challenge which could not be
taken up. 'Excuse me,' I said, 'you, yourself, have written

otherwise in your book. You speak of wives and honest girls injured by immoral and depraved men.' Then he changed his tone and replied, 'Ah, yes, but all that belongs to the region of romance. I am only speaking of what can be recognized and forbidden by the police. They cannot touch the region of romance; nor can the State. You would not desire that it should, would you?' I replied that I desired justice, but that I could not expect justice in this matter at the hands of the police. Then he suddenly assumed a solemn expression and changed his line of argument. He said, 'Madam, ecoutez! Moi, je suis religieux. I am as religious as yourself.' Then he said, as a religious man, he must admire the punishment of vice (in women only), and that where you could not punish, you must regulate; that, among all the plans the world has ever tried, which is of any avail, and the thing of which I would myself become an advocate, when I had had more experience, was his own system — the system of arrests, constant arrests of women. He kept reiterating that he was as religious as myself, and I said rather sharply 'that may be, sir, I did not come here, however, to speak to you about religion, but about justice'. The religion he spoke of was merely a bit of sentiment, unworthy of the name. I brought him back to the failure hygienically, of his system, on account of its injustice. He shrugged his shoulders and said 'but who hopes to see perfect justice established? Who hopes for great hygienic results?' 'Those', I replied, 'belong, I suppose, to the region of romance.'[36]

Josephine left, having obtained his permission to visit the hospital of Saint-Lazare. As an appendix to her account, she noted that Lecour was finally removed from office as a result of an investigation which she among others had instituted. His career, however, was not entirely over. As a reward for services to his country, his God, and womanhood, his friends had him appointed honorary bell-ringer of Notre Dame.

From Paris she proceeded to Lyons, then Marseilles, Naples, Rome, Florence, Milan, Geneva, and Neuchâtel. She travelled not only as an investigator but as a speaker, and reported on her findings at the inaugural meeting of the British and Continental Federation for the Abolition of the Governmental Regulation of Prostitution held in Liverpool in 1875. In the following year

Yves Guyot, the Radical Minister of Public Works and a journalist, recalled Josephine's address to the Municipal Court of Paris.

Mrs. Butler gave me one of the greatest impressions that I have received in my life. Elegant, refined, of an upright figure; she gave quite an original piquancy. She expressed herself with great simplicity; but by this simplicity she reached irresistible oratorical effects. Everybody felt moved in his inmost fibres by this pathetic address, which owed nothing to rhetoric, but was the spontaneous outcome of an intense feeling of justice and humanity. She carried her hearers away from the shabby considerations which form the woof of her conventional morality. When pure woman that she was, bruised in all she had taken up, she denounced — in the name of the sympathy which should unite all human beings — the outlawry to which they are subject, who could have resisted her generous allurement?[37]

This meeting was followed by two in the United States, led by representatives of the British National Association and sponsored by William Lloyd Garrison and Wendell Phillips. These men had seen the achievement of their goal of the abolition of slavery in the United States; their energies were available to combat another tyranny. Josephine Butler had shown them that the cause of 'the new Abolitionists' was an extension of the old, as both derived from the need to fight any system that denied full humanity to a special group.

As always, Josephine placed herself in the thick of battle. In 1880 Alfred Dyer, a Quaker publisher, wrote to the *Daily News* of a young Englishwoman who had been lured into going to Brussels on the promise of marriage and was then kidnapped and held captive in a brothel. Knowing that this was not an isolated case, Dyer sought Josephine Butler's help. As a result of their charges the Belgian Chief of the Special Police, his assistants, and eleven brothel keepers were thrown into prison.

Still, it was one thing for the British to acknowledge that such crimes were taking place on the Continent; it was quite another to admit that they had their origins on British soil. Despite the release of thirty-four British girls as a result of the Belgian investigation, Parliament refused to take action: in 1883 the House of Commons rejected a bill, recommended by the Lords' committee, which would have raised the age of consent from 12 to 16 and severely penalized those engaged in the transport of women for profit.

It seems possible that nothing further would have been done had it not been for the efforts of the journalist William Thomas Stead. Stead was a Dissenter with broad social concerns and a taste for the sensational. He proposed to prove in an extraordinary and irrefutable way that there was traffic in the white-slave trade in Britain; he himself would steal a girl, sell her to a brothel, and then write up the crime for his newspaper. He enlisted Josephine's help in this dangerous and unpleasant venture.

At the time Josephine had living with her Rebecca Jarrett, an alcoholic ex-brothel-keeper, a convert to Christianity who had been brought to the Butlers' by members of the Salvation Army. Since no suspicion would be aroused by this professional resuming her former trade, Stead proposed that she be asked to assume a leading role in the proceedings. Josephine, knowing the trauma that the women would be forced to endure and the possible dangers, felt torn. H. Scott Holland, the leader of the Christian Social Union, who encountered her during this difficult period, has left this description.

A face looked at me out of a hurrying hansom, which arrested and frightened me. It was framed on pure and beautiful lines but it was smitten and bitten into as by some East wind that blighted it into grey sadness. It had seen that which took all colour and joy out of it. . . . Shortly after, all European civilisation shook with the horror of Mr. Stead's disclosures . . . I knew I had seen Mrs. Butler in the thick of the terrible work she had undertaken for God. She was passing through her martyrdom. The splendid beauty of her face, so spiritual in its high and clear outlines, bore the mark of that death upon it to which she stood daily and hourly committed. There was no hell on earth into which she would not willingly travel if, by sacrificing herself she could reach a hand of help to those poor children whom nothing short of such a sacrifice could touch. The sorrow of it passed into her being. She had the look of the world's grim tragedies in her eyes. She had dared to take the measure of the black infamy of sin; and the terrible knowledge had left its cruel mark upon a soul of strange and singular purity.[38]

Rebecca Jarrett contracted to buy Eliza Armstrong from her mother for five pounds and then handed her over to Stead. Under the protection of a member of the Salvation Army disguised as a prostitute, the child was taken to a brothel for a night. She was returned unharmed to Rebecca Jarrett and spent several weeks with the Butlers.

A series of articles exposing the low life of London was published in the *Pall Mall Gazette* in 1885. The final instalment, entitled 'The Maiden Tribute of Modern Babylon', ending with the first-hand report of the kidnapping, created a sensation. The House of Commons was terrified that Stead would proceed to give the names of the wealthy and powerful patrons and partners in crime, names which would undoubtedly include many distinguished members of Parliament. They resolved on immediate action. The Criminal Law Amendment Bill, creating severe penalties for participants and raising the age of consent from 12 to 16, was passed in the same year.

With the enactment of this legislation Josephine's active leadership in public affairs came to an end. More and more she was concerned with personal matters; the affairs of her children and grandchildren, long-deferred holiday trips to the Continent, a move to Winchester where George was appointed Canon. Her husband's health became a constant worry. His death in 1890 was a loss from which Josephine never fully recovered.

Old interests, however, never completely lost their appeal. Visits to friends were scheduled between public appearances on behalf of the 'Cause'. Josephine encouraged two Americans, Dr Kate Bushnell and her missionary friend Mrs Andrews, to make a tour of India on behalf of the Indian women, especially the prostitutes attached to the British Army. She herself went to Italy, and, in emulation of her heroine Catherine of Siena, exhorted a somewhat nervous and diffident Pope. While staying with friends near Geneva, noting that 'the smell of powder is always agreeable to one in a fight on a moral issue', the aging warrior lent her support to the local Abolitionist cause which, being opposed by well-organized and powerful brothel-keepers, was defeated. Increasingly confined, she wielded her pen: her causes now included the Dreyfus case, the Jews in Russia, and the Boer War. From the introspection of old age she wrote long letters to her grandchildren and to old friends, summarizing her religious views and searching for the meaning of a life that had been joyful — and terrible. She died on 29 December 1906.

2 Most Tenacious Christian Faith

Josephine Butler's friends — and indeed her enemies — agreed that religious fervour was the source of her genius. One of the members of the Royal Commission of 1871 admitted ruefully that while the Commission did not enjoy being harangued and preached at by a woman, Mrs Butler had made an extraordinary impression. 'I am not accustomed to religious phraseology, but I cannot give any idea of the effect Mrs. Butler produced, except by saying that the influence of the spirit of God was there.'[1] James Stuart, Henry Wilson, James Stansfeld, William Thomas Stead were alike in acknowledging the spiritual dimension of her personality. The poet F. W. H. Myers attributed his conversion to her. 'Christianity came to me in a very potent way through the agency of Josephine Butler. She introduced me to Christianity, so to say, by an inner door; not to the encumbering forms but to its heart of fire.'[2] Benjamin Jowett disliked Josephine, whose overt femininity was an intolerable threat to his insecurities, yet he confessed that she had 'a touch of genius'.[3] Scott Holland commented 'Men could never be the same after they had known Josephine Butler.'[4]

1   Worldly Evangelical

The Grey tradition which Josephine had inherited centred on faith in a loving and active God, belief in man and woman as made in the 'image of God', and the conviction that society was the stage on which the drama of salvation would be enacted. Ironically perhaps, the very intensity of her faith and its particular social bent separated her from institutional Christianity, even from the evangelical wing of her own Anglican Church, where she might have expected to find a congenial point of view. The issues that concerned many churchmen — the place of the established Church in an increasingly secular society, the threat to faith of rationalism, biblical criticism, and the scientific method, the relations between denominations — seemed irrelevant to the Butlers. Though highly intelligent, they were not primarily thinkers — they were 'doers of the Word'.

In discussing Josephine's faith we are on safe ground in assuming that her views and those of George were very close. Her grandson may be overstating the case when he describes her biography of her husband as really her own autobiography since in all important matters they were 'as one'. Yet Josephine herself, who generally denied that human intermediaries had in any way influenced her relationship to God,[5] made one exception: she gave eloquent testimony to the effect that George had had on her spiritual development, both in the views which he had transmitted and in his sustaining and supportive strength.[6]

Josephine and George were Evangelicals, if this means an emphasis upon personal piety as the mark of conversion, a faith based on scripture and a religiosity centred on social justice.

They were both temperamentally exuberant and life-affirming. It is hard to see them as strict Sabbatarians (though on one occasion George felt the need to apologize to his Swiss host for having so far forgotten his calling as a priest as to have gone fishing on Sunday).[7] They loved music (Josephine was an accomplished pianist), painting, and the companionship of friends. Josephine dressed simply but elegantly. They enjoyed wine, though Josephine, horrified by the devastating effects of alcohol on the poor which she had witnessed, became a tee-totaller in later life. Their letters resound with affirmations of faith and testimonies to the role of God in their lives; yet they are free from the religious haranguing and fussiness, the obsession with sin, that characterize the letters of many Evangelicals, such as Barbara Wilberforce. Josephine was too sensitive, too much of a believer in the integrity of the individual, to indulge in the evangelical passion for analysing the spiritual health of others.

> The abrupt enquiry, 'Is such a one converted or saved', has seemed to me, under some circumstances, as indelicate as the question would be, put to an expectant mother, 'Is the embryo which you bear within you quickened?'[8]

In their dealings with relatives and friends there is a happy free enjoyment of the pleasures of companionship. If the Butlers were Evangelicals, they were worldly Evangelicals.

Deeply committed to the Bible, they seem to have been unperturbed by the challenge to its authority raised by historical criticism. Josephine says of her husband that:

> He was not, strictly speaking, much of a theologian, I suppose. He had little taste for controversial writings, but his Bible was his constant companion. Even in railway journeys — especially in his later years — he almost invariably carried a Bible in his little handbag, and would take it to read during the journey. 'I find', he wrote, 'that the Biblical criticism is too apt to take the place of profitable reading. When I want to derive food and sustenance from the Word of God, I take no commentary, but shut myself up with the plain Word, and meditate on that.[9]

It is hard to believe that the Butlers, with their intelligence and their liberal views, were biblical literalists. After all, they were interested in science and in history and knew many of the scholars whose findings were beginning to question the accuracy of many biblical statements. Given their natural curiosity and their friendship with leading intellectuals, it is surprising that their readings in contemporary theology were, apparently, rather limited. They were friends of Charles Kingsley, Christian de Bunsen, and followed the spiritual trials of James Anthony Froude with great sympathy. F. D. Maurice was an old and valued friend. One would perhaps not expect them to read *Essays and Reviews*, but in the writings of some of the Broad Churchmen they would have found a parallel expression of their views and perhaps help in resolving some of the paradoxes of their faith. They seem to have been untouched by these ideas as well as those of the later Christian Socialists. In 1895, writing to George W. Johnson who had assumed the editorship of the *Christian Socialist*, Josephine seems almost startled to have found a kindred point of view.

> It is strange (and yet not strange when one remembers that the spirit of God works with the same aspiration in human hearts at the same time, even without any communication with each other) that the thoughts expressed in the *Christian Socialist* are just those that I have been preaching and trying hard to press on other people for the last four months.[10]

By then she was an old woman, living in semi-retirement. She would perhaps have been astonished to learn that her example had influenced H. Scott Holland and that her fervent Christian piety and broad social concern had found a new expression in the Christian Social Union of B. F. Westcott and Charles Gore.

Indifferent to contemporary theological issues, the Butlers also refused to be drawn into the arguments on ritual that agitated the Anglican Church. George had been at Oxford during the height of the Tractarian fever. He had listened with admiration to the preaching of Newman, Manning, and Pusey. He was also sympathetic towards the younger men in the movement and deeply regretted the deaths of Matthew Morton and Hurrell Froude. He felt, however, that the original force of the Oxford movement had been lost in the frivolities and attention to superficial detail of the new Puseyites.[11] Josephine recounts their meeting with a young curate who lovingly displayed a long procession of exquisitely embroidered altar cloths, one for every Holy Day of the Church year. Finally, George could stand it no longer.

> 'Do let us get away from this and into the fresh air', he whispered, and we left the Church. As we walked through the meadows he was silent for some time, and then spoke kindly of this young clergyman, at the same time saying, 'I wonder if he thinks that all this prettiness is acceptable to God. Poor young man! We need a revival of spiritual life in our Church, and an awakened sense of the great truths which we have to defend, and of the spiritual warfare in the world around us. There is little reality in all this kind of thing.'[12]

They returned with relief to Winchester and its 'fine old cathedral, grave and grand'.

In Rome Josephine staunchly countered the Pope's assumption that his Church was the only sacramental Church by claiming that 'often I feel that I have the true sacraments in our Church'.[13] Yet the qualifying adverb 'often' is revealing. A faith centred on the response to the social teachings of Christ gave less importance to the sacramental life of the Body of Christ. The traditional Anglican concern with Catholic legitimacy — the Apostolic Succession, the validity of orders, the unity of the Church — held little interest for the Butlers. The arguments over the acts of the early Councils, which drove so many Anglicans over to the Roman Church, seemed irrelevant to George. Both he and Josephine remained convinced that they could find the essential Christianity in the early Church's account of the life of Christ:

> I have been reading the Gospel narrative of our Lord's ministry carefully through and I find it more interesting and wonderful than ever.... The history of the Church during many centuries seems to me to be made up of a mass of heterogeneous elements, but generally full of strife and dissensions and cavilling. One can hardly reconcile the questions of points of doctrine which agitated the Church and were discussed at the several Councils with the simplicity of Christ's own teachings.[14]

Like F. D. Maurice and many of the Broad Churchmen, George had reservations about the Athanasian Creed and its anathemas:

> You have heard me speak of objections that I feel to certain portions of our Church Service. If these weighed very strongly with me, they would drive me out of the Church altogether, but when I look around where do I see any body of Christians, any system on earth, by whomsoever instituted, which is exempt from flaws, the patient endurance of which is a part of the discipline assigned to good men here below. I am sure Mary, who sat at the feet of Jesus, would have been puzzled by the reading over to her of the Athanasian Creed, and the injunction to accept it all at the peril of the loss of her soul; but she understood what Jesus meant when He said, 'One thing is needful' and her knowledge of Him was enough to enable her to choose the better part.[15]

Membership in the 'true' Church as a precondition for salvation was clearly not part of the Butler belief. In their emphasis on individual piety and their 'low' view of the Church they were Protestant. But, unlike many Evangelicals who held a strict view of the qualifications for election, they refused to speculate on the boundaries of the Church. They believed that the Church is 'inclusive not exclusive'. In 1905, quoting Jesus' statement that 'He that is not against us is for us', Josephine remarked that there are 'many outside the Christian pale in whom the spirit of Christ is working'.[16] Some, she continued, had been so repelled by the un-Christian behaviour of so-called Christian governments and the caricature of God drawn in the Creeds that they have 'turned into rebels, or apparently rebels, whose hearts are not estranged from the *true God*'.[17] She compares contemporary Christians (and it seems likely that she would here include the Evangelical with his confidence in his own 'real' faith and the High Churchman and his allegiance to the 'true' Church) with the narrow orthodoxy of the Jews of the first century.

> The contentment which I have heard some Christian people express with the spiritual light and security which is their own portion, while sharing in a great measure the Jewish spirit of exclusiveness and of narrowness of interpretation of God's loving purpose towards humanity, has sometimes filled me with a sad and dreadful fear lest we Christians should in our day be repeating the fatal error of the Jewish people. . . . Such people are in danger of imagining that they have already arrived at 'all truth', and they eagerly build that truth round with a high wall of defensiveness, so that expansion to their view becomes impossible, and the action of the Holy Spirit himself is, for them, restrained. . . . They dare not trust the truth to the care of God.[18]

2 *Inclusive Not Exclusive*

To gain political support for her movement Josephine made the most of her belief in the inclusive nature of the Church. Charles Birrell, the Baptist minister, helped her in Liverpool. Margaret Tanner and Mary Priestman of the Society of Friends in their 'so gentle, so Quakerly' conviction urged her to 'rouse the country'. In giving the history of the Crusade, Josephine provides this listing:

> The religious societies who gave us adherents were, as I have said, first the Friends, then the humblest communities, the Primitive Methodists, the Bible Christians, the United Methodists; then the Wesleyans, who later became a powerful aid to our cause, under the leadership of the late Hugh Price Hughes, a fiery-hearted Welshman, a convinced Abolitionist,

and an eloquent pleader for justice. Then followed, but slowly, slowly, and with divided opinions, the Baptists and the Congregationalists, among whom there were some who remained blind to the meaning of our movement for a very long time. The Scottish Churches slowly followed, the narrowly Calvinistic character of some of them tending to cramp their sympathies. The great leaders of the more enlightened part spoke valiantly for us as early as 1869. I refer to Dr. Guthrie and Dr. Duff, the well-known missionary to India. Nevertheless some few years later, valiant corps of Abolitionists were formed in Edinburgh, Glasgow and Bridge of Allan, men and women, especially women, who laboured with Scottish tenacity and perseverance till quite recent years.[19]

There is no mention of the support of her own denomination, since the intent of her paper is to show the breadth of her support, to dispose of the idea that the Abolitionists were 'a clique of pious people of no width of view'. She may also have continued to resent the reception given George in his early attempt to win over the Church of England to the Cause. In 1872 he had addressed the Annual Church Congress in Nottingham, where his exhortations had been greeted by his clergy brothers with a 'deep and angry howl'. In this speech he had urged the Church of England to assume leadership in a moral cause.

If we constantly take the wrong side, if we are found continually acting in opposition to the conscience of the mass of the people, in public questions; if we walk in the steps of those, whether Baptists or Churchmen, Kings or Parliaments, who burnt the martyrs, drove out Wesley and Whitfield, taxed the American Colonies, upheld slavery, trafficked in Church preferments, supported monopolies, withstood the application of our endowments to purposes of general education, tied up land by vexatious laws, connived at drunkenness and made vice easy and professedly safe, by law — then I think the time is not far off when the cry will come from all parts of the United Kingdom against the Church of England: 'Away with it! Why cumbers it the ground?'[20]

Nevertheless, support from the Church was forthcoming. By May of 1873, 1500 clergy of the Church of England had sent petitions for repeal. The Dean of Carlisle and F. D. Maurice were early converts. By 1883, the year of repeal, Josephine counted Samuel Montague, the MP for Whitechapel, the Jewish section of London, among her supporters. She says:

> It is now evident that our Crusade in England is assuming more of a religious, though not of a sectarian character. While preserving our liberty of conscience, and welcoming all who unite in a desire to see the moral standard of our common humanity elevated, we feel we are engaged in one work, and with a profound conviction that it is God's work.[21]

By 1885 the influence of the Churches was so strongly felt that Stead, before drawing up his plans for the abduction of Eliza Armstrong, met with Archbishop Benson of Canterbury and Dr Temple, the Bishop of London, as well as Cardinal Manning.

The repeal of the Contagious Diseases Acts stands as an impressive witness to the moral power of the Churches. Yet this remarkable event, an outstanding victory in an era of declining influence, has received little attention on the part of Church historians. It does not fit neatly into the conventional categories. It took place not in the Church but in the world. It was ecumenical and inter-faith. It was led, not by a clergyman, but by a layman. And that layman was a woman.

3   Seeking God's Thoughts

For Josephine Butler prayer is the life-blood, the spiritual pulse of the spiritual life. She regarded it as the means by which men and women are transformed into prophets and prophetesses.

> The word, to prophesy, is best translated by the learned as 'to show forth the mind of God' on any matter. What a high gift! What a holy endowment this, to be enabled to show or set forth to man the mind or thought of God! In order to attain this gift, the soul must live habitually in the closest union with God, in Christ, so as to realize the prayer of the saint who cried, 'Henceforth, O Lord, let me think Thy thought and speak Thy speech'.[22]

Josephine's earliest account of her views on prayer was expressed in her memories of an encounter with an Oxford sceptic. A painting by Raphael was being discussed.

> I said I found the face insipid. 'Insipid of course it must be', said a distinguished college tutor; 'a woman's face when engaged in prayer could never wear any other expression than that of insipidity.' 'What'! I asked, 'when one converses with a man of high intelligence and noble soul, if there be any answering chord in one's own mind, does one's expression immediately become insipid? Does it not rather beam with increased intelligence and exalted thought? And how much more if one converses face to face with the highest Intelligence of all! Then every faculty of the mind and emotion of the soul is called to its highest exercise.' No one made any remark, and the silence seemed to rebuke my audacity. The first speaker merely accentuated his idea of prayer as a kind of sentimental, dreamy devoutness of feeling.[23]

From her own experience she believed prayer to be emotional, but not sentimental — the fruit not of fantasies but of discipline and hard work.

> I began to address myself immediately to God Himself. . . . I spoke to Him in solitude, as to a person who could not answer. . . . Do not imagine that . . . I worked myself into any excitement, there was much pain . . . and dogged determination required. . . . I will say nothing of what followed except this — that whereas I doubted before whether there was a God who communicates *directly* with a spirit which seeks Him, *now I do not doubt it.*[24]

As an old woman, looking back on a long life, she tries to summarize her experience with prayer for her friend Miss Forswaith.

> I think it is best to tell you how I feel about it; and also how I have come to regard the whole question, with all its difficulties, as summed up in those words, 'we know not what to pray for, as we ought, but the Spirit helped our infirmities, for God knoweth the mind of the spirit'. . . .

Now it seems to me that, as we get nearer to God, all prayer resolves itself into *communion*. To the Holy of Holies, face to face with Jesus, all perplexities vanish. No difficulties can live. If I may dare to tell a little of what He has taught me, even in days and weeks of bodily suffering, it is this; that in prayer I am *still, silent,* waiting for the Spirit; and the Spirit is granted, so that He prompts every request.[25]

She drew back from recommending a particular technique, yet she gave some hints from her own experience. Prayer, she felt, involved definiteness of purpose, a concentration of energy on this purpose, and a disciplined self-mastery. She wished to speak of something that had played so large a role in her life, and yet she was shy about expressing views which to some might seem sentimental, self-deluding, or to seem to boast of special spiritual gifts. It was only to close friends that she revealed the intimate give-and-take, the conversational quality of her converse with God. During an illness she had

called, therefore, directly on God, sitting up and speaking aloud. . . . 'I appeal to His honour to fulfil His promise of help to those who really believed in Him.' I said, 'Now listen, Lord, in pity, I *do* desire something — that I may get home to England safely, and that I may see all my dear children again before I die, if I have to die.' Then, in the silence in which I sat, a great peace *came to me*. I did not urge myself to be peaceful. The peace *came*, and I felt that Christ is so *honourable*: He would not give that promise and not keep it.[26]

The effect of prayer is more than a renewal of courage and faith; prayer, since it is directed towards a God who is intimately involved with the hopes, and the sufferings, of the world, gives a programme and a plan of action. The present world needed such a plan.

Looking at any of the great questions before us now — the relations of nation to nation, and of the Anglo-Saxon race to the heathen populations of conquered countries; questions of gold-seeking, of industry, of capital and labour, of the influence of wealth, now so great a power in our country and its dependencies; questions of legal enactments, of the action of

Governments, and innumerable social and economic problems — we may ask, How much of the light of heaven is permitted to fall on those questions? How many or how few are there among us who ask, and seek, and knock and wait, to know *God's* thoughts on these matters.[27]

Having found 'God's thoughts', the one who prays is then empowered to put them to work. A mutual relationship between God and man, each responding to the other, is the essence of the divine economy.

With God all things are possible. He can restore power to the paralysed will, even as He can raise the dead. He does it, and we have seen with our eyes these His miracles of power and love.

And how, you ask me, by what means may such a restoration be accomplished? Replying from my own experience, I would say it is brought about very frequently by means of the divinely energized wills of others — chiefly of those creatures so dear to God, those mothers, wives, sisters, daughters and friends who have, through the teaching of the heart and the inspiration of God, learned and embraced that holiest of all ministries, the ministry of intercession.[28]

God is all-powerful and at the same time dependent on man's ability to respond. When man chooses to act in accord with the Spirit, the power of God is released. Man through prayer participates in God's creative energy, bringing it to bear on human affairs.

In holding to God you and He together hold and wield (if you will it) a vast energy and power. ... The day is coming when we shall be astonished and ashamed to think that, for so many centuries, the power possible to man has been limited or denied by the narrowness of human conceptions and the elementary state of our knowledge. ... He has been showing me that, beyond His promises, and beyond Scripture itself, He is God, and that in His *Character* is our great eternal hope and confidence.[29]

4   *The Crusade: Inaugurated by Prayer*

Like all great religious visionaries she heard a call that led her to a specific vocation. In the ensuing years of political struggle, inner conflict and physical hardship, she continued to be sustained by private prayer. It helped her to muster the persuasive energies required to convert a hostile opposition and enabled her to reach difficult decisions. In addition the collective prayer of the movement gave direction and created unity: it was an inner force — and an effective tactic — in bringing victory to the Cause.

In the biography of her husband, Josephine describes her 'call'. Its stages follow the pattern recorded by many spiritual leaders: first dissatisfaction with one's present life and the acknowledgement of the need to hear a call; then the recognition that a call had been made; hesitation and fear of the demands — fear that what seems to be the call of God is in fact the voice of self; and finally, a whole-hearted, and hence transforming, acceptance.

Miss Wolstenholme's telegram, urging her to take leadership of the movement, had met Josephine at Dover, when she arrived home from a summer vacation. She recalls her response.

> Like Jonah, when he was charged by God with a commission which he could not endure to contemplate, 'I fled from the face of the Lord.' I worked hard at other things — good works, as I thought, with a kind of half-conscious hope that God would accept *that* work and not require me to go farther, and run my heart against the naked sword which seemed to be held out. But the hand of the Lord was upon me: night and day the pressure increased.

Her ambivalence continues. She fears the spiritual consequence of her anger.

> September, 1869 — 'Now is your hour, and the power of darkness.' O Christ, if Thy Spirit fainted in that hour, how can mine sustain it? It is now many weeks since I knew that Parliament had sanctioned this great wickedness, and I have not yet put on my armour, nor am I yet ready. Nothing so wears me out, body and soul, as anger, fruitless anger; and this thing

fills me with such an anger, and hatred, that I fear to face it. The thought of this atrocity kills charity and hinders my prayers. But there is surely a way of being angry without sin. I pray thee, O God, to give me a deep, well-governed, and lifelong hatred of all such injustice, tyranny, and cruelty; and, at the same time, give me that divine compassion which is willing to live and suffer long for love to souls, or to fling itself into the breach and die at once.

How was she to know that this was 'perhaps, after all, the very work, the very mission I longed for years ago, and saw coming, afar off, like a bright star?'

Seen near, as it approaches, it is so dreadful, so difficult, so disgusting, that I tremble to look at it; and it is hard to see and know whether or not God is indeed calling me concerning it. If doubt were gone, and I felt sure He means me to rise in revolt and rebellion (for that it must be) against men, even against our rulers, then I would do it with zeal, however repulsive to others may seem the task.[30]

Her ambivalence was resolved through prayer combined with a realistic and growing appraisal of the dimension of the issue; 'I read all that was sent to me.' She became convinced that this issue was a major one, driving the 'most despised' of society into despair and others into 'blindness and hardness of heart. . . . And the call seemed to come ever more clearly.' She could no longer refuse: Miss Wolstenholme had her answer.

Her call had brought together emotional commitment and rational analysis; during the next decades these continued to define her leadership. When tempted to compromise, she sought the religious principle behind every issue. The conviction that God was informing her action gave a certain inflexibility to her stance. It drove her onward, not giving her time to congratulate herself and her companions in their progressive steps toward fulfilment.

A belief that one's will is divinely sanctioned can lead to destructive, even demonic, self-assurance. But Josephine's assurance of divine blessing had not been arrived at in isolation. While it is true that she relied heavily on private prayer, she worked — and prayed — with people. She was responsive to their thoughts and needs. Furthermore, she conceived of faith not as obedience to an inflexible statement of doctrine, but as the response to an ongoing creative spirit, a spirit that was available to all.

> We know that the words translated in our Scriptures, 'Have faith in God', are now more truly translated, 'Have faith of God.' In order to follow our lost sheep *until we find them* — never stopping short of that — it seems to me that we must have, in some degree at least, the faith of the Son of God; His faith in the creative power of the Father of the human race, who can create and recreate, and His faith in the possibility of resurrection for every dead soul.[31]

Josephine's dependence on prayer was shared by the two religious bodies who were her chief supporters, the Society of Friends and the Salvation Army. Given the economic, social and intellectual — even national — diversity among the Abolitionists, and the different goals that drew them into the Crusade, it is extraordinary that the movement held together. There were tensions at times; the Bruce Bill and its half-measures was almost the occasion for division. But the movement held together and pressed forward. A search for religious principles behind thought and action gave the Abolitionists a way of reconciling differences, a compass which guided them through confusing and ambiguous issues. In addition the charity towards each other which they asked for and found through prayer enabled them to deal with their disagreements.

In the year before the crucial vote of 1883 on the Second Contagious Diseases Act, the Society of Friends had organized a convention lasting for two days, offering corporate prayer for the success of the campaign. They invited Christians of every denomination to join them; there were meetings at Devonshire House, the Quaker headquarters; at the East London Tabernacle; and at Exeter Hall. Those who had come from the country were asked to organize local prayer meetings when they went home.

The Abolitionists increased their efforts during the weeks before the critical vote. Soliciting the support of key representatives, one member reported that the amount of pressure 'is unprecedented in the history of any agitation'.[32]

The Butlers took an assembly room in Westminster Palace Hotel. They planned a prayer meeting which would go on as long as the parliamentary debate continued. A remarkable variety of people came, 'well-dressed ladies, some even of high rank, kneeling together (almost side by side) with the poorest, and some of the outcast women of the purlieus of Westminister'.[33] The clergy took turns conducting services. Other groups met in the house of repealist Members of Parliament and in chapels and churches around Westminster. Dr Whitwell, one of their supporters and a Liberal, assured Josephine that her 'persevering prayers will be answered in this matter'. Cardinal Manning, frail and ill, looking 'even thinner than a spider', made a special visit to rally the Irish Catholic vote. Josephine was told that many of the younger members were made quite uncomfortable at the idea of 'all those women' praying for them, and that Cavendish Bentwinck, a seasoned enemy, spoke vindictively of those who 'patronised that woman's praying'. The hope was momentarily deferred by a parliamentary manoeuvre which delayed introduction of the Bill. Finally, on 20 April, the motion was proposed that 'this House disapproves of the compulsory examination of the women under the Contagious Diseases Act'. Josephine describes the final day and night.

> All day long groups had met for prayer — some in the houses of MPs, some in churches, some in halls, where the poorest people came. Meetings were being held also all over the kingdom, and a telegraphic message of sympathy came to us continually from Scotland and Ireland, France, Switzerland, and Italy. There was something in the air like the approach of victory. As men and women prayed they suddenly burst forth into praise, thanking God for the answer, as if it had already been granted. It was a long debate. The tone of the speeches, both for and against, was remarkably purified, and with one exception they were altogether on a higher plane than in former debates. Many of us ladies sat through the whole evening till after midnight; then came the division. A few minutes previously Mr. Gerard, the steward of the Ladies Gallery, crept quietly in and whispered to me, 'I think you are going to win'! That reserved official of course, never betrays sympathy with any party; nevertheless, I could see the irrepressible pleasure in his face when he said this.

Josephine's literary feeling for dramatic tension lends eloquence to her account of the last hours.

Never can I forget the expression on the faces of our MPs in the House when they all streamed back from the Division Lobby. The interval during their absence had seemed very long, and we could hear each other's breathing so deep was the silence. We did not require to wait to hear the announcement of the division by the tellers; the faces of our friends told the tale. Slowly and steadily they pressed in, headed by Mr. Stansfeld and Mr. Hopwood, and tellers on our side. Mr. Fowler's face was beaming with joy and a kind of humble triumph. I thought of the words: 'Say unto Jerusalem her warfare is accomplished.' It was a victory of righteousness over gross selfishness, injustice and deceit, and for a moment we were all elevated by it. When the figures were given out a long-continued cheer arose, which sounded like a psalm of praise. Then we ran quickly down from the gallery and met a number of our friends coming out from Westminster Hall.

It was half-past one in the morning, and the stars were shining in a clear sky. I felt at that silent hour in the morning the spirit of the Psalmist, who said: 'When the Lord turned against the captivity of Zion, we were like unto them that dream.' It almost seemed like a dream.[34]

5   Christ: The Exponent of the Mind of God

In 1869 Josephine Butler was asked to write an introduction to an anthology on the 'woman question'. One might expect to find sociological commentary. Instead, she lays out this premise:

Once more I venture to say I appeal to Christ, and to Him alone, as the fountain-head of those essential and eternal truths which it is our duty and our wisdom to apply to all the changing circumstances of human society. Believing as I do that He is Very God, and that He was in human form the Exponent of the mind of God to the world, I hold that His authority must be higher than that of any man or society of men by whom the Truth which we receive from them, so far as we receive Truth from them at all, can only be transmitted. I believe all His acts to have had a supreme and everlasting significance. The teaching of His great typical acts is not less profound than that of His words.[35]

The call to justice, the equality announced by Christ, went against all wordly principles.

Compared with the accepted axioms of the day, and indeed of the centuries past, in regard to certain vital questions, the sayings and actions of Jesus were, we confessed to one another, revolutionary. George Butler was not afraid of revolution. In this sense he desired it, and we prayed together that a holy revolution might come about.[36]

The Kingdom of God had been established on earth. Josephine exhorted public leaders: they must rise above the wordly practices of parliamentary politics

to the regal conception of justice. . . . Those who profess the religion of Jesus must bring into public life and into the legislature the *stern, practical, social real side* of the Gospel. The religion of Christ must become again what it was when He was on earth.[37]

Through the Resurrection justice has become more than an expendable ideal fabricated by one era in history and discarded by the next. It has become a reality, the incarnation of an eternal principle.

Against this background the Cause takes on special meaning. The proclamation that the well-being of the prostitute is as important as that of the defender of the British Empire can only make sense in a world in which the carpenter of Nazareth is also Lord of Creation. 'The unity of the moral law, and the equality of all human souls before God is the most fruitful and powerful revolutionary principle in which the world has ever known' because it is empowered by God, sealed by the Resurrection.

Yet through man's ignorance and blindness it has been lost. For Josephine the term 'Crusade' became more than a metaphor. She pressed forward with the zeal of the medieval knight who after years of journeying reaches the walls of Jerusalem. An alien in an alien land, she gazed longingly on the Holy City, a city that had once been home.

Understandably then, when she speaks of the principles underlying the Crusade she assumes the ruthless, swinging, militantly marching cadences of the zealot.

And now it is revolt and rebellion, a consecrated rebellion against those in authority who have established this 'accursed thing' among us. We are rebels for God's holy laws. What have I to do with peace any more? It is now war to the knife. In a battle of flesh and blood, mercy may intervene and life may be spared; but principles know not the name of mercy. In the broad light of day, and under a thousand eyes, we now take up our position. We declare on whose side we fight; we make no compromise; and we are ready to meet all the powers of earth and hell combined.[38]

3 A New Dispensation

1 Your Sons and Daughters Shall Prophesy

Man and woman are more than beneficiaries of the 'mighty Acts' of Christ: they have been called to exercise 'the wonderful power with which God has endowed us as social and sympathetic beings, to impart what we know and love, to pass on from hand to hand the torch we bear'. They are human 'mirrors which reflect the character of Christ'.[1] In choosing subjects for two biographies; Jean Frederick Oberlin, the Swiss pastor, and Catherine of Siena, the Italian woman who travelled from city to city exhorting statesmen and shaming a profligate Pope into the resumption of his duties, Josephine describes them as models of the Christian life, 'living and walking by the faith of Christ crucified', conforming their lives to His.

These high expectations are as incumbent upon women as upon men. Women are 'destined' to speak and act for God. They are 'prophetesses'.

> It is an astonishing and a melancholy thing that the churches and their ministers, and the Christian world in general through all these generations, should apparently have ignored or made light of the following blessed fact, the fact that on the day of Pentecost, the great day when the Holy Spirit was poured forth on that multitude of all people and nations gathered in Jerusalem, when the New Dispensation was inaugurated in which we now live, the Apostle Peter, in his magnificent first Pentecostal sermon, proclaimed the actual *fulfilment* on that day, and for all the days to come of the promise of the Prophet Joel. 'I will pour out of my Spirit upon all flesh; and your sons and your *daughters* shall prophesy; and on my servants and on my *handmaidens* I will pour out of my Spirit'.[2]

In tracing the role of women in the new society, Josephine starts with the 'Liberation'[3] announced in the Gospels.

Among the great typical acts of Christ which were evidently
and intentionally for the announcement of a principle for the
guidance of Society, none were more markedly so than His
acts towards women; and I appeal to the open Book, and to the
intelligence of every candid student of Gospel history for the
justification of my assertion, that in all important instances of
his dealings with women, His dismissal of each case was
accompanied by a distinct act of Liberation.

The woman of Samaria and Mary Magdalene were freed from
the 'chains which had been invited by the tradition of the
centuries'. Any honest examiner of scripture, she continues,
must recognize that Christ's life and words announced the principle of the perfect equality of all human beings.

> To some extent this has been practically acknowledged in the
> relations of men to men; only in one case has it been consistently
> ignored, and that is in the case of that half of the human race,
> in regard to which His doctrine of equality was more mark-
> edly enforced than in any other.[4]

Like Mary Wollstonecraft, she was saddened by the greed, the
triviality, the squandering of talent, the false values of a female
existence which was bent toward making a 'good' marriage. The
rejection of the principle of equality had placed women in a
demeaning position.

> What dignity can there be in the attitude of women in general,
> and toward men in particular, when marriage is held (and
> often necessarily so, being the sole means of maintenance) to
> be the one end of a woman's life, when it is degraded to the
> level of a feminine profession, when those who are soliciting a
> place in this profession resemble the flaccid Brazilian creepers
> which cannot exist without support, and which sprawl out
> their limp tendrils in every direction to find something — no
> matter what — to hang upon; when the insipidity or the
> material necessities of so many women's lives make them
> ready to accept almost any man who may offer himself?[5]

To this destructive dependency she contrasts another, the
dependence of human beings, men and women, who help and

support each other in affection. 'That is a wholly different thing from the abject dependence of one entire class of persons on another and a stronger class.' Both sexes are denigrated by a system which sees marriage as the only possible goal for women and in which husbands are chosen not for the affection they offer but for the status they convey. Like many of the other contributors to *Woman's Work and Woman's Culture,* Josephine advocates that the dignity of women, lost in the 'general scramble for husbands', be restored by providing proper education, by opening up the professions, and by the granting of a larger share in social activity and public service.

Using an effective debating technique, Josephine begins her argument by appearing to acknowledge the validity of her opponents' assertion that 'women's place is in the home'. She then enlarges upon this concept, giving it by extension a new and more profound meaning. She understands the statement, not as a limiting factor separating women in a cocoon-like sanctuary, but as an instinct for service that draws them out into the world. She points to the ironies of a society that on the one hand proclaims the family unit as the ideal and on the other supports a social welfare system that breaks up families, segregating members by age and sex.

> I believe that nothing whatever will avail but the large infusion of Home elements into Workhouses, Hospitals, Schools, Orphanages, Lunatic Asylums, Reformatories and even Prisons; and in order to do this there must be a setting free of feminine powers and influence from the constraint of bad education, and narrow aims, and listless homes where they are at present too often a superfluity.[6]

Though admitting that the British home is ideally a stronghold of virtue, she maintains that its goodness has become corrupted by selfishness. 'The French speak of a selfishness *a deux*. I am sure that the prevailing character of many homes is only that of a selfishness of five or ten, as the case may be.'[7] She stresses the need 'to give forth more freely of the strength and comfort and sweetness of family life to the homeless and solitary and sinful'. She says that she had seen children grow more sensitive and considerate after a stranger, 'a harmless lunatic', had been taken into the family. This 'marked elevation of sentiment and growth of Christian feeling . . . dating from the reception into the house of a poor outcast who died among them, instead of in the hospital, tenderly waited upon by them in turns', became apparent in the servants as well.

Like Octavia Hill, Josephine envisioned a society in which all of Britain would become an extended family, whose members were united by ties of love and mutual respect under the benevolent care of a Father in heaven.

While stressing the equality of women and men, Josephine recognized that in some respects their approaches might be different and complementary. She felt that women tend to operate on a one-to-one basis, while men think in terms of institutions and systematic planning. In dealing with social problems each approach when used in isolation from the other will fail.

> We have had experience of what we may call the feminine form of philanthropy, the independent, individual ministering, of too medieval a type to suit the present day. It has failed. We are now about to try the masculine form of philanthropy, large and comprehensive measures, organizations and systems planned by men and sanctioned by Parliament.[8]

Though adequate to the scope of the task, it too will fail because it is based on a false idea of society. It treats the poor as a class to be manipulated. 'The wholesale system tends to turn human beings into machines instead of training them to be self-depending responsible beings.'[9]

While she supported secular feminists in their struggle for civil rights, the right to work and to vote and to be educated, her Christian principles gave a different tone to her affirmations. What some women felt they had to prove — the equality of women with men — Josephine took for granted. Equality was not based on biological fact but upon spiritual principle. It was not something that must be earned, it was freely given. The secular feminists proclaimed that women must wrest the control of their destinies from the men who had subjugated them. Josephine as a Christian feminist held that men and women were equals — dependent on, and subject to, a God-in-Christ who, in the words of Paul, 'did not think to snatch at equality with God, but made himself nothing, assuming the nature of a slave. The divine nature was his from the first.'

2 Our Enslaved Sisters

If Josephine wished to make the theological point that 'the last shall be first and the first last', she could not have chosen a more suitable symbol than the prostitute. In order to understand the revolutionary nature of her Crusade we must learn something of the way in which prostitutes were regarded in British society.

First, we must remember that prostitutes were women, and that women, even the most aristocratic, were not regarded as fully human; their status was a derived one, dependent on a male — father or husband. Their civil rights were limited. Before the enactment of the Marriage and Divorce Bill of 1857 a husband who had deserted his wife could still lay claim to her earnings. Until the protective legislation of 1870 no married woman could own property independently nor did she have the right to make a will or to initiate a suit. As late as 1896 it remained impossible for a wife to obtain a divorce on the grounds of adultery; this option was open to husbands only.

If in the hierarchy of British society as reflected in its legal system women were somewhat less than human, prostitutes were somewhat less than women. They had no social status. Like the garbage sweepers of Hindu society, they were outcasts. The attitude of the gentleman writing from his London Club to advocate that prostitutes must be 'treated as foul sewers are treated, as physical facts and not as moral agents', is typical. Josephine's indignation serves to underscore the barbarism of his view.

> Sewers have neither souls nor civil rights; by admitting into their political theory the idea that any class of human being whatever may be reduced to the level of an inanimate nuisance for political purposes, these writers have demonstrated to us very clearly the intimate connection between a gross material-ism and the most cruel and oppressive despotism. The men who speak thus, and who act in harmony with their utterances, do not believe that the beings of whom they speak have souls; to them any regenerating influence from a Divine source upon the spirit of man or woman is inconceivable.[10]

If Josephine had confined her attention to acts of charity, her work on behalf of these outcasts might have been accepted. But that she, a British Brahmin, should not fear the contamination of associating with them, that she sought them out, calling herself one of them, 'a fellow- sinner, a fellow-sufferer', this was a scandal. 'Can my sister's soul be corrupted without my soul also being attacked?' she asked.[11] She was considered by many to be 'worse than a prostitute' because, by daring to question the assumptions upon which its privileges rested, she had betrayed her class. In addition she had challenged the male view which separated women into two categories: the 'good' but dull virgin-wife and the 'bad' but exciting mistress-prostitute.

She herself recognized that many women would have difficulty in accepting the identification with prostitutes. Her work with middle-class women primarily consisted of showing them that they could not point to the theological base which united women with men until they had demonstrated the spiritual bonds between women.

> Womanhood is *solidaire*. We cannot successfully elevate the standard of public opinion in the matter of justice to woman, and of equality of all in its truest sense, if we are content that a practical, hideous, calculated, manufactured and legally maintained degradation of a portion of womanhood is allowed to go on before the eyes of all. 'Remember them that are in bonds, as being bound with them.' Even if we lack the sympathy which makes us feel that the chains which bind our enslaved sisters are pressing on us also, we cannot escape the fact that we are one womanhood, we cannot be wholly and truly free.[12]

Not content with pointing out that prostitutes were as good as other women, sometimes she even seemed to be saying that they were better. She reminded her opponents that those who are called in the terminology of the police report, 'habitual prostitutes', 'abandoned women', 'recalcitrants', and 'social nuisance', were welcomed by Christ as friends and followers. She speaks of the special force of character of those who have suffered and recalls the last words of a 17 year-old prostitute who, dying with a 'look of heroic and desperate resolve', cried, 'I will fight for my soul through hosts, and hosts, and hosts'! She suggests that such 'lost women', courageous and compassionate, are better equipped to help their sisters than the protected, 'righteous' Christian.

You are women [she tells them] and a woman is always a beautiful thing. You have been dragged deep in the mud; but still you are women. God calls to you, as He did to Zion long ago, 'Awake, awake! Thou that sittest in the dust, put on thy beautiful garments.' You can be the friend and companion of Him who came to seek and to save that which was lost. Fractures well healed make us more strong. Take of the very stones over which you have stumbled and fallen, and use them to pave your road to heaven.[13]

Why were the prostitutes the outcasts of British society? The answer is a complex one, involving sexuality, economics, men's attitude toward women — and toward themselves — conscious and unconscious feelings complicated by the universal and very human unwillingness to confront one's own unresolved problems. A brief analysis shows that, as is often the case, society in resolving one set of problems had created others which might in the long run turn out to be deeper and more destructive.

If prostitution did not 'resolve' the Victorian males' problems with sexuality, it did at least offer an outlet. Here, it seems to me, we must look upon them with some sympathy. It is worth restating the obvious. No society, no matter how 'liberated', is free from some ambivalence about sexuality. Sex is no respecter of reason, or of common sense, or of the social structure that makes possible the orderly transfer of property from one generation to the next. The Victorians were faced with real dilemmas, not all of them of their own making. Venereal disease was increasing at an alarming rate and had proved to be beyond the reach of the current medical treatment. (The Regulationists in giving the ethical reasoning behind their position pointed out that venereal disease not only killed the living: it crippled its innocent victims, the unborn.) Techniques of birth control were rudimentary and highly uncertain. Except among the very rich (who had so much property that it did not matter) and the very poor (who had none), illegitimate children were not readily accepted: middle-class society had no social and economic mechanism by which it could incorporate them. The need for financial self-sufficiency and the requirement that a husband be the sole support of a wife and family, made late marriages a necessity. The prospect of sexual fulfilment in marriage, accordingly, remained a distant and — in the view of the 'good', that is asexual woman — a rather tepid ideal. The Victorian male was told by the medical men that masturbation led to madness and, by the churchmen, that it led to damnation; homosexuality was of course considered to be an even more unspeakable vice. In view of these complicated restrictions one can evoke some compassion for the Victorian male who, finding all other outlets closed, hies himself off to a brothel.

Victorian society's unwillingness to speak of prostitution has usually been explained on the grounds of sexual reticence. The *London Times* in Josephine Butler's obituary is unable to bring out the word; it speaks of her work with the 'moral question'. *The Dictionary of National Biography* pays tribute to her efforts in 'furthering the moral elevation of women'. 'Social hygiene' was another popular euphemism. One wonders, however, if the causes did not go deeper than prudery — if in fact the root was not so much sexual as economic and social.

Prostitution was not only an exploitation of women, but of the poor. Josephine comments bitterly on the double standard of class.

> Those gentlemen who make such a noise about the necessity of prostitution too often forget, I think that in order to satisfy the necessity the *dishonour of the daughter of the people* is indispensable, for till now none of the worshippers of these medical theories have been found ready to declare a willingness that *their* own daughters should be sacrificed.[14]

Prostitutes represented not the 'worthy' poor for whom British society had found a place, but those who had been rejected. The well-coiffed ladies of St John's Wood, the colourful exploits of the Prince of Wales and his female entourage, the beautiful Skittles whose phaeton was drawn through the streets by a crowd of admirers gave prostitution a glamorous façade. The reality was better expressed by the emaciated girl lured into a brothel by the promise of a bowl of soup. Or by the young woman abandoned by the middle-class man who had seduced her, turning to prostitution, the only trade open to her, in order to feed her child.

Prostitution was a symptom of Britain's economic problems. These included declining agricultural prices and a generally uncertain financial picture, as well as the dislocations and unemployment that occur when there is both an increase in population and a shift in density and concentration. Prostitution was one of the unpleasant and indissoluble elements that had surfaced in the muddy turmoil of Britain's adjustment to the Industrial Revolution. Rather than admit the obvious weakness of a system that permitted such a cruel degradation of a growing portion of its population, middle-class capitalist Britain turned away. Invoking a muddled interpretation of Calvinist theology, its proponents claimed that the poverty of the prostitute is a sign that she is not loved by God — and so need not be loved by man. She deserved a fate that she had brought on herself.

Many of the contributors to *Woman's Work and Woman's Culture* singled out the economic factor as the key to the treatment of women. They understood the male prohibition on paid employment for women as one way — patently unfair — of dealing with rising male unemployment. They deplored the divisions between home and work created by the Industrial Revolution, in which their traditional vocations as cook, tailor, agricultural worker, midwife, and teacher had been taken from women and given to paid professionals who were invariably men. Some of them viewed factory legislation, originally intended to protect women, as actually a way of closing the few opportunities that were left to them. With mounting indignation they condemned a society which deplored idleness and exalted the work ethic and yet made it impossible for half its population to find work. The accepted roles of governess and missionary were available to very few. (Florence Nightingale and Octavia Hill would provide two more occupations for women — nursing and social work — but it would be years before their training schools could accommodate more than a very small number of students.) As Josephine saw, full employment for men was bought at the price of enforced idleness for women. If the responsibilities and duties of marriage and motherhood had been available to all women, this might have been tolerable. In a society in which there was a surplus of women, it was intolerable.

The Abolitionists held that most women became prostitutes because there was no other work available to them. This work, however, placed them in double jeopardy. Just as the pious despised them for having been rejected by God and at the same time condemned them for having brought their fate upon themselves, so society attacked them from opposing sides. Condemning idleness as wicked, praising work as virtue, Puritan moralists admitted that prostitutes worked — but they added that the work, and by extension the worker, was depraved. In a final flourish of illogic, they proceeded to classify prostitutes with vagrants and swindlers as 'Those Who Will Not Work' (Mayhew). In addition they called them the evil and depraved corrupters of young men and subhuman carriers of disease. Prostitutes found themselves taking the brunt of a whole complex of male fears and anxieties, arising not from some superficial prudery, but from deeply rooted fears and self-hatred.

It is hard not to hold the evangelical tradition responsible for the Victorians' fear of sexuality. Not merely denying outlets for sexual expression, it maintained that sexual feelings are in themselves debased and sinful. Purity is a matter, not only of chastity of body, but of chastity of mind. The prevalence of flagellation, the 'vice Anglais', and of the sadomasochistic practices that so horrified Josephine Butler and William Stead in their investigation of child prostitution, may be seen as a direct consequence of the evangelical identification which has a long biography in the history of Christian asceticism. They did not have Freud or Jung to tell them that their hatred of prostitutes as depraved beings could be a projection of their hatred of themselves. The very tenacity with which they clung to a narrowly self-serving view, the taboo which they placed on discussion of sexual issues, is an indication of the strength of their fears. In the voice of Lecour and others who claimed that men were the innocent victims of corrupt *femmes fatales*, there is a perceptible nervousness, accompanied by an air of unreality. The reversal of roles in which the aggressor blames his victim is never easily brought about; the pyschological toll is heavy. By the end of the nineteenth century, Lilith had become a popular subject for painters. The first wife of Adam, she was portrayed as a devouring demon temptress. Not surprisingly, sexuality had become associated with darkness, corruption, and death.

The death feared by the Victorian gentleman was the death of his own self-respect. Was it surprising that he did not wish to acknowledge that his pleasure had been bought with the exploitation and degradation of the weak? Was it surprising that he did not want to face the dichotomy in his own nature, the contrast between a man who by day in the House of Lords spoke eloquently on the immorality of the lower classes, and by night whipped and raped young children?

Every now and then history throws up an Iago, an individual who professes a love of evil; but most groups, especially the privileged, like to think of themselves as moral, decent people. The Victorians were no exception. Indeed, as products of Evangelicalism they gave particular importance to moral values. In an era in which the historical and philosophical basis of religion was being challenged, the Victorian gentleman clung with renewed tenacity to its moral precepts, and particularly to a positive estimate of his own ethical sensitivity. He might confine Church attendance to family weddings and baptisms and to a reading of the lessons on Christmas Eve, he would willingly confess to a weakness in theological understanding, but his religion as 'morality tinged with emotion' was dear to him. The fading glow of evangelical Christianity had left a distinct outline of himself as a benevolent, kindly man, a protector of women and children, who in the exercise of legitimate power upholds the social order. While this order might conveniently ensure his privileges as master, he held that it more essentially provided a public service through protecting the lives of those weaker than himself.

He was, by his own definition, kind to human beings; to avoid hearing 'the harlot's curse' that threatened his self-appraisal, he justified his actions by saying that those creatures whom he used were not fully human and therefore had no claim to his benevolence. It might seem far-fetched to compare the plight of the prostitute with the more terrible one of the Negro slave — but the Abolitionists were right in pointing to the common ground. The Victorian patron of the brothel as well as the Southern slave-owner preserved their self-respect by denying the humanity of those whom they exploited. If he began to question prostitution, the Victorian gentleman might end by having to question himself. Josephine saw that in the long run it might be that the master had paid an even higher price than the slave: in a spiritual sense it is perhaps better to be a victim of others than a self-deluding tyrant. The institution of prostitution and the double standard inflicts a double harm: it treats women unjustly, and in assuming that men are weaker and inferior beings who cannot be expected to maintain the same high standards, it deprives them of their spiritual birthright.[15] Only when we understand that can we feel with Josephine that prostitution is 'a poison which threatens the soul of man in its noblest faculties, fear of God, respect for humanity, and love of liberty'. Only then can we understand what her friends meant when they said that 'she and she alone understood the question as a whole'.

3 The Antidote to the Viper's Sting

If the New Dispensation has arrived why do we still hear the cries of a disordered society — a society in which many women suffer hunger, disease, and humiliation, as prostitutes, and many men, as their patrons, suffer lust and the spiritual degradation of hypocrisy and guilt? For Josephine Butler, as for many, the ever-present theological problem of evil stood massive and unavoidable — an ugly protuberance around which flowed the currents of her life. Stated simply it asks the question: if God is all-loving and all-powerful, why does He permit evil?

> That God should *permit* evil seems to some minds as immoral as that he Himself should create and dispense it. This portion of the subject is surrounded with difficulty and mystery. It leads us back to the great unanswered question concerning the origin of evil.[16]

Although sympathetic with those who, like her friend John Stuart Mill, found an answer in the idea that God is all-loving but not all-powerful, Josephine would not admit a solution that denied the active power of God. Like many Christians before and since, in the face of evil she still affirmed her faith in an omnipotent, powerful God. Her whole life was bent towards finding an existential solution to the paradox.

By choice Josephine was not a systematic theologian. She was unimpressed by the claims of logic, and she recognized that, particularly on the problem of evil, a logical solution was impossible. Yet her thoughts on the subject supply a compendium of most of the answers offered in the Christian tradition. She begins by suggesting that much of the evil that we attribute to God is in fact created by man. Admittedly, however, there is a nucleus in natural evil for which man cannot be held accountable. Here she suggests that God has perhaps limited His power for the greater good of man — that in the process of sanctification, suffering may play a redemptive role. Finally, she affirms the way of the mystic, claiming that a vision of God, communion with God, brings a peace and a heightened vitality in which the question is silenced. This vision, prefigured on earth, is more fully experienced in life after death.

Rather than holding God accountable for sin, Josephine first looks at human society. She concludes that most of evil, if not entirely man-made, has been nurtured and reinforced by human complicity.

I feel as if I should like to put on sack-cloth and ashes, and go forth and cry aloud, 'It is you — you professing Christians — who are permitting God's world to become a pandemonium, by your recognition of deviltry, while your eyes are too dim to see the coming of Jesus and the power of the Holy Ghost, which He is waiting and longing to pour forth at this time'! I see some allusion to future leaders. There will never be future leaders, unless some can be inspired with the utmost fanaticism of hope and courage, based on the eternal word.

She does not exempt herself from these charges. She remembers her fears when she was presented with the challenge of the Crusade, and its uncompromisingly idealistic goals:

The stern ethics of Christ — the divine standard — seemed to become impassible as a matter of practical enforcement. Horribly perplexed, I was tempted to give up the perfect ideal. It is in this way, I think *through lack of faith*, that compromises creep in among us, compromises with error, with sin, with wrong- doing — unbelief taking root first in the individual soul, and then gradually spreading, until a lower standard is accepted in family life, in society, in legislation, and in government.[17]

The contribution of human weakness to the power of evil is clear; it does not, however, account for the nucleus that remains: the clearly unmerited sufferings of the innocent from natural disaster. Here Josephine suggests that God may choose to limit His power in order to achieve a more 'glorious' end.

But it is evident to one who studies humbly His Word, and His Providence in the light of His Spirit, that God has been pleased to submit Himself for a season to a certain limitation of His power; and we may be sure that this is for an end that will be much more excellent and glorious than we can now conceive of, when the work of grace in the salvation of the world is fully accomplished.

She speaks of man as an 'allied spiritual agency'.

He *could not* there do many mighty works, 'because of their unbelief'. Here we have a clearly confessed limitation of His power while, at the same time, the words point to that blessed truth and marvel of the appointed working together of God's will and man's will, the union of the divine and the human, for the fulfilment of His loving purposes, and the final triumph of good over evil. If the above words be true, that 'He could not', is not the converse true also, that He could and that He *can* do many mighty works because of the faith He finds in man? It would seem that God needs the faith of man as an allied spiritual agency, for the constant generating of the force by which He will finally 'subdue all things unto himself', when the rebel power, the opposing will, will exist no more.[18]

The implication here is that evil will be the means to a greater good in the process of salvation. Joining with God in the battle against evil, man will achieve a higher spiritual life.

The mystery of the cross stands in a wholly different light when we comprehend, even a little, the law which governs the progress of victory over evil by submission to that very evil in order to its destruction.[19]

Every great reform, every 'holy revolution', has been won because people came forward to suffer willingly for others. Opposing injustice on behalf of those too weak to fight for themselves, the reformers accepted the full consequences and penalties of their opposition, 'even unto death'. In this struggle they were sustained both by the knowledge that God participates in their suffering and that He will ensure victory.

Josephine realizes that while sanctification through the voluntary acceptance of suffering explains the martyr and the saint, it does not account for the sufferings of the innocent. She begins by admitting that unsought miseries are not in themselves a blessing. Afterwards, however,

> we see the inner meaning of it all, and why God allowed it and permitted Satan to take advantage of it. For it has revealed myself *to* myself, as I never saw myself before. It is a *crucible* but the Refiner is standing over it and watching it all the time.[20]

The Butlers' great tragedy was the death of their daughter Eva. From this calamity Josephine was finally able to achieve the serenity of the mystic who is granted a vision of eternal life, prefigured in communion with God on earth, realized in the hope of life after death.

> There were some weeks of uncomforted grief. Her flight from earth had the appearance of a most cruel accident. But do the words 'accident' and 'chance' properly find a place in the vocabulary of those who have placed themselves and those dear to them in a special manner under the daily providential care of a loving God? Here there entered into the heart of our grief the intellectual difficulty, the moral perplexity and dismay . . . which haunts the 'Valley of the Shadow of Death' — that dark passage through which some toil only to emerge into a hopeless and final denial of the Divine goodness, the complete bankruptcy of faith; and others, by the mercy of God, through a still deeper experience into a yet firmer trust in His unfailing love.

In the intensity of their grief the Butlers did not try to find an explanation for their daughter's death. Although perhaps tempted to reproach God for a seemingly arbitrary and cruel act, they prayed together for acceptance. 'O God, look upon the earth, its sins, its sorrows, its wrongs. . . . Give us patience to wait and to watch for the dawn of blessing, as those that watch for the morning.'[21]

This watch was rewarded by the mystic's vision. Josephine found in nature a statement of the majesty and transcendent glory of God. Like Job she found that in the presence of God in nature her anxious questions were stilled. She wrote to George:

> The sun was rising, but we did not see him; we saw only his glory on the mountains. I was not looking out at that moment

but suddenly I saw the faces of my companions flush, and
Stanley cried 'What has happened? The mountains are on
fire!' I looked up. On fire indeed! But it was not like any
earthly fire; it was a strange, celestial glory.

This vision she equates with the glimpses we are offered of life
after death. She could in the end accept Eva's death because she
understood it as a rebirth into life in the Kingdom of God.

The only other transfiguration more beautiful which I ever
saw was that sweet look of holy awe and wonder and peace
which passed over our darling's face when she died, as if she
stood face to face with God. The glory of the mountains
recalled that awful sweetness, and calmed my soul. I felt God
to be so great and high and calm and that earth's longest
agonies are but a moment's pain in comparison with the
eternity of glory hereafter. If God made this earth so beautiful
what must His Heaven be?[22]

This is one of the many references to death as prefiguring of life
in heaven. To death scenes included in the *Memoir* and *Recollections,* Josephine adds her hope of reunion with beloved relatives
and friends in the hereafter, hopes which are also expressed in
other letters and diaries of the period.

The twentieth-century reader has generally been impatient
with the Victorian preoccupation with death, regarding it as
morbid at worst, and sentimental at best. This negative estimate
is, however, superficial. It misses the point. If by 'morbid' one
means a prurient curiosity in the hidden, the Victorians were
not morbid. Unlike us, they were not protected from death by a
battery of professionals and a technology of equipment and
medicines. Death, like birth, was a normal — albeit terrible —
occurrence. It took place at home. The physical details of illness,
suffering, and death were attended to by members of the family.
The interest in death was realistic.

As for sentimentality, it is true that the formal, stereotyped
language of the death scene seems to suppress the expression of
genuine feeling; the emphasis on the 'holiness' of the dying
subject makes one death scene very like another.[23] Yet there is a
profound reason for the observance of the conventions: the eyes
lifted towards heaven, the last words of the dying, expressions of

affection and gratitude, an attitude of resignation and hope —
these were all looked for as indications of sanctification. In the
behaviour of the dying, the living found hints of the life to come.
In the death scenes of an earlier period when Calvinism had
placed the number of the Elect at a very low level, there is a
perceptible nervousness, a straining to demonstrate that the
deceased, through the saintly manner in which he had faced
death, was indeed one of the Elect. For the Greys and the Butlers
the death scene was a confident affirmation.

Of the deaths of her father, her father-in-law, and the many
women who took refuge with the Butlers, Josephine writes with
the conviction that death is the entrance to the eternal. The
fullest apotheosis is reserved for George.

> The moment after his spirit fled and the dear venerable head
> rested on the pillow, and the familiar calm, benevolent look
> settled on his face, the setting sun pierced the clouds and fog,
> and its rays happening just to fall on his pillow and silvery
> hair, made a complete aureole around his head.[24]

Josephine believed not only that individual souls live on after
death, but that there is a link between the living and the dead. To
the dying child prostitute she attributes the words, 'When I get to
Heaven, I will be very busy — I will ask for a place to be got
ready for Mrs. Butler — I will see to it.' She believed that after
her own death she would continue to pray for those she loved. 'So
this is a command from God. I do always pray for you. But when
I am gone out of this world, you will know that I am still praying
for you, and that I will be nearer to you than I am now.'[25]

It is from the perspective of this complex grouping of responses
to the problem of evil that she could look back upon her life as a
long 'incubation'. She fought through to a resolution that
deepened her faith. Nevertheless it seems unlikely that she was
ever completely free from the problem. We may remember that,
as late as 1900, when she was 72, she felt the need to recreate the
conflicts of adolescence. Would she have remembered them so
vividly had they been completely resolved?

> Sin seemed to me the law of the world and Satan its master. . . .
> I could not love God, the God who appeared to my darkened
> and foolish heart to consent to so much which seemed to me

cruel and unjust. . . . I asked of the Lord one thing . . . that he
would reveal to me his one, His constant attitude towards His
lost world; that as I had showed him my heart, he would show
me his heart, so much of it . . . as the finite can receive from the
Infinite. . . . Continuing to make this request through day and
night, through summer and winter, with patience and con-
stance, the God who answers prayer had mercy on me; he did
not deny me my request of his own heart's love for the sinner
and when he makes this revelation, he does more; he makes
the enquiring soul a *partaker* of his own heart's love for the
world.[26]

The final answer had not come from her attempt to deal ration-
ally with the problem, or even from her confidence in life after
death and the mystic's vision. She had become 'a partaker of His
own heart's love' through a commitment which was so demanding
in its requirements that all theological questions had lost their
urgency. The solution had come not in thinking about the
problem of evil but in giving up her whole life to its confrontation.
Like her mother before her she found that 'the healing balm is
ever derived not from an abstract principle but from these very
sorrows themselves'.

4   Hell Hath Opened Her Mouth

Josephine's contention that much of the evil we attribute to God
is man-made could hardly have found a stronger evidence than
in the conditions her investigations uncovered. Her further
belief that evil can become a means to a greater good strengthened
her to endure the sufferings that she witnessed. Her conviction
that heaven could be reached only through a confrontation with
the powers of hell found its fullest expression in the Cause.

It is tempting to dismiss some of Josephine's strong language
as Victorian hyperbole, an indulgence in the martial and biblical
imagery expressed in many nineteenth-century hymns, which
had become something of a cliché. Yet when one remembers the
horrors which this fastidious and finely tuned woman endured
— the sight of children physically brutalized, mentally broken,
and then thrown out to die — the words regain some of their
power. Josephine herself addressed the question of the relation

between symbol and reality. Recalling Dante's response to the Inferno, 'He fell prone as one dead', she continued

> I once replied to a friend who complained of my using strong expressions, and asked the meaning of them, as follows: 'Hell hath opened her mouth. I stand in the near presence of the powers of evil: what I see and hear are the smoke of the pit, the violence of the torture inflicted by man on his fellows, the cries of lost spirits, the wail of the murdered innocents,` and the laughter of demons.' But these, it will be said, are mere figures of speech. So they are, used purposely to cover — for no words can adequately express — the reality which they symbolise. But the reality is there, not in any dream or poetic vision of woe, but present on this earth hidden away for the most part from the virtuous and the happy, but not from the eyes of God.[27]

She herself had visited the padded rooms in which children had been strapped down and forced to submit to the sadistic perversions of the brothel's clients. She knew of the Harley Street physician who in one season had procured one hundred girls for the delectation of the peculiar tastes of his patients.[28] It is worth noting that Josephine's compassion extended not only to the victims but to the perpetrators of crime.

> I doubt if many people have come face to face, as I have sometimes with 'demoniacal possession' in the form of raging impurity and unconquerable lust. I have in a sense, looked into hell. I have been filled with a deep pity for many men so possessed, rather than horror, for I felt they were themselves victims dominated and tormented like the Demoniac of Gadara. . . . The face of some haunt me. You will not misunderstand when I assure you that I have known men of gentle and loveable natures, 'true gentlemen', generous and ever ready to do a kind act, and who at the same time have been 'possessed' by a spirit of impurity and lust so that they were driven to deep despair.[29]

It is no wonder that Josephine found those visions of the battle between good and evil that had for so long held sway over her imagination being acted out in reality. It was Armageddon on England's 'green and pleasant land'.

Like the prophets of the early Church, Josephine believed that she was living in the last days of history and that God's judgement and power would usher in His kingdom. The horrors of child prostitution were signs of the reign of sensuality that preceded the New Day.

It is no proclamation of peace, then that heralds the dawning of the new day, but rather a proclamation of a consecrated rebellion against the rule of materialism and sensuality — that materialism which, creeping into the intelligence of men, had smouldered, scorching and charring the last remains of faith, until sensuality has set on fire that which has been so fully prepared for bursting into flame, resulting in a conflagration more desolating and destructive to the nations of the earth than the fire and sword of material extirpation. We are in times of battle.[30]

The horrors were a necessary accompaniment to, and a means of releasing, the spiritual forces that would be victorious.

The bright rays of the sun of Justice will draw out from the darkness of human nature its most poisonous and fetid exhalations — lust, pride, cruelty, revenge, and hate. . . . We are living amidst the convulsions, a vision of Armageddon that heralds the end of the world. It would appear as if the powers of evil were about to combine, at the hour before dawn, for one last gigantic effort to turn God's dear earth into hell.[31]

The alignment of the faithful with God's purpose is imperative.

Apathy or indifference in such a conflict as this means destruction; to be remiss is to be wounded; to stay the fight is to die. In war waged by flesh and blood mercy may intervene, and life be spared; but principles know not the name of mercy. We are rebels for God's law.

The fury of this passage is somewhat tempered in the next when she speaks again of the battle as one against principles, not against man; and testifying to the power of God to change hearts, she envisions the future in the Kingdom of God. Using the imagery of Isaiah, Daniel, and Revelations, she describes the

New Creation. 'Then shall the mountains bring peace to the people, and the little hills righteousness.'
The love of God working with the responses of the faithful will usher in the Kingdom.

> The groaning and travailing earth shall be released from her bondage, and the rod of the oppressor shall be broken! Fetters shall no longer be wrought out of the intelligence and civilisation of one zone to entrap the unwary simplicity [*sic*] and enslave the generations of another. The light of day will fall upon all the dark places of the earth, now full of the habitations of cruelty, and there shall come forth, at the call of the Deliverer, the thousands and tens of thousands of the daughters of men now enslaved in all lands to cruelty and lust. There will be no more hollow virtues, no more specious and splendid crimes. None shall ever again rejoice at another's expense, or hold advantages bought by the blood and tears of his fellow; but 'rising in inherent majesty, the Redeemer's Kingdom will strengthen and extend, wide as the limits of nature's boundary, far as sin has diffused its poison'. And in the plenitude of His power, when all nations shall serve Him the highest achievement of the blessed Saviour, the Desire of all nations, will be, that 'He delivereth the needy when he crieth, the poor also, and him that hath no helper. VENI, DOMINI, JESU.'[32]

*　　*　　*

Yet from behind the confident words, which in spite of their more florid gestures seem to scorch the page, a haunted face looks out.

In the 1890s George Frederick Watts decided to spend his remaining years in painting portraits of people who 'had made the century'. This gallery he would leave to the people of Britain. He asked Josephine Butler to sit for him.[33] She writes her son Stanley of the encounter.

> It is very cold and dull here. Mr. Watts is eighty; like a small refined wizard — worn and thin — with snow white hair and beard, a black skullcap and a graceful dressing gown; a fine aquiline face, very intellectual.

As he works, the reason for his attraction to Josephine emerges.

> I don't know what he knows about the work I have done, but he
> spoke to me alone, in a curious, sad, self-reproachful tone. He
> said he had never been wakened up to try to do good to
> unhappy people till he was seventy; and he said 'What would I
> not give to be able to look back upon such a life as yours'! He
> does not flatter in the least; but he seemed troubled. I said I
> did not take it up willingly. I was *driven* into it by anger against
> injustice. He replied, 'Oh, yes, I know you were driven into it.
> You were destined for it. But some people refuse to be driven;
> and you did not refuse.'

A few days later Josephine, who must have been familiar with
Watts's studies of aristocratic women and the skilled polish with
which he displayed their elegantly clothed complacency, stood
before her portrait.

> I don't know what to think of it, [she remarked]. It is rather
> terrible. It bears the marks of storms and conflicts and sorrow
> so strongly. The eyes are certainly wonderfully done. You
> know I have no brightness in my eyes now. He said he wanted
> to make me looking into Eternity, looking at something no one
> else sees.

Later she confided to Watts:

> When I looked at the portrait which you have just done, I felt
> inclined to burst into tears. I will tell you why. I felt so sorry for
> her. Your power has brought up out of the depths of the past,
> the record of a conflict which no one but God knows of. It is
> written in the eyes, and whole face. Your picture has brought
> back to me all that I suffered, and the sorrows through which
> the Angel of God's presence brought me out alive. I thank you
> that you have not made that poor woman look severe or bitter
> but only sad and purposeful. For with full purpose of heart she
> has borne and laboured, and she is ready to go down to Hades
> again, if it were necessary for the deliverance of her fellow-
> creatures. But God does not require that descent more than
> once.[34]

Octavia Hill

4 Impressive Stature and Formidable Accomplishments

1 Finchley and Highgate, 1838—51: Daughter and Sister

In 1838 Louisa Hill wrote to congratulate her stepmother Caroline on the birth of a daughter.

> I heartily rejoice that the baby is a girl; you will give her strength to endure and struggle with the evils which are the birthright of her sex. She will add to the number of well-educated women, who, I am afraid, form but a very small portion of humanity. But I forget the difference in age. This little baby belongs almost to the third generation. She will be in her bloom when we are old women, if not dead. Great changes may take place before she attains womanhood.[1]

These expectations, filled with high hopes, yet with a trace of underlying gloom, were fulfilled in every way. The child Octavia grew up to be one of the very few women who had a hand in the 'great changes' that shaped the century.

Octavia Hill, like Josephine Butler, was fortunate in her parents. Her father, James Hill, a corn merchant in Peterborough, was an exceptional man. Civil rights and education were his passion; he was remembered as the man who rode fifty miles to secure the pardon of the last man sentenced to death for stealing a sheep. A liberal in politics and a supporter of the arts, he founded a newspaper and bought up the local theatre so that he could improve its offerings by importing productions from London. Feeling existing forms of education to be unnecessarily dry and tedious he began the Infant School in Wisbech, one of the first schools for young children. He took the motto for the school from Wordsworth:

Of old things all are oversold,
Of good things none are good enough;
We'll try if we can help to mould
A world of better stuff.

It was through his interest in education that he met Caroline
Southwood Smith. Widowed for a second time in 1832, and left
with six children (five daughters and a son) to raise, he looked
for help. Having been impressed by some articles on education
that had appeared in *The Monthly Repository*, he sought out their
author and invited her to take charge of his daughters' education.
She came to the Hills as governess in 1832; in 1835 Caroline
Southwood Smith and James Hill were married.

As James Hill had suspected from reading her work, Caroline
was no ordinary governess. She came from a distinguished
family known for its leadership in humanitarian causes. Her
father was Southwood Smith, a medical practitioner and 'sanitary engineer'. Southwood Smith pressed for reform at a time
when there was as yet no definite proof that overcrowding,
polluted water supplies, and inadequate plumbing were causes
of disease. He contributed to the 1842 Report of the Poor Law
Board on the Sanitary Conditions of the Labouring Population
and on the Means of its Improvement. Having amassed statistical evidence of the correlation between contaminated water and
the 1837 and 1838 cholera and typhoid epidemics, Southwood
Smith worked tirelessly to develop administrative machinery to
regulate the building of sewers and the development of adequate
water supplies. The Report was created over the furious
opposition of the laissez-faire philosophy of classical economists
and greedy landlords. It was a courageous assertion of the right
of the State to interfere on behalf of its relatively powerless
citizens. With Shaftesbury and Edwin Chadwick, Southwood
Smith was among five men chosen as members of the first
General Board of Health.

Southwood Smith's personality and lifelong interest would
have an unusual importance for his grandchildren. James Hill
suffered a series of financial difficulties. Only barely surviving
the national banking crisis of 1832, he re-established himself and
his family at Wisbech — only to be totally ruined by the depression
of 1840. His bankruptcy brought on a severe depression from
which he would never fully recover. Southwood Smith assumed

responsibility for the care of his daughter and her children. In the Highgate house overlooking Lord Mansfield's Park and the Caen Woods, the Hill children heard their grandfather discussing politics, science and international affairs with his colleagues. Octavia, through copying and editing his reports, absorbed his ideas so thoroughly that she was able, thirty years later, to apply them to the current situation. The life was luxurious — 'breakfast in the summer-house, dinner in the garden, dessert in the field where the view was best'[2] — but through their grandfather and his friends the Hills learned that there was a world beyond the beech trees of Caen Woods and that not all of it was beautiful. Octavia was horrified by what she heard of the potato famine in Ireland. She came to feel an interest in, and a responsibility for, those who were suffering far beyond the perimeters of her own life. Once in the middle of the night her friend Margaret Howitt was startled to see her sitting bolt upright in bed. 'What are you about, Ockey?' she asked. 'Praying for Poland', was the matter-of-fact reply.[3]

As Southwood Smith's daughter, Caroline Hill had high ambitions for her children. Practical as well as idealistic, she brought up her daughters to accept domestic responsibilities and to welcome manual labour with no thought as to whether it was 'ladylike' or suitable to a middle-class station. Her 'work ethic' was but a small part of her creed. She believed that young children should be brought up in freedom. Unlike her father, however, she felt that they should be somewhat protected against a too early awareness of suffering and misery. 'A child should be placed in circumstances where it can neither do harm, nor suffer; then it should be left to its own devices.'[4] The protection against suffering — their own and others' — would help them to grow up secure in the conviction that evil is contrary to the mind of God. Feeling that it had no power over them and should have no power over others, they would be strong enough to overcome it. Mrs Hill's Unitarian philosophy, and its benign and gentle rule, were imbued with a high sense of purpose. Her daughter Miranda summarizes it:

It is difficult to express to those who never knew Mrs. Hill what her influence was on those who came in contact with her. On her children it left an indelible impression as deep as life itself, and as lasting. From her book 'Notes on Education' it will be seen how entirely she felt the *spirit* to be everything in education. She seldom gave a distinct order or made a rule; but her children felt that she lived continually in the presence of God. . . . Her children also learned from early infancy from her attitude of mind, that if a thing was right it must be done; there ceased to be any question about it.[5]

Given Mrs Hill's sunny temperament and the nature of her child-rearing philosophy, it is not surprising that the children (Miranda, Gertrude, Octavia, Emily, and Florence) should be 'noble savages'; they became known as 'the young ladies who are always up in the hedges'. A neighbour remembered that 'they know every boy and girl, cat, dog and donkey in the village by sight and a good many of them by name, and for those whose names they do not know they invent one'.[6] Octavia worked in the garden, apprenticed herself to a carpenter to learn his trade, and led her sisters on forays into the countryside. At the age of six, when Emily had fallen into a well, Octavia pulled her to safety.

2   London, 1851–55: Artist and Toymaker

In 1851 Mrs Hill, not wishing to remain dependent on her far from affluent father, began to look for a job. She sought employment not only for herself but for her family. It was part of her philosophy that children, who were strengthened by a happy and carefree childhood, could at an early age move confidently into the responsibilities of adulthood. Along with other Victorians, she did not recognize a transitional stage of 'adolescence'. Her children would find their places in the world, she believed, not through introspection but through action. She hoped that proper employment would bring them companionship as well as financial independence. She sought work among like-minded liberals.

At that time a group of men calling themselves Christian Socialists [7] had started small cooperatives with the object of circumventing the most apparent social liability of capitalism: the exploitation of labour. A manager, paid a small salary, would secure work for artisans. The profits were divided among the workers. A later generation of socialists would dismiss these efforts as amateurish and too limited in scope. The Webbs and the Fabian Socialists were even more sharply critical. They charged the Christian Socialists with having put off the day of reckoning by holding out an illusory hope and thus delaying the millennium of State Socialism. Nevertheless, in their day these modest efforts rescued many from desperate poverty.

The Hills were enthusiastic supporters of the theology from which the cooperatives sprang. More Christian than Socialist, the leaders had little faith in programmes. They found little value in the architects' drawings of hospitals, prisons, and trade schools; the laws, statutes, and economic reports with which the Utilitarians hoped to bring in the secular kingdom. They were repelled by Benthamite psychology which was tied to the belief that a man is merely a bundle of stimulus—response mechanisms. They felt that no economic programme, no matter how altruistically conceived, could solve the most basic problems. The despair of the worker was not primarily due to his poverty, but to his loss of identity. They proposed to concern themselves not only with bread for the body but with food for the soul.

Accepting the position of manager of the Ladies' Cooperative Guild, Caroline Hill felt that she had found worthwhile work for herself and a congenial atmosphere for her family. Housed in the Guild quarters at Russell Place, an awkward but roomy house, the family made friends among both leaders and workers. Miranda joined her mother, helping instruct the workers in painting scenes on glass, which was reinforced and used on tables and decorative panels. Octavia did odd jobs — reading to the women as they worked, taking charge of the supplies, and acquiring some knowledge of the business. Vansittart Neale, noting her executive ability, gave her more responsibility. In 1852, when Octavia was only 14, he put her in charge of his new venture — toymaking.

The work demanded a certain skill in administration and arithmetic and called upon her ability to deal with a variety of people — the child workers, fellow managers, shopkeepers for whom she filled orders, the Christian Socialist leaders to whom she was responsible. She had to supervise the children's work, which was paid by the piece, to assign the various processes to each child, to choose the designs, to price the furniture and see that, when it was finished, it was packed and sent over to the showroom to be sold along with the women's glass work. In addition she kept the accounts and tried to turn a profit.

Although Octavia enjoyed book-keeping and the chance to use her carpentry, she found her friendships with the children particularly rewarding. When she had first come to London, she had been appalled by the poverty around her. Her own experience was reinforced by Mayhew's *London Labour and the London Poor*, a book given to her by a friend at the Guild. Some of her young companions looked as if they had stepped from Mayhew's pages. 'There was poor Denis whose face and neck were terribly disfigured with burns; there was Clara, a tall, over-grown girl from a dirty home, who was half-starved and cruelly treated.' Another child, when she was not at the Guild, 'lived in a dark cellar into which one descended by a ladder, where she sat all day to sell pennyworths of coal'.[8]

It was obvious that the children's needs could not be met by helping them to earn a few pennies, which would be taken home to often uncaring and wasteful families. Seeing the inadequacy of the scraps of food the children brought from home, she suggested that they pool their tiny resources, buy food and cook it themselves. With a white cloth on the dinner table, conversation ranged over a variety of subjects — family life, books, singing, animals, flowers. Once again Octavia found herself at the head of a group of admiring followers. She was distressed to discover that the children had no experience of the outdoors, indeed no recreation of any kind, and began to organize Sunday outings. Hampstead Heath and Bishop's Wood were favourite territories. Gertrude remembered walking there with an older friend, Professor Owen,

> who was quietly explaining something about the mosses on Lord Mansfield's fence — all being very still — when to my surprise, the hedge was broken open, and, with a burst of joy, who should leap down from the bank with a staff in her hand and a straw hat torn by the thicket but Octavia followed by a troop of ragged toy-workers happy and flushed, each with a lap full of blue bells.[9]

After these outings the Hill girls would rise early Sunday morning and walk to the Chapel of Lincoln's Inn to hear F. D. Maurice preach. After a while Maurice noticed the young girls who attended daily and Sunday services so regularly, and sought them out. Often he would invite Emily and Octavia to walk home with him after the service and inquire about their lives and discuss the work at the Guild. Octavia grew to love the services of the Anglican Church and to find in Maurice's theology confirming grounds for her feelings about people and her intuitions about God. She asked to join the Church and was baptised and confirmed at Lincoln's Inn.

When not working, she was caught up in the controversy and excitement surrounding the Christian Socialist leaders. Her letters bubble with adolescent excitement,

> Mr. Furnivall [Frederick Jones Furnivall] I admire more and more, the more I know and read of him and, as to Mr. Ludlow [John Malcolm Ludlow], certainly there is not (excepting Mr. Furnivall) such a person in the whole world. He has the largest, clearest, best-balanced mind joined to the truest most earnest wish to help the working classes I ever met with (of course excepting Mr. Furnival's). [10]

At Guild meetings she listened to addresses by Furnivall, Charles Kingsley, and Thomas Hughes. Thanking Miranda for having sent her Thomas Cooper's *History of the Working Tailors' Association* and Kingsley's *Cheap Clothes and Nasty*, she vowed that reading a Socialist book is 'one of the greatest happiness any one can have'.

While her social sense was being developed through her friendships with the Guild's leaders, her love of beauty and her artistic abilities had attracted the attention of John Ruskin. Her first mention of Ruskin in a letter of 1853, indicates that she was already familiar with his work (Furnivall had given her *Modern Painters*). Characteristically, she is wholehearted and impassioned in defence of her hero.

> If, as I suppose, *The Times* accuses him of affectation of style and want of humility, I entirely deny the first charges; as I think there is never a single word he writes, which could have been left out without loss, or changed without spoiling the idea.[11]

Ruskin paid a visit to the Guild in December 1853. He gave the women some advice about colour, reworking two of the designs and ordering five slabs of decorated glass. Attracted by the vigour and warmth of the Hills, he invited Miranda and Octavia to visit him. Greeting them warmly, he showed the girls some of his manuscripts and sketches and praised their work. 'He evidently thought my designs well done, admired the fir and bramble, blamed my not knowing exactly what colours I should put elsewhere.' He then gave his impressionable young guests one of his whirlwind, somersaulting vaults through the history of civilization, touching on theories of light and colour, the grotesque nature of thirteenth-century art, the ambiguous relation between beauty and happiness. Octavia was dazzled.

This is not half the conversation and we had several others, to say nothing of illustrations and propositions. And now, M. [Emily], do you or do you not wish to hear what I think of it; that *that* which is asked for is given; that, well-used, this friendship, so happily begun, may be a long and growing one; that I have seen a world of beauty and that this might be the opening of a more glorious path.[12]

It is hard to know whether Ruskin's pleasure in the uncritical adulation of his young friends led him to overvalue Octavia's gifts or whether he genuinely believed in her artistic promise. In any case he encouraged her. Mrs Hill reported, 'Ruskin is delighted with Ockey's table, and means to give her employment in illumination. Is this not very good news?'[13] He commissioned her to copy Dürer and Turner and assured her that her work would be used in future volumes of *Modern Painters*. In the companionship of her erudite host, she would forget for a few hours the oppression and misery of the lives of the people with whom she worked. Then left alone, she contentedly studied her surroundings and prepared herself to work. 'A gold frame with eight Turner sketches hung on a shutter before me, all my working things on a nice wide window ledge, and my little book on my knee.'[14]

Ruskin continued to urge her to paint, but he came to recognize that she lacked the artist's singleness of vision. She could not put herself first. He told her that she must paint the faces of the people she saw every day but he foresaw the result. 'If you devote yourself to human expression, I know how it will be, you will watch it more and more, and there will be an end to art for you. You will say, 'Hang drawing I must go to help people'.'[15]

3 Working Women's Classes, 1855—61: Teacher and Administrator

The inner conflicts between Octavia's artistic and social interests were aggravated by severe external pressures. Maurice had offered to teach a class in the Bible to Octavia's toymakers; the year was 1855. Two years before, his *Theological Essays* had created a storm of controversy. It was violently attacked by the evangelical branch of the Anglican Church as possibly heretical and Maurice lost his post at King's College. The chief financial supporter of the toymakers' guild was a Mrs Chamberleyne, whom Octavia described as 'a strict low-church woman who enters a room talking about "the sinful carnal flesh, etc.," who wishes all children to rise and repeat a text whenever she enters a room'.[16] Mrs Chamberlayne threatened to withdraw her support if Maurice were allowed to teach. Maurice accepted her prohibition. Caroline Hill was so angered by the evident relief with which Vansittart Neale and her Committee had received the Professor's withdrawal that she resigned in protest. She knew that this decision, taken as her daughter Octavia said, 'on very high grounds', would have unpleasant consequences for her and for her young daughters. It meant breaking up the family. The girls would be faced with taxing decisions and unless they wished to return to their grandfather's, they would have to learn to live in poverty.

Octavia did not wish to accept her grandfather's protection. 'I detest any sort of dependence. It is almost hard for me even to imagine a person of whom I could, for myself, ask any assistance.'[17] She felt torn. She sided with her mother and Maurice, yet she could not give up her toymakers. In the middle of the crisis she wrote her friend Mary Harris,

> I am working here, where I will continue, as long as ever I have any strength, or as long as I am permitted to do so. My whole life is bound with this Society. Every energy I possess belongs to it.[18]

Emily accompanied her mother to Southwood Smith's. The other girls stayed on. Octavia, then but 17, was placed in charge of the workroom. She handled all the finances and accounting; she ordered supplies and planned the work. Realizing the limitations of toymaking as a career, she started to look ahead for the children, visiting their parents and suggesting vocational possibilities. 'One or two will train as teachers in Infant Schools; others I destine for printing. . . . One should learn some branch of needlework.'[19]

Maurice, though preoccupied with his own professional problems, had not forgotten the Hills. Barred from advancement in the great universities, he determined to build on his earlier success with adult education; he would add classes for working women to the Working Men's College. He offered to Octavia the post of Secretary, at a salary of £25 a year. Octavia accepted the position with the understanding that she would continue with her other work. She assumed responsibility for financial transactions and book-keeping and would step in if there were a problem between teacher and student.

For the first time the colleagues with whom she had to deal were 'ladies'. Many of the teachers were volunteers, educated upper-class women who, bored by the tedium of the parlour, and barred from seeking employment, wished to do something with their lives. It was from among women like these that, in later years, Octavia would draw her workers. But she would first have to overcome her prejudice against 'ladies'.

> I don't know what there is in the word 'lady' which will connect itself with all kinds of things I despise and hate; first and most universally it suggests a want of perseverance, and bending before small obstacles, a continual, 'I would if . . . .'[20]

Characteristically, Octavia kept adding to her responsibilities without being willing to give anything up (though she did confess to her friend Mary Harris that she had to forgo her Latin studies). She spent several happy hours a day in the Dulwich Gallery, copying Turners; she taught drawing to children; she sought out buyers for her toys and negotiated for the best terms; she tracked down jobs for older workers who were beginning to find the work in the toy shop and the £6 weekly inadequate; she helped Miranda with her students; she taught an occasional class in the Working Woman's College and kept administrative order in the ranks. She voluntarily assumed her father's debts and took on extra tutoring to pay them off. Not surprisingly, she exhausted herself.

To her family and to her workers she presented herself as a commanding and fiercely independent person. They thought of her as indomitable, protected by a practicality that made her 'good only to do a sum, carry a weight, go for a long walk in the rain, or decide any difficult question about tangible things'. With Maurice — and occasionally with Ruskin — she allows herself to show her vulnerability, her need for protection, and her youth. Maurice, hearing that she was becoming ill, invited her to visit him after work. He spoke 'very kindly' to her, pointing out that 'it is very self-willed to try to do without rest'. Octavia struggled with her emotions:

> I could not help the tears coming into my eyes, and my voice being choked at feeling so cared for by one so noble, so infinitely strong, so perfectly calm; and a strange sense of perfect peace, such as I have not felt since I saw you, stole over me. And yet I was so hard, so unconvinced, and so strangely bitter; bitter with myself in feeling how much of pride had made me think I could stand without help; and we sat quite silent for a few moments. At last Mr. Maurice spoke in a deep full voice, you felt with a depth of human sympathy in it: 'Will you think about it then, Miss Hill?'[21]

At his suggestion she reduced some of her activities, including church-going, and took extended holidays in Europe and at the country houses of friends. She was warmly welcomed by the George MacDonalds, whom she had met through poetry classes at the Working Men's College. She developed friendships with other members of the College faculty, particularly Jane Sterling, the daughter of the essayist John Sterling, and Sophia Jex-Blake whose wealthy family had permitted her to accept the post as mathematical tutor at Queen's College provided that she was paid no wages. From her Octavia learned that a 'lady' is not always a useless woman.

4 Nottingham Place, 1861 – 65: Schoolmistress

The entire Hill family was reunited in 1861 when they took possession of a large house in Nottingham Place off Marylebone Street. Octavia was asked to prepare two children for the entrance exams at Queens; Emily and Octavia were hired as tutors by Thomas Hughes. Gradually, the need to combine these activities became clear. The Hill family found themselves running a school. A delightfully informal group of teachers and scholars congregated in the old building that housed the Nottingham Place School. They turned a barn into a schoolroom, and in an atmosphere still redolent of horse and with only indirect light from the small, high windows, they conducted three or more classes simultaneously. The school offered the classical curriculum with some additions.

> The subjects we teach are the English subjects, Latin, French, German, music (part-singing but not solo singing), drawing, the elements of Euclid and Algebra, also of botany, chemistry, and natural philosophy.[22]

For the 'in corpore sano' aspects of their education, the girls rowed on the ornamental waters of Regent's Park and played croquet. In this school that was more like an extended family than an institution, the girls were expected to be self-reliant, punctual, neat, and to help maintain the building. In addition they were encouraged to get to know their neighbours, many of whom lived on the edge of poverty.

Once a week mothers of the toy workers gathered under the reproduction of 'The Last Supper' beneath which Octavia had written, 'These are the living men, we the passing shadows on the wall.' They joined in the singing, listened to Octavia read poetry, helped with the cooking, and ate dinner together. In exposing her well-bred young women students to some of the social realities of Victorian life, Octavia was training a future generation of workers, a generation that would combine the political power inherent in their social position with the intellectual qualifications and broad interests of the reformer. Freed by education from the constraints of their class — the snobbism, the materialism, the prohibitions against work — they would be uniquely equipped to become effective leaders.

5   *Paradise Place, 1865 — 69: Manager of Housing*

The early years of the Nottingham Place School marked a period of growth for Octavia as well as for the students. She saw that the poor women who came to visit the school were undernourished. Sometimes they fainted from exhaustion, and Octavia, escorting them home, found that they lived in damp and filthy cellars. She was faced with the inescapable conclusion that, even as she helped these families to achieve a measure of economic sufficiency and gave their children a glimpse of a more humane and joyful life, she must do more. As long as the poor had no access to the comforts of 'home life' they could not achieve the beginnings of human dignity.

Private enterprise had failed to provide decent housing for the poor who were flocking to the city in search of employment. To increase his profit, the owner squeezed whole families into single rooms. For the sake of additional rental property, he closed in the courtyards. Cynical and shiftless, he had no interest in his tenants beyond their ability to pay. One unabashedly admitted to Octavia that his deficiencies as manager of housing actually improved his primary business as funeral director. When asked what he did when rents were not paid, he cheerfully replied, 'Yes, Miss, of course there are plenty of bad debts. It's not the rents I look to, but the deaths I get out of the houses.'[23]

If decent housing was to be found and maintained, landlords must be able to put the well-being of the tenants and the upkeep of the houses first and the profits second. Octavia Hill proposed that she be put in charge of such housing and that John Ruskin provide the initial investment.

It was a natural suggestion, one that she and Ruskin had arrived at together. In 1864 Ruskin's father died, leaving him a considerable sum of money. John's literalist faith had been badly shaken by biblical criticism, but his evangelical sense of duty burned more fervently than ever. In the next decade he was to develop his economic ideas, sharpening his attack on the callousness of classical economists and the brutal effects of unbridled capitalism. Meanwhile he wished to do something useful. Because he was temperamentally unable to deal personally with poor people,[24] he wished to help them indirectly. He sought Octavia Hill's advice. Finally conceding that her social interests should take precedence over her art, he urged her to 'get [her] ideas clear'.

On 19 April 1864 Octavia wrote to Mrs Shaen, the wife of her friend William Shaen who would become the legal adviser to the housing scheme:

> I have long been wanting to gather near us our friends among the poor, in some house arranged for their health and convenience, in fact, a small private model lodging-house, where I may know everyone, and do something towards making their lives healthier and happier; and to my intense joy Ruskin has promised to help me to work the plan. You see he feels his father's property implies an additional duty to help to alleviate the misery around him; and he seems to trust us with this work. He writes 'Believe me, you will give me one of the greatest pleasures yet possible to me by enabling me to be of use in this particular manner and to these ends.' So we are to collect materials to form our plans more definitely; and tho' we shall begin very quietly, and I never wish the house to be very large, yet I see no end to what may grow out of it.[25]

In the spring of 1865 three houses were purchased. To judge from Octavia's description the name of the court in which the houses were located, Paradise Place, was ironic at best.

> The plaster was dropping from the walls; on one staircase a pail was placed to catch the rain that fell through the roof. All the staircases were perfectly dark, the bannisters were gone, having been used as firewood by the tenants. . . . The dust-bin, standing in front of the houses, was accessible to the whole neighbourhood, and boys often dragged from it quantities of unseemly objects and spread them over the Court. The state of the drainage was in keeping with everything else. The pavement of the back yard was all broken up, and great puddles stood in it, so that the damp crept up the outer walls. One large but dirty water-butt received the water laid on for the houses; it leaked, and for such as did not fill their jugs when the water came in, or had no jugs to fill, there was no water.[26]

A year later the walls had been whitewashed, a community laundry had been established, the water supply was clean, and the sewage system had been brought up to the standards of Southwood Smith. Moreover, the houses were bringing in more than the 5 per cent interest that Ruskin had suggested as appropriate. The profit was spent on improvements suggested by the tenants — cupboards and laundry equipment. Some of the men kept up with minor general repairs. The older girls were hired at 6 pence a week to scrub the hallways. On Monday nights Octavia, the landlady, made her weekly visits, collecting her rent, and inquiring 'with perfect respectfulness' about their week.

In the decade following the purchase of Ruskin's houses Octavia found herself increasingly burdened with administrative work and relinquished her responsibilities at the Nottingham Place School to Miranda. Furthermore, the range of her endeavours began to extend beyond the confines of Paradise Place. She recognized that her individual attempts to help a few families could only evolve into a sound basis for national policy if placed in the context of the larger issues. How could one be generous to the poor without making them into paupers? What was the proper relation between classes, between private enterprise and state initiative? In 1869 she read a paper to the London Association for the Prevention of Pauperization and Crime entitled, 'The Importance of Aiding the Poor without Almsgiving'. Her ideas were sought by the framers of the Artisans' Dwelling Act of 1875. In that year her essays on housing were brought together by Louisa Schuyler, President of the State Charity Aid Association, and published under the title *Homes of the London Poor.* HRH Princess Alice, who had visited Paradise Place in 1866, translated the work into German. Octavia had become an important and powerful figure.

6   *Charity Organization Society, 1869 — 75: Policy-maker and Adviser*

While she continued to maintain that the poor must be dealt with individually, and was always wary of legislative 'solutions' to poverty, Octavia found herself increasingly drawn into politics. She campaigned for her old friend and employer, Thomas Hughes when he stood for parliament. (He lost.) She fought to have the licence of a public house near one of her tenements withdrawn. (She won.)

With a hindsight that sees as inevitable the accelerating momentum of Octavia Hill's career, one forgets that the degree of responsibility given to this woman was unique. She, herself, however, did not forget. She speaks of her apprehension before attending the meeting which led to the formation of the first local committee of the Charity Organization Society.

> We are having a large meeting in the parish this week to try to organize the relief given; very opposite creeds will be represented — Archbishop Manning, Mr. Llewellyn Davies, Mr. Fremantle, Mr. Fardley Wilmot, and others. . . . Mr. Fremantle, the Rector of our district, and the main mover in the matter, is to call on me to-day. May some power inspire me with intellect and speech; I have hardly a hope that they will place me on the Committee. I shall try boldly, but I think no ladies will be admitted.[27]

Her apprehension was unfounded. She was not only placed on the committee but invited to take charge of the Marylebone District. This appointment confirmed her as a leading member of what we would call the Establishment. It brought her in touch with policy-makers of national importance and deepened her friendships with a coming generation of Anglican workers in the slums of East London, most especially with Henrietta Rowland Barnett, one of her former managers, and her husband, Samuel Barnett, the founder of Toynbee Hall.

The Barnetts left several impressions of Octavia Hill whom they considered a 'noble influence' and whose philosophy they promoted. Henrietta admitted to occasional exasperation with Octavia's seriousness; she said that some of her husband's best stories had collapsed in the telling 'before her close but irresponsive attention, especially if it occured to him in the middle that the tale would not be up to her moral standard, for she expected high ethics even in a joke'. The following verbal picture of Octavia given by Henrietta Barnett tallies with the bright, birdlike expression of the woman in the Sargent portrait.

> She was small in stature with a long body and short legs. She did not dress, she only wore clothes, which were often unnecessarily unbecoming. She had soft and abundant hair and regular features, but the beauty of her face lay in her

brown and very luminous eyes, which quite unconsciously she lifted upwards as she spoke on any matter for which she cared. Her mouth was large and mobile, but not improved by laughter. Indeed Miss Octavia was nicest when she was made passionate by her earnestness.[28]

After Octavia Hill's appointment to the Central Commission of the Charity Organization Society in 1875, her advice began to be sought on national issues. Many of the charities had been brought to the edge of bankruptcy by the depression of the 1870s and the policy of giving to all who asked without any thought of their needs and capacities. The C.O.S., as it was called, sought to link the efforts of all the relieving societies in London by establishing a common standard. Octavia was among those who insisted that the giving of charity must be preceded by some sort of investigation, it must be accompanied by supervision, and it must always take into account its goal: increased self-reliance on the part of the recipient. The Central Committee looked beyond London. It investigated the relation of housing and state support in Glasgow and Liverpool and other municipalities that had already committed themselves to housing. It became a clearing house for ideas. With the encouragement of members Shaftesbury and Stansfeld, President of the Poor Law Board, it became politically active. It gave the City Council the power to buy land for housing and to offer loans at advantageous interest rates; it recommended a more centralized form of government for London, giving the richer parishes the responsibility of helping the poor and establishing the principle of city involvement in low-cost housing; it insisted that the Railway Extension Act of 1885 contain a clause requiring that the company replace all the housing destroyed by the railways' expansion. (It was calculated that between 1883 and 1901, 76,000 people were evicted by the building of railway lines.)[29]

In these deliberations, the lines of division in the Central Committee were often drawn between the clergy who felt that the Society had become heartless and bureaucratic, more concerned with maintaining itself than with ministering to the poor, and the administrators who accused the clergy of sentimentality and reminded them of the near bankruptcy created by the unbusinesslike openhandedness of a previous decade. Octavia found herself in a mediating position, reminding her colleagues of the imperative need to consider the poor as people, yet advocating fiscal responsibility and warning against the danger that the Society, which was originally designed to seek out the root causes of poverty and advise agencies, would become merely one more charitable society.

> It is of the deepest importance that the C.O.S. should not become a fresh relieving society, for added societies are an evil, and besides it can never investigate cases and organize charities as it ought, if it becomes a relief society. But the C.O.S. must score abundant and wise relief where needed, and it must stop that which is injurious. To accomplish these two ends it must win the confidence of private donors and agencies. Besides this, if its investigations are to be trustworthy and effectual and gently conducted, they must be watched over by people of education, with deep sympathy for the poor. You cannot learn how to help a man nor even get him to tell you what ails him, till you care for him. For these reasons volunteers must rally round the C.O.S. and prevent it from becoming a dry, and because dry, ineffectual machinery for enquiring about people; volunteers must win the support of local clergy and support them in the reform of their charities.[30]

Octavia maintained the pose of one temperamentally unsuited to politics, tripping herself up and sometimes impeding others through her impetuosity and unsparing frankness. Yet during this period her family came to see her as a person who not only had power but the capacity to develop the wiles and subtleties of the politician. Miranda writes:

> I think all went very well; and the deep purpose of Octavia's statesmanship — for which the party was given, that of uniting St. Mary's people somewhat — seemed to have succeeded. I feel frightened when I discover what deep reasons of state Octavia has for her actions. I am afraid of spoiling some political combination (parochial rather than political) by some awkwardness of mine, from being wholly incapable of telling what it all means. I feel as if Octavia were a kind of Cecil in her sphere.[31]

This was the period leading up to the Artisans' Dwelling Bill of 1875 (Cross Act), a bill whose provisions reflected Octavia Hill's work and concerns. She had overcome her antipathy to state control on the grounds that in this case it was needed to do away with the evil of the capitalist landlord. Unlike an earlier bill, it dealt, not with individual houses, but with large areas. It gave the Metropolitan Board of Works and the City Commissioners of the Sewers (London) the authority to make a plan for improvement. (This plan had to make provisions for replacing as many dwellings as it destroyed.) After a long process of confirmation, involving local bodies and even Parliament, the land would be acquired and offered for sale with rigid obligation to rebuild. It is not difficult to imagine the problems arising from this clumsy and impractical act. It did, however, establish a principle — if private enterprise could not house the poor the state must be empowered to do it — and it led to further legislation that more effectively promoted its goal.

Octavia gives a moving account of listening to the Second Reading from the Speaker's Gallery. She was

> leaning back, thinking, when suddenly my own name caught my ear. Mr. Shuttleworth was speaking of the Macmillan article . . . and he read aloud from it the description of the wonderful delight it gave me to see the courts laid out to the light and air. . . . The words recalled vividly the intensity of the longing, and the wonderfully swift realization; a great gush of joy rushed over me. . . . I can't tell how tiny it made me feel.[32]

Her family saw Octavia as continuing Southwood Smith's career and work. As her mother put it, 'the mantle has fallen on her'.[33]

7 *Kyrle Society and National Trust, 1875 — 84; Patron of the Arts and Conservationist*

It had always been the Hill family's belief that people needed more than food and drains. In 1875 Miranda read a paper to her girls at the Nottingham School giving her views on art. She proposed to start a society which should be called 'The Society for the Diffusion of Beauty'. The title actually adopted was the Kyrle Society, after Pope's 'Man of Ross', John Kyrle, who embellished his native town with a public park and an alley of elm trees. Within the decade enthusiastic members of the Society, some of them England's leading intellectuals, were rushing about London setting out window-boxes, painting pictures on blank walls, and teaching slum children to play the violin. Emma Cons, aunt of Lillian Baylis, the founder of the Old Vic Theatre, trained actors; George MacDonald wrote plays and supervised rehearsals; Arthur Rackham painted the sets for Gilbert and Sullivan operettas. Octavia eagerly took part. She handled the Society's finances. Under George MacDonald's direction, she appeared as Piety in 'Everyman'. She offered her advice as an artist to those who were trying to redeem London from the sooty conglomerate of brick and stone that it had become. (One of her ideas — not acted on — was the suggestion that Kingsley's words, 'Do Noble Deeds', be painted in huge letters on the wall next to Waterloo Station.)

The Kyrle Society's purpose was not merely to add man-made decorations to the London scene, but to preserve the beauty that was already there. Octavia was the most powerful and know-ledgeable member of the committee concerned with open space. It was a natural appointment; she had always fought for the preservation of space, starting with her own courtyards in Paradise Place. She believed that they were imperative to her tenants' well-being, not only because they provided clean air, but because people might occasionally glimpse a star or the rough arm of a tree. To the irritation of Emma Cons and some of her executive-minded friends, even — indeed, especially — in middle age and from her position of leadership, Octavia spent many hours trudging about in heavy galoshes, trowel in hand, transplanting daisies which she had brought in from the country and formulating carefully detailed plans for the further improvement of her courts. She wished to cover the blank walls with graffiti of an inspirational nature. Glazed tiles in rich colours would spell out high-minded sayings in letters a foot high. Though losing out on Waterloo Station, she was able to put her idea into execution in two courts. In Freshwater Place the purple, blue and green tiles spelled out the passage, 'Every house is builded by some man but He that built all things is God.' Along the wall next to Red Cross Hall ran the slogan, etched in red and white ceramic, 'The Wilderness shall blossom as the rose.' She spoke of the 'healing gifts' of space and called her courts 'open air sitting rooms for the poor'. They were the smallest unit in a conception of space as 'places to sit in, places to play in, places to stroll in, and space and place to spend a day in'. The members of the subcommittee on open spaces worked at first with immediate problems. Looking at a map, they pinpointed the obvious targets: gardens of the rich, disused graveyards, abandoned ground left over after a subdivision, school play-grounds. They asked the Corporations, City Companies, and the Metropolitan Board of Works, whether in planning for new buildings, they would set aside a certain portion as public land. Most of these excellent suggestions were rejected. When Octavia heard that the Swiss Cottage Fields, one of her favourite spots for day excursions for her tenants at Marlyebone, was to be built on, she tried to raise money to save them. She could not save the Fields but she did become a member of the Executive Board of the Commons and Footpath Association where she continued to press for land reform. 'We tried, oh how we tried, to get the Quakers to devote to the service of the poor their disused burial grounds.'[34]

Always preferring private initiative to state control, the Kyrle Society and the Commons Preservation Society continued to search for land in London. In 1883 Octavia wrote bitterly,

It is strange to notice that though other towns in numbers have had Parks given to them the thousands of rich people who owe their wealth to London, or who avail themselves of its advantages, have not, as far as I know, given one single acre of ground that could have been sold for building over, to Londoners for recreation ground or Park, if we except Leicester Square.[35]

Unable to enlist the support of the rich, the Kyrle Society placed the issue before the people. Octavia trenchantly summarized the situation.

The question before the country, and it is well we should realize its magnitude before important decisions are made, is whether consistently with all private rights there is still any land in England which can be preserved for the common good. . . . Are we, as a nation, to have any flower garden at all? Can we afford it, or will we have beet-root and cabbages only? In other words, is all the land as far as the people are concerned, from sea to sea to be used for corn growing or building over only?

In an age which feels that it has lost not only flower gardens but beet-root and cabbages as well, her words have the sad ring of wasted opportunity.

Although habitually standing for individual rights and limited governmental powers, in this case Octavia Hill speaks like a socialist.

> It must be observed that the nation, as a nation, is not held to possess the open uncultivated unappropriated land of England. True, generation after generation has passed over much of it freely, but it seems that the people are not thereby held to have acquired a right to do so. Perhaps this is because such right has no money value; for rights of way, rights of light, rights of possession of soil, even rights on these very open spaces of pasturing cattle, cutting furze and of playing games are recognized by law where they have long been enjoyed. Had the right to wander freely, and to enjoy the beauty of earth and sky been felt to be a more distinct possession, it may be that these rights also would have been legally recognized.[36]

Octavia and her friends found themselves looking beyond London to the entire map of Britain. There must be an overall plan.

> I was impressed with the fact that unless some very much larger view of the quantity of open space needed should be taken by the authorities, and some really great scheme be adopted for purchasing important land *at once*, the time would go past very rapidly when it would be possible to save what in the future would be felt to be almost essential to the health and well-being of Londoners. To secure the support of the public in pressing forwards large schemes, and that at once, I must use all ways open to me.[37]

The group advocated an approach tailored to the particular political realities of each situation. They sought support from governing bodies and investigated the legal possibilities. The publication of a hard-hitting letter over Octavia Hill's signature was usually enough to arouse public opinion and put pressure on governing bodies. The final move was to appeal to private funds. Some land was saved entirely through private funds, others through matching funds, a combination of private and public money. The tracts of land saved by these efforts include Hampstead Heath, Parliament Hill, Hilly Fields, Vauxhall Park, and sections of Kent and Surrey. It soon became evident that the effort of dealing with each property on an individual basis would quickly exhaust the energies of the conservationists. They must organize ongoing private support. In 1884 Octavia's friend Sir Robert Hunter read a paper in Birmingham suggesting the establishment of a corporation which would hold land and buildings in trust for the people. Octavia began thinking about a name:

> A short expressive name is difficult to find for the new Company. What do you think of the Commons and Gardens Trust? . . . You will do better, I believe, to put forward its benevolent than its commercial character. People don't like unsuccessful business, but do like charity when a little money goes a long way because of good commercial management.[38]

Sir Robert's choice of name, National Trust, was adopted. Canon H. D. Rawnsley, with his love for the Lake Country, was drawn into the scheme. The Duke of Westminster was named the first President and the new society moved quickly to assume wide responsibilities. Octavia wrote of her happiness at procuring Barras Head at Tintagel. 'It is not quite the first, nor will it, I hope, be the last of such places which shall thus become in a new and very real sense the Common Land of England.' She was particularly pleased that this gift of property had come through the cooperative efforts of rich and poor, American and English.

> Bound up with noble thoughts of British history, of British legend, it seems a fitting first fruits of the combined gifts of members and friends of the National Trust which has been founded to keep for her people for ever, in their beauty, accessible to all, some of England's fairest, most memorable places.[39]

8   *Royal Commission, 1884 – 1912, Celebrity*

In 1884 Miranda wrote,

> It has come to a point when two peers and a cabinet minister
> call and consult her in one week. She had Fawcett here
> yesterday, Lord Wemyss the day before to ask what he should
> say in the House of Lords, and the Duke of Westminster on
> Wednesday to ask what the Prince of Wales could do in the
> matter.[40]

She was offered a seat in the Abbey for Queen Victoria's Jubilee.
Her friends got together and commissioned Sargent to paint her
portrait.

While Octavia enjoyed some of the prerogatives of
fame and rejoiced that her work had received national recognition, she never fully accepted the transition from social worker
to administrator and adviser to governments. She was also in
these years oppressed by personal difficulties. Ruskin, who was
now struggling against impending madness, had turned against
her. In 1877 she was briefly engaged to marry one of her workers,
Edward Bond. When he seemed unable to break his ties to his
mother, Octavia saw him in a different light and broke the
engagement. Finally, overwork led to a breakdown. Through an
extended European trip with a new friend, Harriet Yorke, who
was to become her lifelong companion and helper, her health
was restored.

Upon her return Octavia managed to achieve a balance between
her love of working directly with her tenants and the increasing
demands of executive responsibilities. As representative of the
Ecclesiastical Commission she was placed in charge of housing
in Deptford and Walforth, bringing the total number of houses
under her care to between three and four thousand.[41] Some of
this responsibility she of course delegated to other women. For
Southwark she reserved her more personal attentions, building
a central hall and supervising its use as reading room, music
studio, theatre, and men's club.

In 1884 she was asked to give evidence before the Royal
Commission on Housing. She testified against the encouragement
of state-supported housing, predicting that it would paralyse
private initiative and that subsidizing rents would deter

employers from paying proper wages and would add to London's problems by attracting the indigent poor from all over Britain. She warned against surrendering responsibility to government officials whose self-interest in political promotion might take precedence over interest in the poor, and who were already overburdened with other County Council business.

Octavia Hill's career as an adviser to government was advanced by her appointment to the Royal Commission on the Poor Law (1905). This Commission had the job of revising the Poor Law of 1834, whose policies had patently failed. The Majority Report, which Octavia signed, reflected her conservative economic policies: it re-established the principle of outdoor relief, but only on a limited, temporary basis, and it further stipulated that 'the conditions of the able-bodied pauper should be less eligible than that of the lowest class of independent labourer'.[42] That is, the pauper's wages should be lower. She disassociated herself from the Majority Report on the question of work, pointing out that work that is given special economic protection is merely a form of relief. Here she found herself at odds with Beatrice Webb, the only other woman on the Commission and a former student of the Hill system of housing management.

The conclusion of the work of the Royal Commission marks the beginning of the end of Octavia's career as a public servant on the national scale. With increasing age she focused on the job at hand: if England's future depended upon 'faithful servants', she would help find and train them. Her British students included not only Kate and Beatrice Potter (Webb), but Ella Pycroft, who managed the East End Dwelling Company, and Lily Walker, a founder of the Dundee Social Union. Ellen Chase and Jane Addams came from the United States, and Fr Ter Meulen from Amsterdam. At first doubtful of the utility of and need for Settlement Houses, Octavia came to rejoice at their contribution of dedicated, trained workers. She even achieved a kind of respectability among academics when students were sent her from the London School of Sociology. Like Florence Nightingale, she became a model for, and a mentor to, a whole generation of workers.

She spent an increasing amount of time with her family; she was particularly fond of her nieces and she enjoyed digging in the garden with her friend Harriet Yorke. Keeping herself somewhat removed from the administration of the National

Trust, she was thankful for its growing success. Stoically accepting the death of her sister Miranda, she began quietly and deliberately to prepare herself and her workers for her own approaching death. Her last letter is concerned with the planting of the trust property Mariner's Hill. 'Capell met us, and we arranged about various short dwarf-stone walls, curved, and with ivy in the interstices, here and there, to keep up the bank near the lane and preserve trees thereon.'[43] She died on 12 August 1912, and was buried beside Miranda at Brockham on the hillside with the view that had given her 'such a delicious sense of space'.

5 The Ground on Which We Stand

The spirituality which directed this life of great activity and its almost incredible record of accomplishments was deep and, though free from inner conflicts, highly complex.

Octavia Hill was a born pantheist. In the beauty of the countryside at Finchley, she saw the spirit of God: flowers, trees, and other objects of the created world she perceived as tokens of a transcendent reality. At the same time her affections taught her that spiritual reality is conveyed as authentically through human relationships as in the mystic's vision. When she and her family moved to London and undertook the responsibility of working with and for the poor, she found in the Anglicanism of F. D. Maurice a theology that gave concrete form to her strongly felt but dimly articulated views on the value of community and service. Mutual service, the sanctity of personal relationships were given spiritual significance by the sacrificial life of Christ. This vision of Christian community together with her artist's joy in the created world informed her actions as she moved through her life as teacher, artist, manager, and environmentalist.

While Octavia Hill explicitly states her theological views, their fullest expression appears not on the printed page but in her life's work.

Divorced from this theological and spiritual background her accomplishments are something of an anomaly. David Owen admits his puzzlement.

The only enterprise that deliberately sought a less respectable class were those identified with Octavia Hill, a name of immense prestige in the world of philanthropy. Of all the late Victorians few are more baffling to the twentieth-century interpreter. Her achievements were formidable . . . . Though her contemporaries regarded her as an oracle on working-class housing and her accomplishments in the field were, in fact, staggering they no longer command unquestioning admiration. If they were the achievements of a woman of impressive stature, they were also expressions of a social outlook that today is almost incomprehensible and even in the 1880s and 90s was being vigorously challenged. Her own work, placed Octavia Hill not in the vanguard of the main army but, one might almost say, in charge of a diversionary operation.[1]

One could excerpt passages from her essays and letters that would show her to be alternately hard and loving, realistic and idealistic, capitalistic and socialistic, naive and sophisticated, forward-looking and bound to outdated theories. The key to her consistencies, and the explanation of her inconsistencies can only be found by analysing her theology and following each strand — her views of God, Providence, good and evil, Christian sociology — to its place in her vocation.

Determined to create a society that would acknowledge the spiritual meaning of family life and neighbourhood and respect the aesthetic and social potential of all people, she ran up against the conservative implications of her view of Providence. Convinced that God is bringing good out of evil, she minimized the interim suffering caused by the relentless pressures of economic law. Her belief that one is required by God to 'cultivate one's own garden' led to an uncritical acceptance of the status quo. Against a loving, idealistic, forward-looking, sophisticated, and socialist view of society Octavia Hill placed an economics which in its social implications was hard, practical, regressive, naive, and capitalist.

1 God in Turner and the Wheatfield

At the age of 4, Octavia writes, 'I gave Miranda a beautiful piece; it was velvet and the colours were black, purple, yellow, white and green.'[2]

At the age of 14, while confessing to Gertrude her disappointment in her own artistic development, she urges her sister forward. The stumbling haste of her letter, the liberal use of the vibrant exclamation point, reflect her excitement.

Do you go on with your drawing? I hope you do. Oh, Gertrude; is it not a glorious thing to think that a divine thought should descend for ages and ages? Think of Raphael and Michael

Angelo! (though I know but little of them), — To think that
every grand feeling they had they could preserve for centuries!
. . . To think of the thousands of great thoughts they must have
created in people's minds; the millions of sorrows that one
great picture (one truly great picture) would calm and comfort.
Will that never be painted again? Do you think there will?
And when? I am going to see the Dulwich Gallery soon. Is it
not glorious? I wish you could see a bit of hawthorn I have
here, such colours! I am writing a curious letter just what
comes foremost in my mind.[3]

In her opinion Ruskin was not only a great artist, he was, in a
profound sense, a theologian, because he understood the nature
of reality. To those critics who had found him to be 'mad,
presumptuous, conceited, and prejudiced', Octavia indignantly
replies,

if it be prejudiced to love right and beauty, if it be conceited to
declare that God had revealed them to you, to endeavour to
make your voice heard in their defence, if it be mad to believe
in their triumph, and that we must work to make them
triumph, then he is all four, and may God make us all![4]

In an era dominated by the heavy hand of Victorian moralism,
it is a relief to hear joy described as a theological virtue, a 'great
gift' that 'never changes or grows dim'. Like C. S. Lewis she felt
caught unawares, surprised to be 'surprised by joy'.

And when I speak of simple joy I mean a feeling, not a
thought, a spontaneous gust of delight, which may indeed be
the result of a hard long life, which has trained us to see
greatly, but which is, at the moment, no effort, not the result of
definite thought, but a natural gladness of heart. I felt this joy
strongly called up by one or two landscapes by Linnell. One
called the 'Wheatfield'. It is a bright day in late summer, and
over a gentle swell and hollow, the corn grows; the reapers are
already at work, and some of the corn is cut and the gleaners
are there.[5]

In her thinking, as in that of many of the English Romantics,
there is an implicit Platonism. Temporal events point to the
eternal.

It has seemed to me that it is an often forgotten truth, and not a superstition that outward objects and events are all connected with it, that they are meant to be illustrations, and even interpreters of it.[6]

Human nature cannot grasp abstract truths unless they are made incarnate in physical form. With considerable psychological acumen she speaks of the dullness of abstractions, their inability to create emotion. The words 'love', 'gentle', and 'sympathetic' remain inert; yet the word 'mother' conjures up all those feelings, infusing them with life.[7]

This apprehension of the power of the physical has two important corollaries. First, the viewer is constantly reminded of the reality of the unchanging God behind his subjective and changing experience. Octavia contrasts objectivity and the 'God of Truth' with the 'imaginations of men's hearts'. In her struggle to observe more accurately, to translate what she saw into the precision and clarity of drawing, she had felt relief. Confronted with outlines and colours and sizes 'which don't change when we change, nor depend for their power or beauty on our thoughts about them' she felt exhilarated, momentarily rescued from the succession of emotions that buffeted her about.[8]

Second, it provides a balance between materialism on the one hand and asceticism on the other. Octavia acknowledges the pleasure brought by personal possessions. 'I think one is meant to use all the blessings that come to one, not to reject them, but to make them one's own in the sense of their being part of one's life, even after they are gone.'[9] Her own possessions were few. She apparently cared nothing for clothes and her worldly goods consisted mostly of some books, a few paintings, and the crimson curtains that went with her from house to house, yet she did not criticize her more wealthy friends. The rich were blessed; in books, pictures, music they possess the means to read the 'lessons written into the world itself', lessons that 'pour themselves forth to ever fresh forms'. Granted that attachment to possessions may become self-serving and idolatrous, it need not. Ideally, one should prize, even 'cling to', possessions yet at the same time be able to throw them away. The artist and the saint are alike in having this perfectly balanced appreciation of possessions.

I think Gringoire very wonderful. The artist's nature, *alive* from head to heels; that exquisite appreciation of life full of joy, with the utter readiness to lay it down, which comes from holding things, as it were, loosely, because so much by the heart. It gave me a little of the same feeling as St. Francis, against whom everything was powerless, because he was above pain, or loss, or death, or exile, or fear, and yet to whom every bird was a brother. The utter unselfishness and dignity of Gringoire was wonderful.[10]

Events, like possessions, stand outside of time, evoking the eternal. Memory carries the past with us into the present where it continues to shape, not only the present, but our expectations of the future. Anniversaries and birthdays struck Octavia with particular force and poignancy.

'How strangely memories of past years rise in connections with anniversaries, suggesting all the changes that passing time has brought, and all that it cannot bring. The eternal things all safe from power of destruction, seem sometimes the most precious of all.[11]

In the eternal present of the Kingdom memory and aspiration, past and future, find a meeting point. As an old woman, after attending a party at one of the playgrounds, she writes of 'both [Presences], those who are to be, and to inherit the world we are trying to make fitter for them as well as the "wonderful dead who have passed Thro' the body and gone".'[12] All are drawn towards the Kingdom in which after physical death the 'wonderful dead' strengthened and purified, will assume their spiritual identity.

2 To Help Others Love Nature and Art

The careful attention that she gave to the choice of the right colour for decorative tiles, the white-washing of wall, the planting of daisies, the painting of props for a theatrical venture, and most especially her attempts to save the English countryside and the English past for its people — originated in her desire to make available to all the divine joy in nature and in art.

I have tried, as far as opportunity has permitted, to develop the love of beauty among my tenants. The poor of London need joy and beauty in their lives. There is no more true and eternal law to be recognized about them than that which Mr. Dickens shows in *Hard Times* — the fact that every man has an imagination which needs development and satisfaction. Mr. Slearey's speech 'People mutht be amoothed, Thquire', is often recalled in my mind in dealing with the poor.[13]

Her conversion, like Josephine Butler's, came out of her search for a cause that would place her gifts at the service of humankind and God, thus bringing fulfilment. The conflict between her social and aesthetic natures was harmonized, releasing new energies: it was to this that God had been leading her.

If, as now I think, He has been preparing me by multitudes of things, childhood in the country, girlhood in town, hard work, most precious and direct teaching of drawing, sympathy with people round, affection for and gratitude to Ruskin, and an ever deepening admiration for him, and knowledge of his plans — if, I say, God has been preparing me by this, and much more, first to love Nature and Art, second to care that all should love Nature and Art, and third to see how to help them to do so, will He not give me too humility to take the place he ordained for me in this great work, tho' it be lowest of all, — faith to believe I can help, and oh such energy and earnestness.[14]

In creating the National Trust, in helping to preserve the architectural heritage and the beauty of the English countryside, she reflected this world-view that bound together past, present and future, 'clinging to' possessions yet making them available to all.

3 Providence: The Plot of a Book

In the teachings of F. D. Maurice she found a faith that gave new scope to her own views. Affirming the God of nature, he rooted creation in a specifically Christian theology. Like her, Maurice believed that the spirit of God is universal; but he further believed that the source of the 'Light that lighteth everyman' is particular; it is the 'Light of Jesus Christ, the Son of God'. He, too, believed in eternal life but he founded his belief, not in a vague intuition, but in the reality of the Resurrection. The Resurrection as the ultimate statement of the bringing of life from death, of good from evil, showed that the God of the hawthorn, the wheatfields, and the Turner landscape is also the God of history, bringing order from chaos, giving meaning to the human struggle for justice. Furthermore, the sacrificial life of Christ, ending in the ultimate self-giving of death on the Cross, has created the model for human life. The life of the 'joyful creature' who worships beauty is enlarged and deepened through the acknowledgement of the God of society. Life in community — the community of the family and of the nation — is the heart of Maurice's Christian Socialist gospel.

In the evenings the Hill girls, exhausted from work, read aloud from Maurice's *Moral and Metaphysical Philosophy*, a history of ideas couched in two volumes each of which is over 700 pages. Octavia read and re-read the *Theological Essays*, particularly the essay on eternal life that had been responsible for Maurice's dismissal from King's College. She reported that during 1851 and 1854 she had attended all but four of Maurice's sermons, staying in the city even on holidays to hear the renowned preacher. (Many have ranked Maurice with Newman as one of the two greatest preachers of the nineteenth century.) Several of Maurice's sermons appear in condensed form in her letters: the young girl is eager to impart the new faith she has discovered to her family and friends. She speaks with the excitement of one who has found, not a new point of view, but the ordering and articulation of principles which had been the basis of her own beliefs. To Emma Cons, who had some reservations about Maurice, she responds with the indignation of one betrayed; her retort is a capsule summary of Maurice's theology.

I told her I would never tell her anything again; however, instead of that, I told her a great deal more than I ever did before. I told her that it was he who had led me to the Church, who had shown me a life in the creeds, the services and the Bible; who had interpreted for me much that was dark and puzzling in life; how the belief in a Father, a Son, and a Holy Ghost might be the most real faith, not a dead notion; that I might believe not only that God was manifesting himself to each man in the inward consciousness of light and beauty in himself and all around; that those had led to infinite perplexities and doubts, but that a real person had come among us, who had known the Father, whose will had been brought into harmony with His; that He was stronger than doubts and sorrow and had overcome them; that He had declared that we might have life, that life was knowledge of God. From this conversation came a determination that Miss Cons and I should read the *Theological Essays* together.[15]

In a letter to Mary Harrison she describes Maurice as the man who rescued her from 'speculations' and showed her the basis for faith. She enclosed two of Maurice's addresses. She asked rhetorically whether in view of his accomplishments

you could not fail to respect him. But if to this was added the consciousness that he had been the agent of showing you the ground on which you were standing, the sun by whose light alone you could work. . . .[16]

Though Maurice, like Octavia, held that the light is universal, he believed that its source is specific. Christ the source transforms an ideal into reality. Since truth was perfectly realized, not in the formulations of the philosophers or even in the artist's vision, but in a God who became human, the lives of all human beings have been redeemed. As a Christian she commended Thomas Hughes' *Tom Brown's Schooldays*, describing it as 'one of the noblest books I have read', because it is uniquely qualified to counter the 'evil of the day, sadness'.

I speak of that sorrow which eats into the warmest heart, and fights ever against their energy, urging them to hopelessness and despair, the selfish sadness that asks itself continually, 'What have I of joy?' I speak of the sadness pervading all classes, which rushes with sickening force on the young lady who has danced most gaily at the ball, when she begins to unfasten her sash in her own room; which weighs heavily on the comfortable old lady as she sits in her drawing room, to recieve guests; which makes the worker gaze in gloomy despondency on the long long wearying days of toil, and makes the poor man say, 'Nothing but care and trouble, and hard work and the workhouse at last', — each and all saying, 'What is the end and purpose of all this?' I feel the book is a healthy blow at all this way of looking at things.[17]

Christianity, placing human relationships at the heart of the divine economy, had found 'joy' in the human face. 'What is great enough for joy? Not the earth, nor the sea, nor the sky .... I think Heaven and people's eyes must be alike .... for there is room for any amount of joy in them.'[18]

Belief in a central meaning bound together the events of life. She compares providence to the plot of a book.

> Is there not a strange binding up of first and last in life which gives one a sense of government in it, not of warning, not of chance, but of distinct plan, as when in a noble book the beginning explains the end, and the end gathers up the beginning .... There is a certain height of noble passionate enthusiasm, a grasp of a grand ideal, a faith in the possibility of even here attaining to it, which ought to accompany us through life, like a scale at the side of a picture by which we may measure things later on.[19]

Providence, however, is more than an ideal and a scale of measurement; it is also the means by which the ideal is realized. The circumstances and events of life, properly understood, are the means by which God educates the human race. To a God who, though all powerful, has chosen the path of humility, suffering an ignominious death, we can trust ourselves, our lives and the lives of those we love.

> What one would desire for those one loves would be as much knowledge as can be obtained to the right rules of life, and such entire trust in God that all outward things may be felt to be in His keeping, so that we may be content in whatever state we are, and walk calmly above all loss.[20]

In the context of this absolute trust in God and the assurance of the Resurrection, the problem of evil is greatly reduced. Josephine Butler had wrestled with the powers of darkness, 'shrieking aloud to God'. Only after this long and painful struggle had she reached her conclusion that evil is necessary for a greater good, part of the drama of light and shade that gives life a spiritual dimension. Octavia's latent Platonism and confident nature, nurtured by a mother who believed in protecting young children from the knowledge of the world's tragedies and sorrows, provided her with a ready answer. Like her teacher Maurice who had been charged with a superficial and un-Christian understanding of the problem of evil, she believed primarily that evil is an absence of good; it is equated with ignorance and has no independent ontological life of its own.

When she arrived in London as a young girl she had been appalled by her first experience of poverty.

There where the Christmas tree stood, I had sat and watched, through the great window, the London poor pass in rain and fog. There I sat and cried thirteen years ago at the remembrance of Tottenham Court Road on Saturday night with its haggard faces. There the first awful wonder about why evil was permitted came to me, and I remember well saying, 'Miranda, I don't believe in a resurrection, or that if there were one it would be a blessing, because a little rest for one's brain would be the best thing. It would be very hard to get up and begin questioning and wondering again.'[21]

This shock, however, was mitigated by her emerging faith. The evolution of her views is apparent in her conversations with Ruskin. In 1858 Ruskin, despondent over his failed marriage, his strained relationship with his parents, and his growing religious scepticism, sought out the Hills. He confessed his difficulties with Christian doctrine. He claimed that when he did what he believed to be right, it turned out badly; God did not bring good from evil. The Hills asked for an example.

Well, I will give you a small crumb of an instance. When I was traveling a great many years ago, at a time my father was ill, I met with a picture of Turner's, one of the finest he ever did. I did not quite know the value of it myself; and I knew that it would vex my father if I bought it without his leave; so I wrote back to him.

While he waited for his father's reply the Turner was sold to someone who later allowed it to be destroyed.

It is always the way when I do right. Miss Edgeworth [Maria Edgeworth] would have made the picture go to a round of people, converting them to Turner, and come back to be crowned with laurel. I was brought up on Miss Edgeworth's principles but I have not found them at all true in my case.

The girls seemed momentarily daunted by this story, but Mrs Hill, whose optimism matched that of her daughters, suggested that good had come from Ruskin's life. Ignoring his Turner story, she pointed out that Ruskin's views on art had been misunderstood, he had suffered; yet in the end he had achieved the power of 'exciting noble and beautiful emotions'. She concluded by saying

> that she thought when people did right, the good they expected often did *not* come . . . but that, tho' they had to suffer for want of judgment, in the end they were always blessed; but in different ways from those that they had expected; that, as long as people calculated results, they could not do right; they must do right for right's sake.

The conversation turned to other matters. Ruskin listened to a letter from Miranda in Florence. He showed them some of his sketches. Once more the subject of suffering was broached. Emily said that it was comforting to look back 'and see how things which had seemed so sad turned out as blessings'. Ruskin said, 'It may be so with you good people, but if I look back it is to find blunders. To remember the past is like Purgatory.'[22]

Five years later the debate took a somewhat different form. Ruskin, his energies further depleted by the collapse of his faith, had spoken despairingly of being abandoned by God. Octavia's answer described suffering as one of the means by which we know God; since Jesus experienced loneliness and abandonment, by identifying our isolation with His we can also participate in His love and its triumph in the Resurrection. Paradoxically, experience of the loss of God attests to the existence of God.

> I said the sense, of course, was most terrible, most real, but that I could not believe that any one was ever really left. I spoke of the cry on the Cross: 'My God, My God, why hast Thou forsaken me?' of the certainty we all have that God was near then, that, whoever was or was not left, one was quite sure that the imperfect and weak would be the last to be left; of the

sufficiency for all purposes of life of perfect trust in God, of our power to live in that when all other faiths shook and crumbled.

Ruskin presses her further, speaking of all the doctrines that 'may be shaken' and asking for 'all the help you can give me'. Octavia, using not only the arguments of her teacher Maurice but even his patterns of speech, acknowledges the validity of Ruskin's doubts while she searches out the truth which lies beneath them.

Doubt immortality if you can. Dare you not trust yourself, and even all men, to Him who made and taught them? Doubt the Old Testament, and does not life remain? I cannot interpret mine, or those I watch, without such a God as it shows. Doubt even the Gospels and what remains? I cannot lose from out of me the knowledge of the supreme sufferer and His infinite love; no other character can be that of the Father, Whose love is near us.[23]

These two themes — God bringing good out of evil, and human suffering as sanctified by the suffering of Christ — remained of central importance to Octavia. As an old woman, after the death of her beloved sister and companion Miranda, she wrote,

In every deed there is a fellowship of suffering. Our modern way of looking upon suffering as a thing which by good arrangement, we can get rid of, misses often that solemn sense of its holiness, which those who live in constant memory of our Lord's suffering, enter into.[24]

4 *God and the Rent*

Her friends compared her to Hercules; Octavia's hero was St Christopher, the man who carries the Christ child and his burden, the sins of the world. While her work did not involve her in the soul-searing confrontations with desperate misery and the acrimonious political conflicts that so taxed Josephine Butler, the scope of her interests placed a heavy responsibility upon her — the saving of open space and historic monuments all over England, the management of thousands of homes. Alongside these far-reaching and endlessly demanding professional concerns, she maintained close relationships with family and friends, co-workers and tenants, carrying on a voluminous correspondence.

The disciplined zeal with which she went about her daily tasks (albeit punctuated by bouts of prolonged illness), her fearlessness in attacking the highly placed and powerful, she attributed to her faith in providence. It sustained daily life, making it possible for her to find satisfaction in unpleasant circumstances and work that went against her temperament. Essentially a country woman, she was never reconciled to the ugliness and barrenness of London. Yet on her nineteenth birthday, she had written to Minnie:

> It is good to be *here*, good to learn to love the beating heart of London life, that throbs with vast desire, and great purposes — good to learn to turn our looks above all beauty and comfort, while our feet are upon stones; good above all to learn to say 'That Thou hast placed me here, Lord', implies that I have a work to do here.[25]

The conviction that she was acting as an agent for God gave her not only energy but authority.

> 'Break out a window there in that dark corner; let God's light and air in' or, 'Trap that foul drain, and shut the poisonous miasma out'; and one has the moral power to say, by deeds, which speak louder than words, 'Where God gives me authority, this, which you in your own hearts know to be wrong, shall not go on. I would not set my conviction, however strong it might be, against your judgment of right but when you are doing what I know your own conscience condemns, I, now that I have the power, will enforce right![26]

Social critics have differed in their responses to this confidence. Enid Gauldie finds it on the whole beneficent.

> This enviable Victorian certainty about what was right gave Miss Hill and others like her the strength to go among the poor without being discouraged, to display her own behaviour,

with the whole back-ground of culture which induced it, as undoubtedly right, undoubtedly superior.[27]

Beatrice Webb understood it as a negative; she found Hill's legislation of morals to be arrogant and hypocritically self-serving. Henrietta Barnett admired Octavia Hill, yet she criticized her 'exaggerated cordiality'. It was, she believed, an outgrowth of the false relationship implicit in any form of *noblesse oblige*.

There is another side, however, to Octavia's faith in God's plan. While on the one hand God was 'directing' her work and supporting her efforts, He was also teaching her that she was a means to a greater end. Since her authority was derived, it was not unbounded. Speaking to her friend Janey Senior, the first woman to be appointed as inspector of schools, she describes their work as the 'out-of-sight piers driven deep into the marsh, on which the visible ones are carried, that support the bridge'.[28] There were times when she drew back from asserting her presence and her ideas. Although her friends tried to persuade her to move from Marylebone and take up the larger responsibilities of running the newly established settlement houses, she declined.

> I can't help thinking it would be turning my back on the principles of a life-time. My sister and two of my friends here have all their work in this neighbourhood; it has gathered around this home and will continue centred round the new one. . . . So, if we moved, I should uproot and alter the whole character of three people's work. . . . It would not all be gain. . . . For, I ask myself, is not this work a new one? Is it not right that it should develop much in accordance with the aspirations of a younger generation? . . . Will not this very limitation of not living there keep my rather over-powering presence just far enough away to foster native growth? [29]

The picture evoked by some of Octavia's critics of the strong-jawed insensitive woman bent on getting her way at any price, is not confirmed by a close reading of the letters. Her system, far from being the rigid programme of a dictatorial nature, gave scope and flexibility to her fellow-workers. 'I have therefore usually said, "Look for yourself, but look with the sound of my words ringing in your ears".'[30]

She belittled her accomplishments; her ideals, however, she hoped would live on. The words with which she thanked her friends for the portrait presented to her in 1898 serve as a fitting testament to her modesty and the grandeur of her vision.

When I am gone, I hope my friends will not try to carry out any special system, or to follow blindly in the track which I have trodden. New circumstances require various efforts; and it is the spirit, not the dead form that should be perpetuated. When the time comes that we slip from our places, and they are called to the front as workers, what should they inherit from us? Not a system, not an association, not dead formulas. We shall leave them a few houses, purified and improved, a few new and better ones built, a certain record of thoughtful and loving management, a few open spaces, some of which will be more beautiful than they would have been but what we care most to leave them is not any tangible thing, however great, not any memory, however good, but the quick eye to see, the true soul to measure, the large hope to grasp the mighty issues of the new and better days to come — greater ideals, greater hope, and patience to realize both.[31]

Octavia Hill's management may not have been a 'special system'; it was, however, based on specific principles. Convinced that there was no situation 'in this, God's earth' where right is impossible, believing that mundane 'circumstances' are vehicles through which the love of God is conveyed, she urged her people to 'cultivate their own gardens'. She exalted the value of work and condemned the almsgiving of well-meaning philanthropists which, she believed, destroyed the very order it was trying to create. She accepted the ruthless pressure of economic law as part of the created order. In addition, she advised women to keep their place, at least in the realm of politics.

The 'quiet, regular, orderly management of affairs; the habitual obedience to the right rules of life', which she enjoined upon herself, she believed should be made possible for her tenants.

A practical woman, she found spiritual meaning in plumbing and the coin tucked under the mattress. The cause-and-effect relation between dirt, over-crowding, a contaminated water supply and death and disease was a God-given reality. She required that her tenants maintain a modicum of cleanliness and order. Financial obligations were equally exact; the work for pay that would be spent on food, clothing and rent was required as a moral duty. It ensured the independence and self-respect of the tenant as well as the acceptance of obligation, the acknowledgement of dependence upon economic laws which, as much as physical, govern the world. Octavia Hill offered no apology. She made her housing available to the 'respectable', that is the working poor,[32] because she felt that only those who had shown themselves capable of holding a steady job could begin to understand the 'circumstances' of God's plan. The man who worked, supported his family, put aside a portion of his earnings to tide him over, was already on his way.

Financial accountability was important even in the initial selection process. Ellen Chase, one of the managers, expressed the Hill philosophy when she advised other workers to be tough-minded in their scrutiny of applicants for tenancy. With a realism born of experience and a remarkable degree of psychological insight, she offers the following suggestions:

> Learn what is necessary as incidentally as you can. Note what furniture they have, how the home is kept, how the neighbours appear. It is best to see both man and wife, the more presentable of the two is apt to apply . . . . An offer to pay a month does not especially recommend an applicant, as a man in constant work would fall into the usage he found without question, one to whom a half-sovereign is more of a rarity, feeling uncertain of his next, or too weak to trust himself, urges it on one.[33]

The new tenant was required to pay the rent on a weekly basis.

There is firstly, the simple fulfilment of a landlady's bounden duties and the uniform demand of the fulfilment of those with the tenants. We have felt ourselves bound by laws which must be obeyed, however hard obedience might often be.

Though this system, as we will see, was tempered by 'individual friendship' between tenant and landlady which sometimes deferred — or even excused — the payment of the rent, financial accountability remained the linchpin of the Hill management. If the tenant failed to meet his obligation he was eventually evicted. (Miss Chase is explicit in describing the means of extracting rent from a reluctant tenant before going on to furnish the process and details for eviction: the first notice, the second notice, the role of the broker, the legal rights of the tenant and the owner, etc.)

Octavia contrasts the anarchy of the pauper to the ordered life of the working poor. Drifting on the surface of society, without direction, without the means of sustaining his family, the pauper has been cast outside the cause-and-effect relationships that hold the universe together.

A man accepts underpaid work; a little is scraped up by one child, a little begged by another; a gigantic machinery of complicated charities relieves a man of half his responsibilities; not once and for all clearly and definitely, but — probably or possibly he gets help here and there. There is no certainty, no quiet, no order in his way of subsisting. And he has an innate sense that his most natural wants ought to be supplied if he works; so he takes our gifts thanklessly and then we blame him or despise him for alternate servility and ingratitude; and we dare not use his large desires to urge him to effort; and, if he will make none, let him suffer; but please God one day we shall arrange to be ready with work for every man, and give him nothing if he will not work; we cannot do the latter without the former, I believe.[34]

Octavia Hill's system provided no place for the disordered and the desperate, not because she felt that they were 'unworthy' but because she could think of no way to reach them.

Her attitude towards the almsgiving that helped create pauperism is implicit in her description of the pauper himself. Her objections were both practical and theological. She realized early that if she offered housing without ensuring adequate returns she would soon lose her business, and hence her ability to serve the poor; the open fist would become the empty hand. (While this might seem an obvious point, there were philanthropists who did not recognize it. In the 1880s there was a series of bankruptcies among large charitable organizations; some found themselves the first among paupers.) Octavia meant to hold her returns to a low rate, but one that would make a small profit, most of which would be put into improvements decided on by the tenants. The figure she arrived at was 5 per cent, a good

7 to 10 per cent lower than that required by the profiteering capitalist landlords.

Octavia Hill's theological objections to almsgiving, shared with most Victorian philanthropists, are complex. Given the role that almsgiving had played in Christianity, they seem astonishing. The Early and Medieval Church had blessed both begger and giver. The mendicant, in renouncing possessions and casting himself utterly on the providence of God, displayed an enviable depth of faith. In addition he had opened an opportunity to his neighbour: the passer-by fulfilled the cardinal duty of charity in dropping a coin into the cup. Yet beginning in the sixteenth century the practice was discouraged. By the end of the nineteenth it was passionately condemned. Kindly Samuel Barnett, who did as much for the poor of London as any man, said, 'Indiscriminate charity is among the curse of London.' 'Nothing was more difficult to deal with than the soft-heartedness which could see nothing but hard-heartedness in the refusal to give', wrote Henrietta Barnett.[35] She reported that Samuel had caught an old gentleman red-handed in the act of dispensing charity. The guilty party had been sitting at the end of the table next to an applicant. While appearing to listen with close attention as Octavia Hill explained to the woman that the C.O.S. could not give her money, he had slipped her six-pence under the table. Canon Barnett gave him a dressing down that reduced the old gentleman to tears.[36]

The explanations for the reversal in attitude, as presented in the classic studies of R. H. Tawney and Max Weber, depend upon the convergence of Protestantism and capitalism on two points: the importance of the individual and the evidence for sanctity to be found in the life of the successful worker. Octavia Hill did not share the Puritan suspicion that poverty is, if not actually a sin, at least a mark of God's disfavour. She did, however, believe that work — with or without pay — is a virtue, a 'joyful occupation' which must be made available to all. It is a protection against chaos and anarchy, the acknowledgement of human dependence on economic law and since most work is done in company, the context of the mutuality and self-giving that are at the heart of the Gospel. She hated almsgiving because she felt that it perpetuated unemployment and encouraged passivity and dependence.

Octavia Hill opposed almsgiving: she did not oppose philanthropy. She suggested that the old forms of charity, suitable to a feudal and agricultural society, had been rendered obsolete by the Industrial Revolution. Society has a duty to create new forms.

> Never let us excuse ourselves from seeking the best form in the indolent belief that no good form is possible and things are better left alone nor, on the other hand, weakly pleading that what we do is *benevolent*. We must ascertain that it is really beneficent too.[37]

She suggested that in the nineteenth century work in society and gifts of land would have been more effective than the handout.

Octavia Hill's philanthropy was not laissez faire; her economics was. She accepted uncritically the conventional economic wisdom, which probably reached her through Jane Hughes Senior and the Nassau Senior family. Almsgiving or any other tampering with a part of the economic system would have immediate and disastrous effects on every other part of the system. The poor would be the first to be hurt; if rents were subsidized, wages would drop. Almsgiving would lead to increasing unemployment and 'demoralization'. Yet she must have placed her own experience against these theories. She had known first-hand the destructiveness of financial failure. Her father, a 'deserving' man, had been devastated by a bankruptcy brought on through no fault of his own; it had destroyed his health and broken up his family. Octavia felt his unhappiness deeply and after each visit admitted to feeling severely depressed.[38] She herself had been forced to give up her venture in toymaking. Though well-managed and filling an important social need, it did not pay.

One might wonder why, believing capitalism to be a fragile mechanism and knowing the damaging effects of its failures, she did not consider the alternatives. Where was the eager girl who spoke of reading a socialist book as 'one of the greatest happiness any one can have'? Did she not read Ruskin's 'Unto This Last'? She seems, however, to have had little interest in the later developments of socialism. She considered William Morris to be an appealing but impractical man. Her early social ideals had been eroded by the growing left and right wings of anarchism and state socialism. Anarchism held no attraction for this woman who hated bloodshed and had given her life to creating harmony and order; state socialism went against her belief in freedom and individualism. Deploring Beatrice Webb's faith in science, objectivity, and programmes, she foresaw a nation in which the ideals of socialism would be destroyed by bureaucratic power, greed, and sloth. In her view, 'state' and 'socialism' were opposed concepts. Socialism would never be brought about through legislation and social engineering; true socialism was life in a community that respected the individuality of its members and acknowledged its dependence on God — its basis was spiritual, not economic. Government by its very nature lives by the manipulation of power and the jockeying for position of different interest groups. It could in no way embody the 'self-giving' which was the basis of Octavia Hill's Christian Socialism. In choosing to accept an unbridled capitalism Octavia Hill found herself 'in charge of a diversionary operation'. As David Owen says, she placed herself outside of the mainstream of history. Looking at England today, however, and at the competing forces that have brought it to a standstill, who can say that she placed herself outside the mainstream of truth?

Having noted her conservatism in economic matters, we are not surprised to find it in the social sphere — not surprised, but nevertheless, disappointed. After all Octavia Hill was a forerunner of the women's movement, stepping off the pedestal to become a national leader, a leader who, not disdaining to roll up her sleeves and scrub floors, went on to initiate policies that affected the lives of thousands. Yet in words that seemed to belie her actions, she cautioned women to limit their goals. She wrote *The Times* in 1910, urging her opposition to women's suffrage.

> I feel I must say how profoundly sorry I shall be if women's suffrage in any form is introduced into England. I believe men and women help one another because they are different, have different gifts and different spheres, one is the complement of the other; and it is because they have different power and qualities that they become one in marriage, and one also in friendship and in fellow work.[39]

The traditional views on the different spheres of men and women had never prevented Octavia from stepping across the prescribed limits for 'ladylike' behaviour. It seems more likely that her real objections are expressed in the following paragraph.

I think, also, that political power would militate against their usefulness in the large field of public service. This service is, to my mind, far more valuable now than any voting power could possibly be. If you add two million voters, unless you secure thereby better members of Parliament, you have not achieved anything, but you have used up in achieving nothing whatever thought and time your women voters have given to such duties. Whereas if they have spent this time and heart and thought in the care of the sick, the old, the young, and the erring, as guardians of the poor, as nurses, as teachers, as visitors, if they have sought for and respected the out of sight silent work which really achieved something, a great blessing is conferred on our country.[40]

Once again, she employs the idea of being placed by God in a small corner of the world and of being asked to 'cultivate one's own garden' as an argument against seeking change.

Her biographer, E. Moberly Bell, further suggests that she cared little about extending the franchise because she had no confidence in the political process. Here again, as with state socialism, fear of centralized government influenced her most. An effective strategist in promoting private philanthropy, she was always suspicious of national politics and state interference. She favoured reform on the local level; she hated bureaucracy with its inhumanity and inefficiency. Perhaps disillusioned by her experience in the unsuccessful campaign of Thomas Hughes, she tended to regard the activities of Members of Parliament as relatively unimportant. It is true that she had seen the need for state involvement in housing and stood behind the Artisans' Dwelling Act. Yet she had had second thoughts. Did not the dismal edifices created by it bear witness to the inability of legislation, blueprints, and the paper schemes of planners to meet the real needs of people?

She justified her conservatism in political and economic matters by enshrining the status quo as providential, the expression of God's will. She seems to have been unaware that she was arbitrary in applying this justification. Why legislate for sewers but not for state-supported housing? If the poor were required to bear the inequities of an economic system that could not provide for them, why were they not also required to endure dysentery and cholera? Similarly, why say that a nurse or a housing estate manager is 'cultivating her own garden' but a female voter or politician is trespassing upon someone else's? She herself had difficulty in deciding upon the size of her personal garden. In the matter of housing it confined her to the perimeters of the property she controlled; the political dimension she tried to ignore. When it came to open space, however, the whole of England became her garden.

Revolutionaries have evoked the name of God. Joan of Arc, Florence Nightingale, Martin Luther King, Gandhi, Josephine Butler, like Octavia Hill, believed that 'circumstances' of the world are agents of God. Yet using those 'circumstances' they fought not for the status quo but against it.

Accordingly, Octavia Hill's conservatism, her avoidance of controversy, cannot be completely explained by her doctrine of providence. Its roots lie deeper. Her belief in the critical impor-tance of family and neighbourhood drew her attention away from the problems of a larger society. She held to this belief with the tenacity of one who acts out of a deeply felt early experience. With her father's illness she had lost the steadying comfort and support of a 'home' life that had been unusually happy. Throughout the rest of her long life she helped create homes and gardens for others, in this repeated and tireless endeavour recreating the home she had lost. Perhaps she cultivated her own garden and did not look over the wall towards the wasteland of indigent London because she was afraid that she would find the view too appalling.

6 A Universal Family

1 The Prototype of Divine Love

Charles Kingsley, whom Octavia greatly admired, had attacked the celibacy advocated by many High Churchmen on the grounds that it implicitly denied the importance of family relationships undercutting an essential insight into the divine. He felt that his ability to respond to God the Father was deepened by his own human experience of fatherhood. Octavia's other Broad Church friends, Thomas Hughes and F. D. Maurice, were devoted fathers and endowed family relationships with spiritual significance.

Octavia Hill shares this view. Though she herself never married, she rejoiced in the marriage of her sisters Emily and Gertrude. Throughout her professional career she maintained a home for herself, her mother, and her unmarried sisters. She looked to family relationships for the understanding and affection that would sustain her in her work.

> What we all need most, is to be able to enter into the hearts of others. If we see here love, truth, strength, we can realize a Father of love, truth, strength. I am sure there is no other way. ... Therefore, I believe that one must always work from the known and strong up to the unknown and weak. We must seize as most precious the vague memories of loved ones, the feelings that have bound us in families, and strive to strengthen them, and then work upwards.[1]

Observing a friend who from the balcony had watched the confirmation service for his daughter, she felt that she saw in his intent look a 'type' of the loving concern of God who watches over human persons, however unaware they may be.[2]

The nuclear family is the smallest circle in the ever-enlarging pool of relationships that widens towards universality. Next

143

comes the class, then the nation. Each unit has a particular character, fitted for its work in the world. Each builds on the smaller, the nation standing midway between the family and universal society.

In defending what might seem to be a parochial nationalism Octavia points out that our experience is perforce limited by time and space. We experience the universal only through the circumstances of our particular life. National life, in spite of its obvious limitations, serves a purpose. At least it calls people out of their own individual selfishness and their family-centredness; at best it helps them understand the patriotism of other nationalists. It leads to a respect for the differences of national character, those 'fragments that make up the mighty humanity which [is] Christ Himself'.

In the context of family and national life there is little that distinguishes the role of women from that of men. Granted that women as wives and mothers and keepers of the Lares and Penates have special responsibilities; yet men as well as women are called to be cultivators of the domestic virtues. The assuming of family responsibilities, the care of children and the elderly, are incumbent upon all.

While Octavia gave lip service to the conventional belief in the 'complementary' natures of men and women, more often she showed herself unwilling to divide psychological characteristics into groupings marked 'feminine' and 'masculine'. Like most women of her period, she knew that intelligence and strength were thought to be male prerogatives. Flouting the risk of being labelled masculine, she went her way, speaking her mind freely, accosting the highly placed. Shaftesbury and the clerical members of the C.O.S. recalled that they quailed before her attacks. While she gives a lukewarm tribute to the 'silent self-control and sweet temper' enjoined upon the female, she describes with enthusiasm her growing involvement:

> I used to think that time would soften passionate engrossment, and leave me leisure to perceive the little wants of others, but I think I pant with almost increasing passionate longing for the small things that I see before me.[3]

Lacking empathy with the more passive martyrs of the Church, she admired the activists: St Christopher and St Michael; their maleness did not hinder her from identifying with them. She claimed for herself the name 'Loke'. ' "Loke" is my name with which is associated all my strength; it is Florence's own invention; whenever my sisters call me their brother then I am "Loke" '.[4]

In a sparring match with a wealthy and opinionated Captain, exasperation gets the better of Octavia's caution.

First the man talked such intolerable complimentary stuff, and hardly more interesting boasted of his own performances. And then suddenly he became serious and interesting. He defined a woman's duties, with which I did not dare to quarrel, but threw out half scornful suggestions as to her gentleness and amiability, etc. He patronizingly enumerated little offices she might fulfil if she could find suitable objects. 'Oh, certainly', I said, 'if the real, solemn, large business of life does not demand too much of her thought and strength.' 'What should I point out and suggest?' 'Oh, nothing certainly for other people, but to keep their eyes open, and do bravely what they saw was wanted. I knew nothing of other people's duties, only I thought, God having made them, He had meant them to be of some use at all times of their life.' 'Then if I couldn't tell him about other people's work would I tell him about my own. I had spoken of the homes of the poor. Had I a district? because he supposed there was work to be done if people knew how to do it.' So I told him a little about the houses, rather ashamed of having got so deep as to talk of personal work. He had found fault with women speaking in public, and I told him that 'I thought he would not at all approve of my work, for certainly there was much in the business and in the stern determination required, which might really make a woman mean, ungenerous, and hard, but if the work is at all worth doing we must fairly estimate and bravely meet the risk.'[5]

The responsibility of human beings to concern themselves with the 'real, solemn, large business' of life was as incumbent upon women as upon men. The temperament, the psychological characteristics of women, were formed in part by their response to the call to service. Before such a challenge the feminine virtues of 'gentleness and amiability' were not only irrelevant; they were downright demonic, standing in the way of commitment and action. Octavia had no sympathy with the self-protective ideals and limited scope accepted by aristocratic women. Like Mary Wollstonecraft, Josephine Butler, Florence Nightingale, and many others she deplored the superficiality and selfishness of such lives. Brought up by a mother who had welcomed her need to work outside the home, Octavia had at an early age affirmed its value. She saw work as a right, not a need. In the tradition of her mother, her father, and her grandfather, she hoped to take part in the affairs of the world. Scrubbing courtyards, pulling out weeds, importuning Cabinet Ministers and heads of Royal Commissions, making speeches at testimonial banquets was 'women's work' when it was undertaken in joyful response to God.

This call to service helped resolve the confusion about woman's nature by shifting the emphasis to woman's role. Admittedly there is some tension between her belief in self-development and self-sacrifice, partly because we tend to see them as opposites. On the one hand she stressed the importance of self-expression and self-development — physical and aesthetic — and on the other the more essential value of self-giving. The ambiguity is resolved when one recognizes that one has first to develop a 'self' — and to recognize it as an important self — before one can offer it to others. Octavia called for self-giving, not for self-denial or self-effacement. Giving and receiving are united, two faces of the single coin of self-esteem.

As young children Octavia and her sisters were taught this lesson by their mother in an unforgettable way. On their birthdays each girl not only received gifts but was expected to give gifts to every member of the family. This mutuality, acknowledged between members of a family, should also, according to Octavia, be recognized as the foundation of marriage. To a friend who is engaged Octavia writes in congratulation:

I cannot defer writing to tell you how entirely and heartily I hope that a very happy and full and whole life may be opening for you both. . . . As to sacrifice, I don't know; perhaps there is a great good possible without it; but what one feels is the immensely deeper meaning and joy which comes when, as Ruskin says, one gets the equality, 'not of likeness', but of giving and receiving. . . . And of such interchange all noble life has much.[6]

Like many strong-willed people she was often painfully aware of her tendency to take credit for her own gifts and of the spiritual sin which accompanies the self-congratulation of the giver.

Have I often fancied that I alone was the giver? I believe I often have. Oh, how false, how blind, how ungrateful! I remember Mamma as she nursed me when I was ill. I remember all the little things she does daily, weeks of momentary self-sacrifice that make up a life of devotion, that I with all my boasted strength and generosity never live for a day. I remember Minnie's intense gentleness, Miranda's determined self-sacrifice and feel with bowed spirit that they have done infinitely more for me than I have ever done for them, because the gifts are of a nobler kind. Oh, it is easy to work early and late, to keep accounts, and manage housekeeping, etc., but the gentle voice, the loving word, the ministry, the true, tender spirit, these are great gifts, and will endure when the others have perished. The first are the works of strength, the others of goodness. If I had used that strength always nobly, if I had recognized the goodness as divine, if I had been ready to be made in Christ's likeness, then I should have no cause to bow my head, as I do now.[7]

If the tendency, born of selfishness, to become aware of and take pride in one's 'unselfishness' undercuts the purity of intent, does this mean that sacrificial giving is impossible? Is what Octavia calls 'unselfishness' merely a kind of enlightened self-interest?

Octavia does not admit this: self-giving, she claims is opposed to selfishness. She faulted Guinevere for having been unwilling to put aside her self-interest; a purer love would have enabled her to help Arthur achieve his ambitions for the Round Table. She faulted a friend who described love as an extended form of selfishness. She argued that true love cannot be selfish since it is willing to give up the loved one.

The self-sacrifice here enjoined, however, is based on self-esteem: it is, though generously given, a last resort. In Octavia's Christian humanism, masochism, which is based on self-hatred, a self-serving though pathological impulse, is not a spiritual virtue. There may be occasions, however, when self-sacrifice must be offered even when it brings harm to self. If one must make a choice between 'self-fulfilment' and 'self-deterioration' for the sake of others, one must choose the latter.

> Sometimes among the crowd of small cares and worries here I feel the old fear that they may make me small and mean . . . . Of course, I believe that neither angels nor principalities nor powers can separate us from the love of God, neither can small annoyances or intercourse with people of low standards of morality. But, were it possible, I suppose one would unhesitatingly choose self-deterioration for the sake of raising others. I suppose such experience throws light on the words, 'He who will lose his life will save it.'[8]

A theology that on the one hand stresses the importance of self-expression and on the other asserts the greater value of self-sacrifice, necessarily raises some difficult questions. How is one to know whether one is acting from selfishness or in self-sacrifice? Octavia herself admits the dilemma. In 1869 she expressed her confusion to Maurice.

> I must not mistake self-will for conscience, nor impatience for honesty. No one on earth can distinguish them for me; but He will. It so often seems to me as if two different courses of action were right or might be right; and this is what puzzles me, even tho' it is a blessing as binding me to people of different opinions.[9]

The answer can only be reached when one takes the question out of the merely psychological and puts it where Octavia believed it belonged, in the theological. She resolved the problem not through introspection but by looking away from the self towards God. Since sacrifice ultimately concerns not the isolated self but the self united with God and with other selves, she could put aside her confusion.

> Mr. Maurice has been speaking today of sacrifice as the link between man and man, and man and God. It was such a sermon! One feels as if all peace and quiet holiness were around one; everything appears to have a beauty and calm in it; to which we can turn back in times of storms and wild noisy

rivalries, as to the memory of sunny days, and to shed a light on all dark and difficult things, on sorrow and loneliness.[10]

Through Christ, sacrifice has become more than a moral pronouncement concerning the way people should — but do not — behave; it has become a living principle, the proclamation of what in fact *is*. In the Incarnation God has given His life for man and so established a model of reality. Since the God-man Jesus Christ comprehends not only the historical Jesus but the Christ of eternal life, His sacrifice is the foundation of all other sacrifices throughout history. Pagan, Jewish, and Greek sacrifices are anticipations, imperfect and partial, yet important, of the atoning ('at-one-ing') sacrifice of Christ; they are, accordingly, linked with eternity and through this link unite men with each other.

It is the end of all God's acts and dispensations towards men, to make them righteous; to bring them out of that condition which they have chosen for themselves, — the condition of distrust, alienation, sin.

Like Josephine Butler, Octavia felt that the disorders of society were caused by blindness. Refusing to recognize redemption, mankind had rejected the reality of the Kingdom. In the 1880s she expressed her discouragement.

The days are full of difficulty, the temper of the poor is difficult, the old submissive patience is passing away, and no sense of duty has taken its place; the talk is of rights, not right. The ideal the poor form for themselves is low, and the rich support them in it. The rich, on the other hand, while they are continually coming forward more and more to help the poor, are thoroughly cowardly about telling them any truth that is unpalatable, and know too little of them to meet them as friends, and learn to be natural and brave with them. We have great relief funds, and little manly friendships, idleness above and below an admiration for what is pleasant, which degrades all life. This temper makes work difficult and sometimes fills me with wondering awe about the future of rich and poor.[11]

This 'temper' will be transformed when people acknowledge that through the Resurrection they have been brought 'into that state for which He has created them, of dependence, trust, union with Him'. Along with other Christian Socialists she envisioned a society in which the uniqueness of the individual would be respected, while the unity of the family of man would be restored through work — the great equalizer — and mutual self-giving. She set herself to bring it about.

2   Charity Begins at Home: Tenant and Manager

Octavia Hill said that the purpose of her system of management is to 'make individual life noble, homes happy, and family life good'.

In view of the complexity of the economic and social problems now afflicting the Western world, such faith in the redeeming power of home life seems naive — at once too idealistic and too limited in scope. Nevertheless, in advising planners and architects to forget their own need for artistic aggrandizement and to study carefully the needs of those for whom they built, Octavia Hill's common sense spoke prophetically. As she warned, large schemes of state planning and philanthropy would fail; they had ignored the essential nature, which is social, of their clients.

Today the terms are new. No one wants to be called, or to call others, 'poor'; 'low-income' is the preferred euphemism. Those architects who sculpt concrete and steel to their vision, revealing the ganglia of heating ducts and pipes, are labelled, somewhat unfairly, 'New Brutalists'. Those who muddle along, making do with a Neo-Georgian arcade here and there, accommodating the wishes of the shop-keepers, the lorry driver, and the gardener, call themselves 'New Empiricists'. The debate is often conducted in twentieth-century jargon and stupefying abstractions; yet the issues are the same, proceeding from differing views of human nature.

The Utilitarians had said that man is a rational creature with physical needs; conditioned by pain and pleasure, he could be taught to accept simple accommodations. The apartments built by their descendants, the Radicals — Early Brutalists, if you like — were tough, relentlessly antiseptic, designed to render misuse difficult. The water supply, the sewers and the ventilation were adequate; there were no courtyards, no gardens. The flats had separate entrances for each family; often the only public space was the latrine. Nicholas Pevsner, describing them as the 'grim and grimy barracks of the poor' credits them with having destroyed any chance of the block of flats becoming popular with the class that needed housing most desperately.

In contrast Octavia Hill, Ebenezer Howard, and the philanthropists gave less importance to man's rationality and physical needs; they believed that man is essentially a spiritual, aesthetic and social creature. Octavia Hill's recommendations for water, sewer, and ventilation were restricted to the minimal needs of hygiene. She shocked some of her supporters by suggesting to the Royal Commission in 1885 that water and drains for individual families were not necessary; it was enough to make clean facilities available for the use of the whole building. She placed the need for community at the centre of her architectural plans. For this reason she generally preferred to work, not with new buildings, but with old houses that already had a garden or a courtyard. These she would renovate around two public centres, one indoors and one out-of-doors.

Today's visitor who walks past the dilapidated warehouses, picking his way over gritty heaps of trash, past empty pubs and parish halls, will recognize the Hill houses in Southwark before he reads the street sign. In this industrial wasteland seven or eight small houses with irregular gables and gingerbread roofing lean towards each other for comfort. Their children's book-illustration Victorian-Gothic eyes look out over a small park. Now sparsely planted, it contains a bench where a few old women sit talking. It is easy to imagine the spread of laundry, the animated exchange of small-talk and gossip, the shouted warnings to children, the heckling of a stranger, of 80 years ago. Octavia's description of the property which housed 500 families shows the care and attention to detail that went into her planning. The ruins of a paper factory that stood on the land were cleared by burning. A low wall was placed around the property and a covered playground was built. She paved part of the clearing with red bricks

set diagonally as a pattern. At one end a drinking fountain of plain grey granite. Immediately in front of this arcade is a space of gravel, in the centre of which an octagonal bandstand is being created. Walks wind about between lawns and flower beds. Two plane trees are planted on the larger space and a small pond has been made, crossed by a little bridge. We have planted bulbs in plenty, and 1,000 yellow crocus, which thrive better than most flowers in London.[12]

On the edge of the park, right next to the houses, stands Red Cross Hall, until recently occupied by the Society for Liturgical Drama. The Walter Crane murals have been painted over but the inscription of dedication to the young servant girl who gave her life to rescue two children remains. From its pleasant propor- tions, the pitched roof and high windows, which give it both intimacy and spaciousness, one can catch glimpses of its former use. Serving alternately as library, gymnasium, school-room, art centre, dining hall, music studio, and theatre, it was once a community centre not only for Octavia Hill's tenants but for much of Southwark.

> On Sunday afternoons we have opened the Hall free to all grown-up people who like to come; by the great kindness of friends we have been able to provide really beautiful music, Sunday after Sunday. . . . Always we have been supplied with flowers and the Hall looks really lovely all lighted up, with its three great cheerful fires, which are a great attraction, especially when one turns in from the mud, fog, and general dinginess of Southwark.[13]

In the context of Octavia's views on community her fondness for parties takes on a different light. On the surface there is something a little absurd in the child-like zest that this woman of affairs brought to a party. In 1886, when she was 48, she describes a 'triumphantly successful party at Southwark'. Fifteen years later she writes to her mother at length about another Southwark fete.

> At the end it was really most impressive, to stand on the balcony and see the great group of children fall into line, and march singing to the accompaniment of the band, three times round the garden, making lovely curves over the bridge, and the bandstand, the sunlight streaming on them, till they filed into the Hall, where each received a bunch of flowers and a bun.[14]

These parties were more than diversions and entertainments. Just as in the services at the Chapel at Lincoln's Inn the choir, the stained-glass windows, the flowers on the altar, and the procession of priests honoured God, so at Red Cross Hall, the singing, the marching of cadets, the giving of prizes, the crowning of child-kings and queens on floral thrones, were religious ceremonies, paying homage to God the Father of mankind. One can hardly fault Octavia Hill, who stood looking out across this animated scene, if she felt some pride. She had after all helped bring to life the inscription she had placed on the wall; in bold red and white letters it read, 'The Wilderness Shall Blossom as the Rose'.

The blossoming of this community in the desert of Southwark was husbanded by Octavia Hill's managers. The ideals by which she trained them were lofty, their responsibilities heavy.

You have taken on yourself the wants, longings, desires of people, you are bound not only to let them live, but to let them live happily; you must throw open to them stores of amusement, especially if they work hard, you must give them the power of learning; they must see friends, make presents, have holidays, and they will have the right to look to you for the power to do all these things; and if you do your duty, you will give it them, without their seeing it is any trouble.[15]

The ideal manager combines two principles: she is to participate as 'a volunteer', that is 'a spontaneous undertaker of tasks' (*Oxford English Dictionary*) and she is to be trained as a 'professional', a worker whose knowledge of hygiene, sociology, and economics enables her to reconcile the care of individual tenants with the needs of the community.

In her *Letters to Her Fellow Workers*, Octavia Hill speaks of the growing recognition among landlords of the need for trained estate managers.

There is growing up a certain number of ladies capable of representing them and possessing certain knowledge. So that in the years to come, as they will have lawyers to do legal business, surveyors and architects to see to the fabric of their houses, so they will have managers to supervise in detail the comfort and health of their tenants, so far as these depend on proper conditions in the houses in which they live, managers who will be interested in the people and will have time to see thoroughly to the numerous details involved in management.[16]

Unlike the lawyer, architect, and surveyor, however, the manager's competence depends not merely on her ability to master and apply technical details of special knowledge; she must also be raised to be a volunteer. This can best be done at home.

In later life Octavia Hill expressed reservations about the division of workers on the basis of age and sex in the settlement houses; it seemed to stifle the diversity that she found so rewarding in family lfe. She also deplored the increasing tendency of social workers to specialize. The worker who concentrated on one thing — trips to art museums for the elderly, the schooling of young children, or the engineering aspects of sanitation — was in danger of losing her sense of purpose. Emphasis must remain on '*knowing* people with whom you work' not on exercising skills.

It is but a feeble effort to bring, according to the special need of the moment, one human being into near touch with others in their homes; to lead the new and wiser thinkers of today to occupy themselves not with the problems pondered in the study, but with individuals in their homes and daily life. What the result of such intercourse will be must depend solely on what our visitors are and what their flocks are, and this must vary infinitely.[17]

The professional status of the visitors might be considered to make them superior to their clients, yet as volunteers they can be equals. Octavia Hill's great abilities, her forcefulness, and her commanding position set her apart. Occasional references to 'my own dear poor' have an unpleasantly condescending ring. Yet she never thought of herself as a superior. Here her anomalous social position was an advantage. As a single woman of competence, authority and considerable education, she held her own with aristocrats and Members of Parliament. Yet her own background was middle-class: she had known poverty; all her life she had worked, receiving a salary as a teacher. (For her work in housing she took no pay.) Like her tenants she had repeatedly moved her belongings — the Turkish rug, the family pictures — from place to place. She knew the merciless exhaustion, the tension and tedium of the daily routine. 'It is with me here almost as with the poor themselves, a kind of fight for mere existence — references, notices, rents, the dry necessary matters of business, take up almost all time and thought.'[18] She felt that she had got back more than she had given, and thanked her tenants for the help they gave her.

In short when the equality of all and the common responsibility of work are recognized, both rich and poor benefit.

Because her tenants were working people, independent, they would not be corrupted by receiving gifts; they would not succumb to the 'helpless indolence of expectant selfishness' that demoralized the pauper. In the last analysis the Octavia Hill of mercy took precedence over the Octavia Hill of law and order. She urged her managers to see people as individuals, rather than as cases or as members of a class.

For the rich as well, egalitarianism and work brought its rewards. In Octavia Hill's view, as in that of Josephine Butler and Florence Nightingale, the lives of aristocratic women were as demeaning, as restricted, as those of the pauper poor. She accused the rich of shutting up their hearts 'in cold dignified independence'. In creating a profession for women, Octavia Hill felt that she had done more than find them employment; she had given them a sense of themselves.

Octavia Hill would be the first to admit that a theory is only as good as its practice. Studying her complex ideal, one constantly has to push aside a rising murmur of unanswered questions. How did the tenants really feel about the Monday evening visit with its settling of accounts and inquiries about the health of the children? Did they believe that the manager's friendship was limited by the notice for dismissal, which lay concealed in her pocket? How did the manager decide whether to apply the requirements of justice or of mercy? Were some relieved of their duties because they were too generous in forgiving debts — or not generous enough? Did Octavia Hill wake up in the middle of the night, stricken with a vision etched for her by Gustav Doré and George Frederick Watts of bodies huddled together in the mud with the underside of a bridge for a roof? Did she wonder whether among the bodies there were some whom she had turned out of her houses?

Most of these questions cannot be answered. The tenants left no accounts. Many of Octavia's co-workers' comments, both the critical and the adulatory, were based more on philosophical differences and affinities than on the specific merits of the Hill system. Beatrice Webb's Fabian Socialism led her to criticize the

Hill method as superficial and too individualistic to deal effectively with national problems. The Barnetts, on the other hand, thought Octavia Hill's way of dealing with people extremely impressive.

One volume is invaluable, however, because it is unique. Ellen Chase came from Boston to London to work as a manager for Octavia Hill. She returned in 1891 after five years and wrote an account of her apprenticeship, *Tenant Friends in Old Deptford*. It is a delightful book and of special importance to any student of the Hill system. Not only is it the only record we have of the system, but its point of view is particularly revealing. By Octavia Hill's own acknowledgement it describes her management, not at its best, but at its worst.

Among the various sections administered by the Ecclesiastical Commission of the C.O.S., Deptford was notorious. Year after year Octavia Hill's annual charge to her workers and her report on progress contains lengthy scoldings, admonitions, and exhortations concerning 'poor Deptford, our black sheep'. In her introduction to Ellen Chase's book she apologizes for Deptford, adding that only Miss Chase's 'deep human sympathy enabled her to see all that lay below the squalor and violence of the inhabitants, and to realize how much family life redeemed even the most degraded'.[19]

Exactly how 'low' was the Deptford level? To what extent did Deptford incorporate the caring community, the mutually sympathetic relationship between worker and tenant prescribed by Miss Hill?

The community which Miss Hill had described with such evident distress emerges from these pages as far from squalid. There is poverty — the 'furnishings' which the tenants bring are often no more than packing crates and a couple of mouldy mattresses; the week's pay is hardly enough to buy food for the children. There is tragedy — women die in childbirth; consumption and cholera take a heavy toll; men responsible for supporting large families are fired without notice; the old are carted off to die in London hospitals; adolescents disappear into the low life of London. There is crime — the fighting among the tenants over the stealing of laundry and the more brutal Saturday-night brawling and wife-beating.

On the whole, however, the reader is left with the impression that the Deptford people are individuals with a good sense of self-respect, supported by a strong commitment to each other. The women, as they hang out the wash and weed the flower-beds, keep an eye on the children playing in the court. Their solicitude includes not only their own children but those of the women who are absent because they are working or ill — or in a few instances, drunk. (One old woman observed to Miss Chase that 'God made the babies, and the Devil their mothers'.) They break up fights, listen to the old people's complaints and run errands for them. In a community in which everyone is known they are quick to spot an intruder. Near the Foreign Cattle Market, Deptford was frequented by peddlars and the petty thieves that dog large crowds. Established by Henry VIII as a royal dockyard, it continued to attract those who made their living by the sea. To create a stable community, an oasis for English family life, out of this great flowing procession was no easy achievement. Ellen Chase gives her people credit.

> Our people, sadly thwarted as they were in many ways, we saw could still claim freely the great possessions, the spiritual qualities of courage, patience, and faith, wherever they please to lift up their souls and desire them. And hence it was not the bareness of living, but the richness of life, that struck me most in Green St., since what really matters was there as everywhere else, within the reach of all.[20]

Her tenants' feisty optimism is evidently contagious and Miss Chase describes daily events with relish. She was less interested in having her people moral than in having them in high spirits.

> Another day, toward noon we were startled by a series of sharp cries, 'Ow! Ow! Ow!' resounding from Vicarage Lane, and rushed out to find the Bottom filled with men, women, and children surging toward Creek Road, and in the midst a woman under arrest for breaking a publichouse window after having been locked out. . . . Green Street was always unexpected in its revelations, and I remember Mrs. Coster, a much respected tenant, said to us proudly in the heat of the moment, 'Oh, it used to take eight or nine to lock up my man.'[21]

If relations among the tenants were quite open and, in a rough and ready way, caring, tenant and manager seem to have had an equally constructive association. Ellen Chase, along with the Barnetts and Beatrice Webb, believed that the mutual respect created by a businesslike relationship was the proper foundation for charity.

The embarrassing sense of intrusion which sometimes accompanies the other forms of visiting is escaped by a collector who goes naturally as agent for the landlord into the homes of all the families in her charge. Then, too, the tenant has for his part a helpful sense of self-respect, when he turns to his collector, assured that having fulfilled his duty to her he has a right to expect that she will do her duty by him.[22]

Her relationship with her tenants is not unlike that between tenant and tenant. She visits the elderly in hospitals, settles arguments in and out of court, finds jobs in service for adolescent children, provides work (some of it improvements on the property in response to suggestions from the tenants) for those temporarily unemployed. She arranges holidays for old pensioners and fetches them at the station. To some, perhaps, Miss Chase was a rather formidable mother figure — oppressive in her demands for cleanliness and financial rectitude. To many of the older people she was a daughter figure. They petted her and fussed over her. They asked to have their pictures taken with her, and in a caricature of Victorian domesticity with her in their midst, they sat, stiffly holding buns, behind a row of cups and saucers placed with military precision.

Others regarded her as someone to be got around, an attractive challenge to their highly skilled abilities at evading responsibilities. (Miss Chase writes feelingly on the subject of forged testimonials, the prevalence of piously respectable — and false — identities, and clothes and furnishings hired by the hour to impress a prospective landlady.)

Miss Chase brought energy and good humour to her specific tasks as rent collector. She seems appreciative even of the tenants' forthright attempts to hang on to their rent money. These were, after all, indications, if negative ones, of the independence of spirit she hoped to develop.

A little farther on I met old Egan taking a circuitous route toward the Top. Generally speaking, he was in constant work and a credit to the 'property'. Just now he was much the worse for celebrating, and stopped me to remark with a confident smile, 'The world is full of temptation. Everywhere you turn a public-house'! So far I could assent but I was utterly taken aback by his ending, 'A man would need the "res-olution" of a carthorse to pass by, and, thank God, *I* am a man and not a beast'! Certainly Deptford has a logic all its own! With entire self-approval, he continued, 'I have three times the rent in my pocket, but you shan't have a farthing of it. I am going to be happy to-day and to-morrow and drink it all. And I shan't have a poor time to-morrow because I could not say "no" to you to-day. I give you my best compliments. May you soon have a handsome husband, and a happy married life; but as for giving you my rent, that I shall not do!'[23]

The following week his rent was collected — by another collector.

The intimate knowledge of the family gained through the Monday visits could be put to use when they were beset by special difficulties. Tenants who owed rent were in fact kept on for months beyond the traditional 'warning' period, while attempts were made to tide them over through loans, the procuring of temporary work, and negotiations with the pawnshop. Countless families in financial trouble were held together and given hope through the encouragement, the suggestions, the 'sympathetic entering into of circumstances' enjoined by the Hill theory of management.

It is of course true that not all were amenable to Miss Chase's influence. She is not afraid to face her failures. She entitles chapter four of her book with the telling phrase, 'Go She Must.' Her failures were not the victims of unemployment, disease, and bad luck — these she could help. They were the habitually and competently manipulative, those who refused to accept the 'middle-class morality' enveighed against by Eliza Doolittle's father and upheld by Miss Chase, those who insisted upon their own irresponsible way. Miss Chase felt no compunction about evicting these determined transgressors of the financial law. She knew that the same energy and imagination that went into the successful attempts to evade the Hill management would be used with equal success in finding new housing — and in getting around the new manager. This 'middle man' of capitalist housing was, in the Hill estimation, a worse villain than the landlord.

No one would feel sorry that he would have to deal with the forged testimonials, the furniture-by-the-hour, the broken promises, and all of the complicated shenanigans of Miss Chase's ex-tenant.

Here one must admit that special circumstances protected Miss Chase against one of the limitations of her system — its inability to provide housing for the destitute poor. While the general population was increasing, the distribution was uneven. Many sections in the south and east, among them Southwark and Deptford, were actually losing population. A clever vagrant would be able to keep some sort of roof over his head indefinitely

To those who wondered whether eviction had not pushed families from the 'respectable' into the 'outcast' category and who criticized a system that turned people out at the point when they most needed help. Deptford offered no answer. To those who valued housing for the working classes, Deptford provided evidence of a system that for many had prevented the desperate slide into General Booth's 'darkest England'.

3   *Believing and Doing: A Holy Society*

Octavia Hill, like Josephine Butler, believed that she lived in a divided world. In one sense church and society are co-inherent, one and the same, since Christ, 'the Light of every man', is the head of that body which is the community of mankind. Yet in another sense the church is a spiritual outpost. Through refusing his spiritual citizenship man has made of society a wilderness; the church has become a tiny gathering of believers, men and women who recognize and claim their birthright, opening the gates of their city to those beyond the walls.

Nor is this process of fragmentation simply a division between church and society. The church has itself become a victim, cut off from its true nature. Churches — prideful, self-centred groups of people — war with each other, each setting up a particular idea of truth in place of the universal truth of God. Octavia claimed her citizenship in both churches. She remained an Anglican because she believed that only by belonging to a particular sect could she witness to the universal Church. Her artist's nature was drawn by the power and beauty of the Book of Common Prayer. Unlike many who shared her latitudinarian views, she was not frightened by the liturgical elaborations of the High Church party. In 1857 she wrote excitedly of attending an evening service in a house chapel located in a very poor part of London. She described, appreciatively, the stained-glass windows, the singers, the organ played by their host, a wealthy printer, the blue and gold gas lamps.

The congregation consisted of workmen and their families, the employers and theirs, the clerks and servants. I should guess about 70 in all. The clergyman who entoned the service, was evidently a Puseyite, which Miranda in her bigotry had been mourning ever since I came in, but I saw too much in the large, sad, earnest eyes to care whether he preached in black or white, or to doubt that in more important points, he, too, is being led home. See him, then, a pattern Puseyite, a pale worn face (wasted with fasting), evidently with fears and sorrow about the intense wickedness of the world and its ways, probably a believer in the superior righteousness of celibacy. Great dark eyes, large forehead, very small chin, smooth short black hair parted in the middle, and so smoothed and pressed that evidently no hair could have a will of its own. Strange type was it of the complete subjection of the man's spirit, all human nature, good and bad alike, subdued and kept in order, and still his great dark eyes saying how wicked he thought himself.[24]

Speaking warmly of her acquaintance with the Watsons, she describes them as 'very High Church, but not foolishly so', adding that it is undoubtedly 'the refinement and beauty which attract them'.[25]

She sympathized with those who were repelled by the narrowness and conservatism of the Anglican Church, and its identification of sanctification with doctrinal conformity and intellectual consent. But to her friend Janey Hughes Senior who is considering leaving the Church she makes a case for reform from within.

As to the points on which you and I equally differ from so many clergymen and churchmen, if we think Maurice's interpretation of the creeds the true and simple one, is it not doubly incumbent upon us to uphold it in the Church? Leaving it would be like saying we could not honestly stay in it. Then does not all the best, most thorough, most convincing, most peaceful reform of any body come from within? in family, in business, in nation, in Church?

In the spirit of F. D. Maurice, she points to the truth of the things which unite, rather than those which divide, as the springs of action.

Is there not almost always a right at the root of the relationship, which may be asserted and vindicated, and on the recognition of which reform depends? *That* body must be corrupt indeed, which must be left by earnest members of it. Surely there are abundant signs of growing healthy life and reform in the Church; all the vigorous and new things nearly are signs of good. Why should you set up the decidedly old fashioned interpretation of doctrine, and *that* held by a certainly decreasing number in the Church, and feel hardly honest in differing from it and remaining in the Church?[26]

As an Anglican she did not feel separated from her fellow-Christians. When Margaret Howitt asked her to join the Society of Friends Octavia replied simply that she already felt herself to be a member.

It feels to me that all people who are obeying the best part of the nature that has been given them, more or less belong to it — that those who know from Whom the light proceeds 'that lightest every man that cometh into the world', know themselves to be bound into a society by that gift, by being children of God and heirs of Christ.[27]

She sometimes expressed herself in ringingly evangelical terms. Addressing the children at the Nottingham Place School, she surprised herself.

They ask me questions that make me feel, in answering, as if I were speaking almost like a prophet of the things that are and will be . . . . The old fire, that is gone for action, often flames in me. I can feel it almost burning my eyes, when I speak to them of the faith in God that may be a sure rock to them from the shame and sins of this age. And . . . sometimes . . . when I sit there all wearied and worn, and they tell me of their day's doings, and we fall on some great subject of principle or spiritual fact, I wonder at the might of this strange, spiritual life we lead that can glow and burn, while the face grows paler, and the frame weaker. [28]

Generally, however, she refrained from preaching. She disliked those who 'try to *force* their notions, their *faith* on everyone; who decidedly set to work to convert people'. She was exasperated by those who regard a person with greater affection when they learn he is a member of the Church. When the question arose as to whether it was proper for a Christian to teach in a school based on agnostic principles, she replied in the affirmative.

I never have stopped, I hope I never shall stop, to consider what sect or sects of people are at work, if I thoroughly and entirely approve of the work. I may think the work incomplete; but, if it comes in my way, and I think it good, as far as it goes, I will help it with the power I have.

In a profound sense the goal of her system of management was religious. But because faith grew primarily out of experience, it could not be communicated by merely didactic exposition. 'One fact about God well burnt into a heart with life's fires, and pressed into it with life's pain, conforms a child more to His likeness than colder acceptance of facts'.[29] She wanted to show that 'we care for men as men, we care for good as good'. She was awed by the mystery of faith and the complexity of human nature and she believed that no person should pass judgement on another's faith or lack of it. She steered away from talk.

Florence Nightingale

7 Eminent Victorian

Of the three women discussed in this book, Florence Nightingale is the best and the least known. For Josephine Butler and Octavia Hill biographical facts provide both a record of their accomplishments and an insight into the inner life that gave birth to those accomplishments. For Florence Nightingale, however, the facts speak less clearly.

The difficulty does not arise from lack of interest or material. Miss Nightingale has been immortalized in Staffordshire china; her portrait has its place in Lytton Strachey's gallery of 'eminent Victorians'; she appears as a paper-doll cut-out in a feminist colouring book; in the company of Luther and Plato she has talked her way through an American television show. In addition she has captured the imagination of talented and scholarly biographers, most notably Sir Edward Cook and Cecil Woodham-Smith. This interest has fed on a voluminous collection of documents: official papers, letters and diaries, many of which have been annotated by Florence Nightingale herself.

These sources give evidence of a woman of considerable complexity. Rebelling against her parents, she remained in their household for 17 years. Devoting herself to the saving of military lives, she never questioned the policies that sent them into battle. A woman for whom faith was the overriding concern, she confessed that she didn't believe her own convictions. The weight of her accomplishments and the speed with which she brought them to fruition attest to her energy; yet she remained for 40 years a prisoner of her invalid's sofa. Proclaiming the rule of reason, she was destroyed by her emotions. Creating 'a new life for women', she rejected many contemporary feminist causes.

If the subject is a relatively unified personality, the biographer can let the facts speak for themselves. Actions, words and feelings tend in the same direction, supporting and complementing each other. If, however, the subject is a divided person, the unanalysed facts appear anomalous. Even with interpretation, Florence Nightingale remains a puzzle; without it, she would be an enigma.

1   *Lea Hurst and Embley, 1820—47: Rebel Daughter*

Florence Nightingale, daughter of William Edward and Frances Smith Nightingale, sister of Frances Parthenope Nightingale, was born on 12 May 1820.

On the surface the household in which she was raised was not unlike that of the Northumberland Greys. Her father, William, a well-to-do country squire, was a man of liberal persuasion with a taste for languages and metaphysics. He took over his daughters' education when Florence was 12, instructing the girls in Latin, Greek, French, history, composition, and mathematics, as well as his beloved Italian. He was delighted by Florence's quickness of mind and took particular care in the upbringing of this daughter who so resembled him in her interests and abilities. Fanny Smith, Florence's mother, was endowed with a gregarious nature and the advantages of wealth inherited from her father, William Smith, a philanthropist and Member of Parliament. Florence's only sister, Parthenope, judging from her accomplishments (she wrote an effective antiwar tract, essays on agriculture and land-ownership, and several novels), was a girl with brains and spirit.

Like the Greys and the Hills, the Nightingales lived in beautiful surroundings. As a child Florence went to sleep with the sound of the Derwent river in her ears; in the harsh and arid plains of the Crimea she remembered with longing the purple hills seen from her window at Lea Hurst. To satisfy Fanny's social ambitions the Nightingales acquired a second house in Embley, a handsome Georgian building which they embellished in an ornate Elizabethan manner. After the London season, they returned to spend their winters there. Parthenope, writing to Hilary Bonham Carter, describes it as 'il paradiso terrestro as depicted in the 25th Canto, stanze 40 something' and Florence speaks of the garden as 'a blaze of beauty'.[1]

The Nightingales did not lack for company in their Garden of Eden. There were some famous names among their visitors: the Palmerstons with their son-in-law Shaftesbury; Julia Ward and Samuel Gridley Howe. The house was often filled with relatives:

the Smiths — Aunt Mai, Uncle Sam, and their son Shore — the glamorous Nicholsons and Bonham Carters.

This country house setting that Josephine Butler found so nourishing was to Florence Nightingale deadly and oppressive. To the end of her life she continued to rail against the tedium and stupidity of its conventions. How can one account for this reaction?

Florence was an unusual child, a child who might have had difficulties in accepting the restrictions of any family, even an ideal one. She combined remarkable gifts of analysis and imagination with a passionate heart and a dominating will. It was a nature that cried out to be taken seriously, needing on the one hand the security and balance that comes from discipline and on the other the freedom to develop a powerful intellect.

This challenge was beyond Fanny Smith Nightingale. Her marriage was not particularly happy. Prevented from marrying the man she first loved by her father's opposition, she had accepted the offer of a childhood friend and neighbour six years her junior. Unlike Caroline Hill and Hannah Grey, she had no special affinity for children. Like many women of wealth and position, she occupied herself with the running of her houses — Lea Hurst, Embley and a rented house in London. Her time was taken up in looking after the comfort of her guests and an exacting social circuit that included the London season, foreign travel, and house parties. She assumed that her daughters would unquestioningly follow in the aristocratic tradition, enhancing her own social success with their brilliant marriages. Drawing up menus for dinner, shopping for gloves in London, and steering the tea-table conversation away from any subject that might invite controversy or an unseemly display of emotion, she could never provide a model for a daughter with an ardent nature, uncompromising integrity, and a consuming need to assert her will.

Then there was Parthenope. Her attractive qualities as a companion were vitiated by implacable jealousy. Unlike her younger sister in taste and temperament she resented Florence's special place in her father's affections. She resented her sister's suave good looks, her social charm, and her gifts as a conversationalist. The bitterness of her jealousy was intensified by the realization that Florence, the embodiment of their parents' conception of the perfect daughter, thought little of her gifts and

d to make use of these advantages in the conventional
sband. In later years when Parthenope had been
ppy marriage, the two women came to appreciate
...er. They were never entirely able to transcend the
competitiveness of their youth, however.

The relationship that had the most damaging effect on Florence
was that of her father. Dominated by a wealthy and insensitive
wife, he gave his affections to, and shared his interests with, his
favourite child. To the education of this daughter whose abilities
were so closely attuned to his own, he brought intellectual
energy and imagination. He was a student of Bentham, friend of
Wilberforce, and follower of Palmerston, a Whig and Unitarian.
He discussed politics and religion with both girls. Deeply
appreciative of the education that he himself had received at
Edinburgh and Trinity Cambridge, he encouraged his daughters
to think, to argue, to speak and write clearly and effectively.
Walking through the woods, a daughter on either side, he would
argue the comparative merits of classicism and romanticism.
Once a week he assigned them a written theme based on the
College Essay. Florence was the better student of the two. He was
delighted with her as a mathematician, as a student of classical
and European history, and as a translator of Plato's Dialogues.
He urged her to make use of her talents.

He was, however, a weak man. Eventually Florence, applying
the training and principles he had given her, announced that she
wished to have something worthwhile to do; she would become a
nurse. Naturally, Fanny was horrified. Parthenope had hysterics.
Her father was the only one who might have secured for Florence
her right to choose her life. He refused to take her part. Frightened
by family outbursts and conflicts, he simply withdrew. Through
his silence he conspired in her defeat.

Florence's reaction to her father's withdrawal is significant.
With Parthenope and her mother there were violent scenes —
bitter denunciations and recriminations, even physical battles.
Later in life she had the dubious satisfaction of denying them
access to her company. But with her father, the person she loved
most,[2] she remained mute. The letters she continued to write
throughout the course of her long life are affectionate and
even-keyed. It seems likely that she had never been able to bring
herself to face the tremendous ambivalence — the great hostility
towards, and the yearning for approval from, a father she deeply

loved and could no longer truly admire. Her curiously flawed life with its invalidism and withdrawal from normal human relationships, her seesawing between dominance and helplessness, love and hate, rationality and irrationality was the outward manifestation of this conflict. It is conceivable that, rather than acknowledge her wrath towards the father on whom she remained psychically dependent, she turned it upon herself, condemning herself to a lifetime of debilitating self-destruction.

The tension within the family soured Florence's view of the country house and its upper-class inhabitants. While sorting the china she asked, 'Can reasonable people want all this? Is all that china, linen, glass necessary to make man a Progressive animal?'[3] She was bored by the routine of walks in the garden, embroidery, reading aloud, a succession of heavy meals.

On excursions to the village and to the parish church she desperately searched for signs of a more vital life. She noted that the assertions on eternal damnation of the unbaptized uttered from the pulpit by clergymen seemed at total variance with the readings from scripture which described God as loving and forgiving. She noted too that her companions attended church for reasons of convention rather than deeply held belief. Young women took hours over their appearance, and expressed sentiments on Sunday that they appeared totally to ignore the rest of the week. Young men dragged themselves out of bed and followed the family to church, not because they wished to worship God, but because they hoped to win favour with a future mother-in-law.

All children are single-hearted; Florence was exceptionally so. She determined to search beyond the contradictory and lukewarm witness of the parish priest and the casual irreligion of the congregation. The injunction to pray was automatically taught by a mother and governesses who saw it as a part of the heritage of all well-brought-up children. She took it with a literal-minded seriousness.

When I was young, I could not understand what people meant by 'their thoughts wandering in prayer'. I asked for what I really wished, and really wished for what I asked. And my thoughts wandered no more than those of a mother would wander, who was supplicating her Sovereign for her son's reprieve from execution. The Litany was not long enough for me. I wished for all those things, and many more; and tried to cram in as many requests as I could before the *spell* at the end came in the form of St. Chrysostom's prayer. I liked the morning service much better than the afternoon, because we asked for more things. In private prayer I wrote down what I asked for, specified the time by which I prayed that it might come, continued in prayer for it, and looked to see whether it came. It never did. I have papers upon papers, 'by the 7th of July, I pray that I may be' so and so. When the 7th of July came, I looked, and I was not.

Like the young Octavia Hill who prayed for Poland, Florence extended the scope of her prayerful concerns to include political prisoners and travellers. Royalty was a special interest.

I could not pray for George IV. I thought the people very good who prayed for him and wondered whether he could have been much worse if he had not been prayed for. William IV I prayed for a little. But when Victoria came to the throne, I prayed for her in a rapture of feeling, and my thoughts never wandered.[4]

To a serious examination of the life of prayer, she added a commitment to service. In 1845 she helped care for her grandmother Nightingale.

I am very glad sometimes to walk in the valley of the shadow of death as I do here; there is something in the stillness and silence of it which levels all earthly troubles. God tempers our wings in the waters of that valley, and I have not been so happy or so thankful for a long time.[5]

Although she had seen that the rich also are under the shadow of death, Florence found in confronting the sufferings of the poor a reality which, though terrible, held deep meaning for her. It swept away the cardboard scenery of her life in the country house with its Chinoiseries and pseudo-Greek nymphs and fauns; it called upon her to see life as it really is. She was depressed by the indifference she saw around her, 'all the world putting on its shoes and stockings every morning all the same'.[6] She was moved by pity; 'my life is so filled with the misery of this world that the only things in which to labour brings any return seems to me helping or sympathizing *there*'. [7] She had found a purpose: to relieve the suffering of others.

To her experience of the sickroom Florence brought belief in a God who gives ultimate meaning to life and death. On 7 February 1837 she received a 'call' from God to a life of service. The implications of this call were not immediately apparent. 'I desire for a considerable time only to lead a life of obscurity and toil, for the purpose of allowing whatever I may have received of God to ripen; and turning it some day to the glory of His Name.'[8] Eight years later she had decided on a plan. To Hilary Bonham Carter she wrote:

> Well, my dearest, I am not yet come to the great thing I wanted to say. I have always found that there is so much truth in the suggestion that you must dig for hidden treasures *in silence* or you will not find it; and so I dug after my poor little plan in silence, even from you. It was to go to be a nurse at Salisbury Hospital for these few months to learn the 'prax'. . . . I thought something like a Protestant Sisterhood, without vows, for women of educated feelings, might be established. But there have been difficulties about my very first step, which terrified Mama. I do not mean the physically revolting parts of a hospital, but things about the surgeons and nurses which you may guess. Even Mrs. Fowler threw cold water upon it; and nothing will be done this year at all events, and I do not believe — ever.[9]

The reasons behind the Nightingales' rejection are indicated in this letter, and are in any case well-known — the danger and degradation of work that dealt with the most dangerous, unpleasant physical diseases and the lascivious desires of fellow-workers of a low class. Fanny Nightingale's objections are understandable: no mother would desire a course that would bring hardship to a beloved child. Yet there was a pathological element. Fanny seemed determined to break her daughter's will. She almost succeeded.

'How the soul dies between the destruction of one and the taking up of another', Florence wrote to Hilary. The years between 1845 and 1851 were difficult. Anger towards her parents alternated with self-doubt. 'There is no pure thought in me.'

Perhaps she had been right to accede to her parents' wishes. On the other hand in failing to act she might be renouncing a lifegiving opportunity. 'It seems to me that there are great turning points in people's lives — when one error of judgement, one act of selfishness, is the beginning of a long downward course.'[10]

The prayers of the child for specific gifts have been supplanted by the prayers of the penitent for spiritual guidance.

> I never pray for anything temporal, even for my lad [her cousin, Shore Smith], but when each morning comes, I kneel down before the rising sun and only say, Behold the handmaid of the Lord — give me this day my work to do — no, not my work but thine.[11]

2   London, Rome and Greece, 1847—51: Pilgrim and Penitent

Fortunately for Florence's sanity the perquisites of an upper-class young lady included the London season, the larger society of the salon, and travel in Europe, as well as the country house. In London she felt herself to be in touch with human needs and concerns.

> Life is seen in a much truer form in London than in the country. In an English country place everything that is painful is so carefully removed out of sight, behind those fine trees, to a village three mile off. In London, at all events, if you open your eyes, you cannot help seeing in the next street that life is not as it has been made out to you. You cannot get out of a carriage at a party without seeing what is in the faces making the lane on either side, and without feeling tempted to rush back and say, 'These are my brothers and sisters.'[12]

Her acquaintance with London, however, was not limited to the painful sights of urban poverty. She delighted in music, the theatre, and the excitement of political intrigue. The letters she wrote as a young girl to her friend Mary Clarke bubble with excitement. 'We are revelling in music all day long.' She describes Pauline Garcia's debut in *Otello*. She speculates on the composition of the next cabinet. With an adolescent's delight in the foibles of important people, she gives an account of Melbourne's relationship with Queen Victoria's dog. Her information, an equerry to the Queen, had said

> that Lord Melbourne called the Queen's terrier a frightful little beast, and often contradicted her flat, all of which she takes in good part, and lets him go to sleep after dinner, taking care that he shall not be waked. She reads all the newspapers and all the villifying abuse which the Tories give her, and makes up her mind that a queen must be abused, and hates them cordially.[13]

Florence had met Mary Clarke in 1838 when her family had taken her to Paris. Of all the privileges of aristocracy, travel and the Grand Tour most appealed to Florence. Here was a context for her studies in history, art, and the classics. Here at last she became acquainted with a group of people who shared her interests fully. Their leader, Mary Clarke, was kept in Paris by her mother's invalidism, and had become a close friend of Madame Recamier. The men who attended her Friday night salon included Claude Faurel, the medievalist; Chateaubriand; and Julius Mohl, the Oriental scholar whom she later married. A tiny woman with huge eyes and a mop of tangled curls, she was noted for her wit and spontaniety. In her company Florence could give a free rein to her own humour and directness of speech — qualities which in deference to her mother she had suppressed in the sober social intercourse at Embley. To her delight she found that far from scandalizing her companions she charmed them. She enjoyed the heady excitement of being admired and sought after; throughout her life she regarded the desire to shine in society as one of her besetting sins.

Another privilege of the aristocratic life — the company of attractive young men who sought her hand in marriage, brought her less happiness. Henry Nicholson was perhaps not as devastatingly attractive as his sister Marianne, who was the object of the adolescent passions of both Florence and Parthenope. At any rate Henry was kept waiting for six years for his negative answer. His successor Richard Monckton Milnes, witty, rich, intelligent, and kind, is regarded by many of Florence's biographers as the man she would have married had she not felt called to renounce the pleasures of this world for the life of service to God. Perhaps — yet somehow it is hard to believe that a woman of so strong a will, with instincts and feelings of a compulsive honesty and primitive intensity would have been drawn to a man whom Carlyle described as a 'semi-quizzical, affectionate, high-bred, Italianized little man'. In any case they did not marry and Monckton Milnes became one of the many men who, alternately drawn by the positive currents of Florence's approbation and impelled by the negative shocks of her threats and chastisements, helped her achieve her ambitious goals.

The prospect of making a good marriage had not deflected Florence from her private concerns; Mrs Nightingale now held out the lure of foreign travel. In 1847 Florence was permited to set out for Rome with her friends Mr and Mrs Bracebridge. To her parents' delight she wrote happily about her visits with the Sidney Herberts and the Christian von Bunsens, walks through the streets of the Eternal City, encounters with the monuments that she had first seen in the history and Latin books of her childhood. These excursions did not, however, distract her from what she felt to be the essential purpose of her life: the development of her spiritual calling. As she had always admired the Roman church for its serious and professional attitude toward spirituality, she went to study with Madre Santa Colomba, Lady Superior of the Dames du Sacre Coeur, the convent attached to the church at Trinita dei Monti. She went on retreat at the convent; she followed the spiritual exercises expected of novices and the forms and disciplines of self-examination; she made extensive notes on her readings in devotional literature and she accepted Madre Santa Colomba as her spiritual director.

Three years later, the Italian trip was followed by a more extensive voyage to Greece and Egypt. The manuscripts from this trip are of particular interest to biographers since they include her diary as well as letters to her family. The reader finds two Florences: the calm dutifully affectionate, scholarly daughter of the letters, and the passionate, distraught penitent of the diaries. When one correlates the entries in the diary with the dates of the letters, one realizes the degree to which the inner self that tormented her was kept hidden behind the outward self she displayed to her parents. The isolation and the ignorance of each other, which she deplored in British family life, had with the Nightingales reached its most extreme manifestation.

Our position to one another in our families is, and must be, like that of the Moon to the Earth. The Moon revolves around her, moves with her, never leaves her. Yet the Earth never sees but one side of her; the other side remains for ever unknown.[14]

At the same time as she was writing long and rather pedantic essays on art and architecture to her parents, she was desperately trying to hold together the fragments of a disintegrating psyche. In June 1850 she writes calmly and appreciatively to her parents, describing her love of the Greek 'principle of fatalism'.

Yesterday morning I sat a long time in that cave of the Eumenides, though the overhanging rock is broken and torn away and lies in the other side, the deep black spring is still there. And you sit in the cleft and look out between the rocks upon the Acropolis, the Temple of Victory, and the Propylaea, . . . I sat and thought of poor Cowper's sufferings, but not bitterly. I like to think how the Eumenides' laws work out all things for good — and I would not be such a fool as to pray that one little bit of hell should be remitted, one consequence altered either of others' mistakes or of our own. How true the Greek feeling of the suffering of Orestes for his mother's murder. Poor Eumenides, your cave is blasted, and your worship destroyed — but the feeling which dictated it is as true as it was one thousand years ago, as it was in the beginning is now and shall ever be. I love the Eumenides better than almost any part of the Greek worship and I love the spirit, which we have miscalled fatalism, which so nobly acquiesced in it, without understanding the reason why.[15]

In her diary she records quite different feelings. Thwarted from pursuing the life to which she had felt truly called, exhausted from trying to cut and shape herself to fit a society that she could not respect, she felt that she was going mad. She visited the cave of the Eumenides, not because she wished to gather material for an essay on Greek religion but because she sought salvation.

During her childhood Florence had been disturbed by the demands of her imagination; her fantasies distracted her from carrying out family duties. 'We talk and we dine and we dress as if the tadpoles, our hopes were not feeding in thousands in silence and abandoned in despair.' By 1850 the frustrations, the repressed hostility, that 'tadpole world of restless activity which swims around the glassy surface of our civilized life'[16] had brought her to the edge of an abyss.

Her prayers are no longer for specific things, or even for guidance, but for life itself. On Pentecost, 19 May, she writes, 'God, I place myself in Thy hands', and on the following day:

> All the afternoon a voice was saying to me, 'If thou know the gift of God and who it is that saith unto thee, "Give me to drink" thou wouldest have asked of Him and He would give thee living *water*.' Lord, thou askest me to do Thy will and I am to ask of Thee life.

Besides these words, she has added in small, unsteady letters, 'but I am dead'.[17]

Unlike Orestes, she was not guilty of murdering her mother nevertheless, she thought of herself as a murderer. She believed that beneath the decorum of the country house matricide and infanticide were regular occurrences. She spoke of mothers murdering daughters. In heated encounters Fanny and Parthenope had warned Florence: if she persisted in going against their wishes, she would kill them. After one scene Parthenope had become violently ill; in 1852 she suffered a complete breakdown. Of Fanny Florence wrote, 'Oh dear good woman, when I feel her disappointment in me it is as if I were going insane. . . . What a murderer am I to disturb their happiness.'[18] For a psyche that had been formed by parents who viewed filial independence as a personal and wounding affront, the guilt was unbearable. Given the choice between a self-assertion that seemed like matricide, and self-denial she chose the latter.

In June and July the entries in her diary record the alternation of hope and despair. On 10 July she wrote:

> All plans — all wishes seemed extinguished . . . I had three paths among which to choose. I might have been a married woman; a literary woman, or a hospital sister. Now it seemed to me as if quiet with somebody to look for my coming back was all I wanted.

The diary ends with her return. 'Wednesday, August 21st. Surprised my dear people, sitting in the drawing room and not thinking of me with the owl in my pocket.' There are a few other desultory entries. 'Sat with Mama and Papa in the nursery', followed by blank pages. On the back cover there is a careful listing of purchases made while abroad — 'bronze knife, tobacco pouch, bracelet.'

3 Kaiserswerth and Harley Street, 1851 — 54: Nurse and Administrator

For a time at least the nightmare ended in 1851 with Florence's visit to Kaiserswerth, where she went to learn the skills of nursing. While her parents could with some degree of legitimacy refuse Salisbury Infirmary for their daughter, it was more difficult to find objections to a training offered in the protective environment of a hospital ordered by Protestant Deaconesses. Kaiserswerth had, furthermore, the recommendation of some important people. While in Rome Florence had been encouraged by von Bunsen, the Prussian ambassador to Britain, who was an Egyptologist and an amateur Protestant theologian. His wife recalled that Florence had discussed with them the essential question of her life, 'What can an individual do towards lifting the load of suffering from the helpless and the miserable?'[19] Realizing the depth of her theological commitment and hearing of her long interest in nursing, Bunsen suggested Kaiserswerth.

When the ailing Parthenope was granted a cure at Carlsbad Florence insisted that she be allowed to spend equal time at Kaiserswerth, which she had briefly visited the previous year. For the first time in years her letters crackle with vitality. Released from inertia and inner conflict, she felt that she had become the person she was meant to be. The training was minimal, but the work itself and the people were admirable. On 16 July 1851 she wrote to her mother:

> The world here fills my life with interest and strengthens the body and mind. People here are not saints, as your courier calls them, though that was a good hit, but good flesh and blood people, raised and purified by a great object, constantly pursued.

The schedule was very demanding, 'breakfast at a quarter to six, work in the hospital until a lunch of ground rye at two and supper at seven'. It suited her.

In everything here I am so well, body amd mind. This is life. . . . I know you will be glad to hear, Dearest mother, this — life rich in interest and blessings and I wish for no other earth, no other world than this.[20]

Invigorating though it was, her new life did not completely free her of dependence on her family and her need for their approval. Her letters seeking their support are pathetic in their pleadings.

I wish I could hope that I had your smile, your blessing, your sympathy upon it, without which I cannot be quite happy. Very beloved people, I cannot bear to grieve you — life and everything in it that charms — that you would sacrifice for me — but unknown to you is my thirst, unseen by you the waters which would save me. To save me, I know would be to bless yourselves. . . . Speed me on my way to walk in the path which the sense of right in me has been pointing to for years.[21]

In her three-month interlude at Kaiserswerth Florence felt that she had achieved the first step towards a life of independence. Her mother and sister saw it differently. They entertained hope that the rebel, having had a taste of the fresh air she sought, would be content to return to her accustomed life. Fanny Nightingale proposed somewhat facetiously that she and Parthenope should be objects of Florence's new ideas and missionary zeal. She suggested that

Florence will be able to apply all the fine things she has been learning, to do a little to make us better. Parthe and I are much too idle to help and too apt to be satisfied with things as they are.[22]

Not surprisingly the return home brought Florence the renewal of conflicts, the depression of frustration. She asked permission to study with the Catholic Sisters in the Maison de la Providence, a large Parisian orphanage to which a nursery and a hospital for women were attached.

Her sojourn with the Sisters more than fulfilled her expectations. In addition to hospital training in Paris she was able to collect reports and comparative statistics from the major medical facilities in France and Germany. As a relief from the demands of her work she attended *soirées dansantes* in the Rue du Bac with Mary Clarke Mohl and renewed her acquaintance with French culture and ideas.

In July 1853 Florence returned to a place in England that she had prepared for herself before leaving. In a compromise with her parents' values, which encompassed respectability as well as a life of service, she sought and obtained the job of Super-intendent of an 'Establishment for Gentlewomen during Illness' in Harley Street.

It immediately became evident that while her skill in nursing was considerable, her real talents lay in administration. To her father, himself a hospital trustee, she writes:

> When I entered the service here, I determined that, happen what would, I *never* would intrigue among the Committee. Now I perceive that I do all my business by intrigue. I propose in private to A. B. and C. the resolutions I think A. B. and C. most capable of carrying in committee, and then leave it to them, and I always win. I am now in the hey-day of my power.

She goes on to describe her manoeuvres with relish.

> All these [resolutions] I proposed and carried in Committee, without telling them that they came from *me* and not from the Medical Men; and then, and not till then, I showed them to the Medical Men without telling *them* that they had already passed in *Committee*.
>
> It was a bold stroke, but success is said to make an insurrection into a revolution. The Medical Men have had two meetings upon them, and approved them all nem. con. [no one contradicting] and thought they were their own. And I came off with flying colours, no one suspecting my intrigue, which of course would ruin me were it known, as there is much jealousy in the Committee of one another, and among the Medical Men of one another, as ever what's his name had of Marlborough.
>
> I have also carried my point of having good, harmless Mr. — as Chaplain; and no young curate to have spiritual flirtations with my young ladies. And so much for the earthquakes in this little mole-hill of ours.[23]

Fanny could not directly appeal to this zest and energy. Instead, she disguised self-interest as concern for Florence's well-being. She fears that the Harley Street work will be too tiring; she regrets that her daughter is 'sacrificing her peace and comfort'; she suggests that while the family is in London she could live at home. Florence remained calm in the face of these overtures. In a letter written to Mary Clarke Mohl in August 1853 she indicates that she feels that she has now, after 33 years, won her struggle for freedom.

I have not taken this step, Clarkey dear, without years of anxious consideration. It is the result of the experience of years, and of the fullest, and deepest thought. It has not been done without advice, and it is a step, which, being the growth of so long, is not likely to be repented of or reconsidered. I mean the step of leaving them . . . . To serve my country in this *way* has been also the object of my life, though I should not have done it in this time or manner . . . . So farewell, Clarkey dear, don't let us talk any more about this. It is, as I said before, a *fait accompli.*[24]

4   *The Crimea, 1854-56: Purveyor;* Dea ex Machina, *and Legend*

In March 1854 England and France declared war on Russia. In June a British Army landed at Varna on the Black Sea. On 30 September the Battle of the Alma was fought with heavy British losses. Pride in the courage and gallantry of the British soldier and confidence in ultimate victory was soon replaced by other emotions. William Howard Russell's despatches to *The Times* became increasingly critical of those in command. On 13 October he wrote,

It is impossible for anyone to see the melancholy sights of the last few days without feelings of surprise and indignation of the deficiencies of our medical system. The manner in which the sick and wounded are treated is worthy only of the savages of Dahomey.[25]

It became evident that more British soldiers were being killed through their leaders' incompetence than by enemy bullets. Readers of *The Times* were indignant; it was galling to hear that their old rivals the French were able to provide their forces with excellent provisions, medical arrangements, and nursing care; fifty Sisters of Charity had accompanied the expeditionary force.

> Why have we no Sisters of Charity? There are numbers of able-bodied and tender-hearted English women who would joyfully and with alacrity go out to devote themselves to nursing the sick and wounded, if they could be associated for that purpose, and placed under proper protection.[26]

Sidney Herbert, the man who had befriended Florence Nightingale in Rome in 1850 and had been to some degree responsible for her going to Kaiserswerth, was now in a position of high responsibility. As Secretary of War he had control over certain financial aspects of the conduct of the war. With the self-confidence — and the connections — that enabled him to go beyond the prescribed limits of his authority, he wrote to Florence Nightingale, suggesting that she organize a band of women to go to the Crimea.

> There is but one person in England that I know of who would be capable of organizing and superintending such a scheme and I have been several times on the point of asking you hypothetically if, suppose the attempt were made, you would undertake to direct it. . . . Your own personal qualities, your knowledge and your power of administration, and among greater things your rank and position in Society give you advantages in such work which no other person possesses.[27]

On 21 October a party of forty-one left London. It consisted of fourteen nurses recruited by Miss Nightingale, ten Roman Catholic Sisters, fourteen Anglican Sisters, Mr and Mrs Bracebridge, and Florence Nightingale.

The account of Florence's time in Crimea is well known — the chaos which she found — the shortage of supplies, the lack of sanitation which turned a hospital into a mortuary. It immediately became apparent that the Army needed more than nursing care. If Florence Nightingale was to be helpful, she would have to attack the root causes of suffering and death. She became a kind of General Dealer in works, shirts, knives and forks, wooden spoons, tin baths, tables and forms, cabbage and carrots, operating tables, towels and soap, small tooth combs, precipitate for destroying lice, scissors, bedpans and stump pillows. I will send you a picture of my Caravanserai, into which beasts come in and out. Indeed the vermin might, if they had but 'unity of purpose', carry off the four miles of beds on their backs, and march with them into the War Office, Horse Guards.[28]

She handed out 50,000 shirts; she planned, built and paid for a hospital which accommodated an additional 800 patients. She surveyed the ground for a cemetery. As Cook says 'In fact, and by force of circumstance, she became a Purveyor to the Hospitals, a Clothier to the British Army and in many emergencies a *Dea ex machina.*'[29]

It is not difficult to empathize with Dr John Hall and the medical men in their admiration, fear, and jealousy of the 'Nightingale power'. Theoretically her authority was limited; she had been sent to supervise a group of women under her charge. To some degree she seemed to accept the limits of her power, seeing to it that the nurses were scrupulous in their obedience to the medical orders of the surgeons. Her furious objection to the arrival of Mary Stanley with her band of forty-seven untrained women arose in part from the fear that these women, who were not under her direction, would threaten the fragile relationship that she had finally been able to develop with the medical men.

On matters of importance, however, Florence enraged the doctors by simply doing as she pleased. While the doctors were hampered by bureaucratic rules and regulations and by the incompetence of some of their superiors, Florence as an amateur and an outsider had no such constraints. Furthermore she had powerful weapons at her command; an able mind, a strong will, access to Cabinet officials, a sympathetic press waiting to publish words from her articulate tongue and pen, and — perhaps most important of all — money. Sidney Herbert had correctly assessed her advantages and had known that she could use them with extraordinary effectiveness. Much of her later life would be spent in administrative reform, but her contribution in the Crimea was largely improvised and outside the structure of the Army.

The heroes of war are generally military leaders; the glitter of medals, the glow of scarlet and blue uniforms seems designed particularly to appeal to the portraitist. Nevertheless, in recording the Crimea War history has rejected the claims of Lord Lucan, Lord Cardigan, and Lord Raglan, and substituted the portraits of two unlikely candidates — one a cook and the other a small grey-eyed woman. It was not merely that the military men were not the stuff of heroes (such consideration had in the past been no obstacle to the myth-making process) but that the circumstances of the recording of war had been changed by two events — the development of the camera and the presence of a war correspondent. The mock-heroics and the unreality of sketched illustrations that concentrated on the distended nostrils of the horses and the choreographed symmetry of raised sabres, had been replaced by Roger Fenton's record of the life of the ordinary soldier. The camera did not lie: swathed in tattered animal skins, their faces dulled by cold, boredom, pain, and privation, against a desolate landscape of stone and dirt, the men huddle around a tiny flame which burns in a metal can. Instead of the carefully modulated declamations of the War Office which once accompanied the cannons' roar, the readers were confronted with the first-hand observations of *The Times* correspondent, William Howard Russell. In his view Alexis Soyer, the ex-chef of the fashionable Reform Club, with his skill in replacing the foul 'boil-and-trouble' vats with salubrious soups and stews, was the hero of the day: the other hero was Florence Nightingale.

While Russell did justice to Florence's stringent and complicated personality, his readers were already involved in the myth-making process. In picture and in verse she was extolled as 'the lady of the lamp'. Sitting with eyes demurely downcast she wrote down the last words of a dying soldier to his mother and his sweetheart. Gliding noiselessly through the dark wards, holding a cool hand to a fevered brow, she became the ministrering angel of Longfellow's poem, 'the very type of good, heroic womanhood'. Queen Victoria was a leader in the making of the legend. In fact Florence Nightingale carried the Queen's hopes and wishes to the men; she became the incarnation of the Queen on the battlefield. In December 1854 the Keeper of the Queen's Purse wrote to Florence Nightingale:

The Queen has directed me to ask you to undertake the distribution and application of these articles, partly because Her Majesty wished you to be made aware that your goodness and self-devotion in giving yourself up to the soothing attendance upon these wounded and sick soldiers had been observed by the Queen with sentiments of the highest approval and admiration; and partly because, as the articles sent did not come within the description of Medical and Government stores, usually furnished, they could not be better entrusted than to one who, by constant personal observation, would form a correct judgment where they would be most usefully employed.[30]

The legend was indeed built on fact. Florence Nightingale did write hundreds of letters describing the final hours of her dying patients for their grieving relatives; without thought for her own health; she spent whole days and nights in 'soothing attendance'. Yet, like all legends, it sentimentalizes and restricts reality, finally doing justice neither to her virtues nor to her faults.

The legend is still very much alive today. Every school-child has heard of Florence Nightingale while almost none has heard of Octavia Hill or Josephine Butler. Why was Florence Nightingale's life, during these few years in the Crimea, so memorable, while the lives of the other two women are almost forgotten? The answer lies in the power of the legend and the deep psychological needs that it filled.

Josephine Butler never became a legend in her lifetime because no one wished to hear what she had to say, no one, that is, except for her constituents the prostitutes — a small band of powerless women. No-one wished to be told that the society that they believed to be founded on the Judeo-Christian ethic of love of neighbour and the Anglo-Saxon charters of civil liberties in fact incorporated gross exploitation, cruelty, and injustice. Octavia Hill is a little better known; her constituents were the working-class family, a group which middle-class England acknowledged had some claims on its attention.

The legend of Florence Nightingale contained much that people wanted to hear over and over again. It centred on two folk heroes — the British soldier and the woman who serves him. It shows each in a noble light. Furthermore, it epitomized what the Victorians believed to be the ideal relationship between man and woman. The man to whom England owed her power and her wealth was long-suffering, brave, patient, and kind. The woman was hard-working and gentle; furthermore, she reached a final fulfilment and happiness in a life of service, offering herself wholly to caring for the male. Florence was the perfect mother, comforting and soothing her suffering children, the perfect sweetheart and daughter, ever-agreeable, acquiescent, and solicitous. The legend conveniently ignored the headstrong woman known to Dr John Hall, just as the myth-making process centred on Victoria recognized the adoring wife of Prince Albert without really acknowledging the Sovereign Queen. It made no mention of the resolute woman who demanded to read every document in the boxes that Lord Palmerston laid before her and infuriated prime ministers by trying to exercise a royal authority that they hoped had been buried along with George III.

If the legend brought reassurance to the Victorian male — and encouragement to the common soldier whose qualities had long been unappreciated — it also brought hope to the Victorian middle-class woman. Without disturbing the underlying assumptions in the male—female relationship, it showed a woman, living in a setting of danger and excitement, making important decisions, taking on important responsibilities. It showed, perhaps, that you could have your cake without eating it; it provided a halfway house between dependence and independence. It seemed to offer the best of two worlds, change without revolution, progress with security.

Florence Nightingale returned from the Crimea in August 1856. She soon realized that in peace, as in war, she would have the backing of the nation's leaders. 'The diamond has shown itself and it must not be allowed to return to the mine', wrote Sidney Herbert. In September she went to Balmoral. Queen Victoria and Prince Albert, paying homage to the canonical Victorian female virtues, praised her modesty. They were, however, more impressed by her intelligence and her determination. 'She put before us all the defects of our present military hospital system, and the reforms that are needed', wrote Albert. Noting her keen mind and sense for administrative order the Queen added, 'I wish we had her at the War Office.'[31]

Throughout the rest of her long life, particularly during the long nights of the insomniac, Florence was haunted by the memories of the suffering of the soldiers in the Crimea — and the needlessness of much of it. 'Oh my poor men, I am a bad mother to come home and leave you in your Crimea graves — seventy-three per cent in eight regiments in six months from disease alone. Who thinks of that now?'[32] Her goal was the reform of the entire Army medical service. The means would be a Royal Commission with appointments controlled by Florence Nightingale. Through encouraging and dominating its members and the Commission's chairman, Sidney Herbert, she would get her way. She was prepared to use all of her strength as a woman and all of the magical power of the legend to achieve her goal.

While Florence protested against the fame that she had accrued and professed to dislike any special attention, she deliberately and with great skill used the legend to promote her work. In 1856 the 'Nightingale power' was at its height. Children were named after her; the Staffordshire potters put out a figurine entitled 'Miss Nightingale', showing her standing resolutely beside a soldier whose arm is sportily encased in a polka-dotted sling; poets eulogized her. The money that had been showered upon her during the war was now formally set aside in the Nightingale Fund; a sum of £44,000 was invested; the members of the controlling Council were nominated by Florence, assuring that she could use the income to promote any cause that appealed to her. Furthermore, she had the press at her command. Until the end of her life any letter from Florence Nightingale on any subject was bound to receive immediate and wide attention. If she felt that her ideas were not being put to good use by those in high office, she knew that she could always put her case before the public. Her fellow-workers from their positions of political responsibility knew privately that though she held no office, her power was greater than theirs; she had access to a public who would believe anything she said; she had access to the Queen. They were afraid of her.

The 'Nightingale power' had in fact grown with her return from the Crimea. The saint had become a martyr; the fever that she had contracted during the war left her permanently damaged; she must rest; she must avoid excitement. There were several times when the doctors gave up hope. Even when her symptoms subsided, they continued to insist that her life 'seemed to hang on a slender thread'.

The doctors were wrong. The thread sustained Florence Nightingale for an extraordinary 90 years. Although she was encouraged by her advisers to believe that her illness was physical, there are indications that she sometimes felt that its genesis was emotional. Had she not accused parents of 'murdering' their children? Did she not remember that she had first suffered from palpitations during her confrontations with Parthenope and long before the Crimea? Had she not said that there was scarcely a house in England in which there was not an invalid daughter?[33] Did she not tacitly admit that she was the first and most famous of these invalids?

Her biographers, while attempting to be open-minded on the nature of her illness and its genesis, have commented on the way in which she used it to further her work. In the first place it meant that she was always in the position of a commandant, never that of a supplicant. People came to her; she did not go to them. Furthermore, they came only by appointment and only if she were well enough to see them. It put her in control of every social situation; she saw only one person at a time, thereby dominating any relationship and keeping a tight control over the conversation. It provided her with a ready excuse for not seeing those who might distract her from her work, most particularly her family.

Florence Nightingale's illness laid a heavy burden on her fellow-workers; it gave her an excuse to demand the most. If she, a small woman without professional position, irreparably damaged by suffering incurred while serving her country, could muster the energy to undertake radical reforms, how could her co-workers — strong and able-bodied men committed by profession and position to the welfare of Britain, do less? There were times when, as after the death of Sidney Herbert, she bitterly regretted the consequences of her demands. Nevertheless, she continued to make them. By appealing to the pride and the guilt of cabinet members, Viceroys of India, generals, and prime ministers, she spurred them to emulate the implacably high standards of devotion-unto-death set by the Lady of the Lamp.

They were, furthermore, bound to treat her with deference because of the gravity of her illness. They were told that they must accede to her wishes; disagreement might bring on a fatal attack. The normal exchange between policy-makers of agreements and disagreements, open hostility and reconciliation, conflicts and compromises, was denied them. Who was strong — or foolish — enough to take the risk of being remembered as the man who through callous opposition had brought on the heart attack responsible for the death of Florence Nightingale? It is hardly surprising that her co-workers chose acquiescence, or sometimes retreat, rather than risk conflict. Lord Panmure, known as Bison, because of the magnificent dimensions of his nose, his swinging gait, and the massive stubbornness of his personality, retreated to the rivers of Scotland with his fishing rod rather than oppose Miss Nightingale. From a safe distance he wrote affectionately, apologizing for having called her 'that turbulent fellow'.

Her illness had the further advantage of allowing her to develop one interest at a time. Since her invalidism protected her from social obligation, and since she could not assume a full professional life, she was able from the confines of her bedroom to expend her energies on the subject that most engrossed her. Unlike her male colleagues who had a wide range of family and professional responsibilities and distractions to deal with, and for whom a particular cause — no matter how important — was but one among a plethora of interests, Florence Nightingale fixed the beam of her interest on a single spot. First it was the reform of the Army medical services, then hospital architecture, then the establishment of a school of nursing, then the health of the British soldier in India. Each of these topics in its turn absorbed her entire interest; having dealt with it exhaustively, she would move on to the next.

In all this she depended heavily upon her family. Here again her illness gave her several advantages. It enabled her to make excessive demands without fear of the hysterical battles which she remembered with such horror from her youth. By holding them at bay, by being 'too ill' to see them, she won for herself the appearance, if not the reality, of independence. And in partially freeing herself, she had bound them to her more closely. As a famous woman she could make demands on the world; as a frail and ailing daughter and sister she could make demands on her family. As the years went by and family tensions relaxed, Aunt Mai Smith, Hilary Bonham Carter, Parthenope and her husband Sir Harry Verney, all waited on her. To Aunt Mai's husband Sam Smith she delegated the enormous task of answering her mail. Her directions to him, obviously not intended to be made public, reveal a peremptory and sharp-tongued character. 'I give one pound for Mrs. Sutherland's sake, *provided* they don't send me any more of their stupid books.' 'Please answer this fool but don't give her my address.' 'These miserable ecclesiastical quacks! Would you give them a lesson?'[34] Sam Smith also handled her financial and legal matters. Faithfully and patiently, the family dealt with her changing housing demands, moving her from one lodging to another, soothing the complaints of fractious cooks and overworked housemaids.

Her illness was of course pathetic. She had paid an enormous price for small and bitter advantages. We will never know what her life would have been like if the doctors had urged, not rest and the seclusion of invalidism, but a full and active life. If she had accepted the responsibilities of a professional life with the tensions, conflicts, compromises — and companionship — that came from working with people as equals, would she have accomplished more, or less? As it was, having inflicted upon herself a retreat from the world she was an easy prey to fantasies. Tormented by images from the past, by disappointments and regrets, by anger, by the devouring needs of her own ego, with no outlet for her physical energies, she destroyed herself. Besides the notebooks of research, pioneer examples of the use of statistics as a means of analysis, and persuasive arguments for important reforms, she left her diaries and her frenzied jottings on the backs of letters: the noting of the anniversaries of the deaths of friends — and the death of hopes, the self-accusations of an unstable mind. This turmoil was finally ended by the soothing advance of age; the invalid began to gain weight; she left her sofa to visit Benjamin Jowett when he was ill; she posed for her picture, taking the central place in a group of Nightingale nurses. Over the rounded cheekbones the hooded eyes gaze squarely at the camera with the implacable unseeing detachment of a Buddha. Finally, there was the long descent into arteriosclerosis of the brain. Once she had put her passion for statistics and for list-making in service to the world; now her horizons were limited to the trays that were brought to her bedside. The diary trails off . . . . Her last entry notes the quality of the meat on her plate — 'roast not tender. Tough. Hard though minced. Not nice.'[35]

*5 Little War Office, St Thomas's and India 1856 — 1910: Chief, Founder
of Nursing, and Governess*

In 1856, however, Florence Nightingale was still on her feet, still
in command of all her formidable faculties. With the ambitious
goal of the reform of the health of the entire British Army in
mind, she set about gathering research and planning the complex
political manoeuvres that would enable her to accomplish this
task. She visited barracks hospitals; she compiled comparative
figures of mortality rates. She decided which of her friends
would make effective members of the Royal Commissions and
saw to it that they were appointed. She coached the witnesses; she
prodded the Bison out of his slow pace by threatening to publish
her own report should the Committee be tardy or partial in its
findings.

Her case was presented in a volume of 500 pages entitled *Notes
affecting the Health, Efficiency and Hospital Administration of the
British Army.* To the twentieth-century reader, it is astonishing
that the research behind this volume had been compiled and the
ideas distilled from it in the space of six months without the
helping technology of the computer, the tape recorder, the
typewriter. Florence had the editorial help of her friend Arthur
Hugh Clough, the secretarial help of Aunt Mai, and the
contributions of many specialists, but it is essentially the work of
one woman. It is sweeping in scope, incorporating analysis with
suggestions for reforms.

Florence had correctly assessed the effect of her threat to
publish. Lord Panmure accelerated the pace of the Commission;
he agreed to accept Florence Nightingale's figures for mortality
rates, with their shocking revelation that the death rate in
military hospitals was five times that in civilian hospitals. He
included thirty-three pages of testimony by Florence Nightingale
which is in effect a summary of her *Notes* and he presented
evidence and arguments suggested by her.

Before the Commission's Blue Book was published Florence
and Sidney Herbert were already working out the means of
implementing the suggestions. There would be four Sub-
Commissions; Mr Herbert would be Chairman of each. One
would be in charge of barracks, the second would organize a
statistical department, the third would found a medical school,
and the fourth would reorganize the Army Medical Department,

revise hospital regulations, and work out a plan for the promotion of medical officers. Exhausted by the demands of their 'Chief', Sidney Herbert and Lord Panmure once again took refuge in the Highlands. Florence worked even harder; she thought that she was going to die. 'I am sorry not to stay alive to do the "Nurses", but I can't help it.'[36] During the fall and winter her advisers' visits succeeded each other without pause. Florence's quarters at the Burlington became known as the 'Little War Office'. 'Mr. Herbert for 3 hours in the morning, Dr. Sutherland for 4 hours in the afternoon, Dr. Balfour, Dr. Farr, Dr. Alexander interspersed.'[37]

The movement came to a temporary halt with Sidney Herbert's tragic death from cancer. For Florence the sense of loss was enormously compounded by guilt. She felt, with good reason, that she had been too hard on her Master. She was bitterly aware of the irony involved. By pleading her own poor health and imminent death, she had persuaded the dying man to redouble his efforts. Now she was still alive and he was dead. Her remorse was deep and genuine, but she was also able to use Herbert's death to political advantage. Her *Memoir* of Herbert in effect summarizes their joint work and urges the British people to effect the only appropriate memorial to the great man by the rapid enactment of the reforms that he had advocated.

The death of Sidney Herbert marked the beginning of a new era in Florence's life. Her withdrawal became more complete. She left the Burlington, where she had received her series of advisers, and retreated to a sofa in a room in Hampstead. From now on the material she gathered would not come from first-hand observation, but through correspondence and the amassing of statistics.

Using this material she produced treatises on medical problems. In 1859 she advised builders on hospital architecture in *Notes on Hospitals*. The following year she published *Notes on Nursing: What It Is and What It Is Not*. Beside the sense of detail and fact that one expects it shows another side of Florence Nightingale. With deep compassion and rare sensitivity to the psychology of the sick, she advises her nurses:

> People who think outside their heads, who tell everything that led them towards this conclusion, and away from that, ought never to be with the sick . . . . Apprehension, uncertainty,

waiting, expectation, fear of surprise, do a patient more harm than any exertion. Remember, he is face to face with his enemy all the time, internally wrestling with him, having long imaginary conversations with him. ... Rid him of his adversary quickly is a first rule with the sick.

Notes on Nursing was an immediate success in England, on the Continent, and in the United States. Its principles became the basis for the Nightingale Training School for Nurses, started in June 1860 with money from the Nightingale Fund. Nursing would be recognized as a high calling and an art; its practitioners were to be trained in the scientific basis of medicine and the personal needs of the ill. Under Florence's direction Mrs Wardroper, the Matron of St Thomas's and director of the Training School, imposed demanding standards upon her fifteen students. The 'Monthly Sheet of Personal Character and Acquirements' took into account the Moral Record (punctuality, quietness, trustworthiness, personal neatness and cleanliness, and ward management) and an equally exacting Technical Record. The employment of the first graduates marks the beginning of the end of 'private', that is, untrained nursing.

With the nursing school launched, Florence turned her attention towards the British Army in India. In May 1859 she had written to Harriet Martineau:

For eight long months I have been 'importunate-widowing' my 'unjust judge', viz. Lord Stanley, to give us a Royal Sanitary Commission to do exactly the same thing for the Armies in India which the last did for the Army at home.[38]

India, however, was not Britain. The job of acquiring the necessary statistics appeared impossible. The Army of the East India Company had not been fully absorbed into the Queen's Army, there were thus two armies and two sets of statistics. Florence dealt with this by bypassing the leaders and writing directly to every medical station — over 200. It is a tribute, not only to her genius, but to the competence of the British Army and the Indian civil servants as well, that without ever leaving a small room in London, she could make a fairly accurate analysis of the conditions in an enormous, primitive country halfway around the world.

Once again Florence made the best political use of her material. To the official report published in 1863 totalling 2028 pages, she wrote a companion piece; a 23-page summary of the station reports, illustrated with the effective woodcuts of Hilary Bonham Carter. In her covering letter to Buckingham Palace, Florence, with a somewhat artificial simplicity, expressed the hope that the Queen would 'look at it because it has pictures'. This short work and its popularity ensured that the recommendations of the weighty, and for obvious reasons, largely unread report would be adopted. With public opinion behind her she pressed a succession of Viceroys for sanitary, economic, and agricultural reform, earning for herself the nickname of 'Governess of the Governors of India'.

During the latter part of the 1860s she occupied herself with England's domestic affairs. She advocated research in the causes of pauperism and criminality and developed a scheme for workhouse reform. On her advice Agnes Jones, her favourite student, was sent to Liverpool. While Miss Jones's responsibilities did not take her into the oakum sheds that so distressed Josephine Butler, she was able to reorganize the Brownlow Hill Infirmary before her death from typhus in 1868.

As old friends and members of her family died, the visits from students meant more and more to her. In 1882 she was asked to help select the nurses who were to accompany the British forces to Egypt under one of her trained supervisors, Mrs Deebles. In this task Florence relived her Crimean days, sending flowers to each nurse's cabin with the message, 'God speed from Florence Nightingale', and following them onto the battlefield with letters of encouragement.

But there were few now to remind her of the accomplishments and hopes of her youth. John Farr, Mary Mohl, Monckton Milnes, John McNeill, John Sutherland, Parthenope had all died. In 1893-4 she lost Sir Harry Verney, Benjamin Jowett, and Shore Smith. The wishes of the sentimentalists who made use of the Nightingale legend in the Diamond Jubilee meant little to her. 'Oh, the absurdity of people and the vulgarity. . . . I will not give my foolish portrait (which I have not got) or anything else as relics of the Crimea. It is ridiculous!' By 1907 when the King conferred upon her the order of Merit, the bright mind, the caustic temper had been so damaged by senility that she could only murmur the conventional, 'Too kind, too kind.'

She died on 13 August 1910 and was buried beside her father and mother at East Wellow, near Embley.

8 Her Stuff: Suggestions for Thought

The faith that drove Florence Nightingale, the theology that shaped her vocation, were, not surprisingly, a strange mixture of the naive and the sophisticated, the unexamined and the rational, the eccentric and the orthodox. Benjamin Jowett, commenting on her theological treatise, warned, 'The enemy will say, "This book is written by an Infidel who has been a Papist." '[1] He pointed out that she worked from two seemingly unrelated bases — that of a spirituality based on the writings of the saints of the Early Church and that of nineteenth-century rationalism. Her attempt to harmonize these opposing views was far from successful, yet it offered along the way some interesting results — insights into the nature of man, a vision of a life sustained by a high sense of purpose, a sometimes unfair, yet often disturbingly accurate critique of society and of the popular religions of the day.

In spite of inner inconsistencies, her thought provided strong supports for her vocation. It gave her a criterion by which she chose her cause and a method of procedure. Believing that God's plan reveals itself in creation, she gathered facts in order to analyse the evidence for the laws of nature. She then chose issues of social importance. Nursing, the health of the British soldier, hospital architecture, India, Poor Law Reform — each one of these she selected because she felt it her duty to help 'man create mankind'.

Her theological views appear throughout her writings — in letters to her family, to Aunt Mai, to Benjamin Jowett, in jottings in the notebook she kept beside her bed, in diaries — but they receive their fullest expression in a three-volume work that she referred to as her 'Stuff'. This she presented in 1860 as *Suggestions for Thought to the Searchers after Truth among the Artizans of England*. The title and the introductory remarks strike a tentative and elliptical note, unusual to Florence Nightingale. 'Fellow-searchers, I come to you not to declare the truth; I come to ask you . . . to join in seeking it with those capabilities which God has given to us.'[2] The three volumes total over 800 pages. Before embarking on the final volume Florence offered the reader an apology for the length of her treatise. In hope of

> reaching different minds the same subjects have been differently (and not always consecutively) dealt with in the several portions of this book. A feeling of their extreme ignorance has dictated, and it is hoped will excuse, this course, which has rendered repetition, even to the frequent use of the same phraseology, unavoidable.

These volumes, along with two brief articles published in 1873 in *Fraser's Magazine*, and some notes on the spirituality of the mystics, represent her principal writings on religion.

She sent copies of the first two volumes to John Stuart Mill and Benjamin Jowett. Mill urged her to publish, saying that there was 'much in the work which is calculated to do good to many persons beside the artisans to whom it is more especially addressed'.[3] Although disagreeing with some of her metaphysical conclusions, he praised her critique of British middle-class society. Benjamin Jowett, along with his 'Infidel-Papist' remark, answered rather guardedly that 'he felt that he had received the impress of a new mind', but advised against publishing it in its present form, pointing out that the overall design of the book needed recasting. The friendship between the two, which developed largely through correspondence, lasted until Jowett's death in 1893.

The reason that so little has been written on the theological views of this woman for whom religion was a central and moving force is clear. Cook says without specifying the number that 'a very few copies were struck off'. The British Museum owns a copy. Undoubtedly, the work lies hidden in several libraries and nursing schools in the United States, its rarity unknown to its owners. The Union Catalogue of books available in the United States lists only two sources; the Massachusetts Historical Society and the Yale Medical School. The copy has disappeared from the library in Massachusetts and the Yale Medical School possesses only the first two volumes, now under lock and key.

The perseverence of the reader who finally obtains the prize is rewarded by some of Florence's best writing — witticisms and sharp images, pungent descriptions of contemporary Christianity, a devastating critique of family life among the upper classes — alongside of some of her worst. The issues with which she deals are highly complex; their solution has defied the greatest minds over the centuries; nevertheless, Florence Nightingale's own abilities could have been used to better advantage. The promise of an elaborate table of contents, the supportive security of summarizing notes in the margin are given the lie by the text itself. Ever intrepid in doing battle for the 'Spirit of Truth', Florence tilts her lance at all of the targets of classical philosophy. Her aim is off the mark. Frustrated by the imprecise contours of the targets she moves in a frenzy, without stopping to judge the effect of each blow. In naming the topics she has substituted the grandeur of the capital letter with its implication of transcendent importance for the precision of the definition. 'Truth', 'the Perfect', 'Law', 'Will','Eternal Life', 'Free Will', and 'Necessity', the 'Problem of Evil' whirl about, their shapes and sizes changing, depending upon the angle from which they are attacked. There is no fixed horizon and the reader is in danger of succumbing to vertigo. Florence herself said that she could not read the book. Carlyle, commenting on the summary of Florence's religious views appearing in *Fraser's Magazine* said that she was like 'a lost lamb bleating on the mountain'.[4] Jowett objected to her 'scream style', adding that he would refrain from more detailed commentary because 'it is like pouring water upon red hot iron and makes a terrible hissing'.[5]

The overall argument lacks cohesion. There are, however, flashes of insight and the general approach, which anticipates some of the twentieth-century process and 'death-of-God' theologians, is original and, indeed, important. Using the concise and more coherent presentation from *Fraser's Magazine* as a key to the larger work, it is possible to get a fairly clear idea of Florence Nightingale's theology.

1   A Critique of Contemporary Thought

In *Suggestions for Thought* she attempts to work out a philosophical position that will support and enlarge upon the faith of her early life. First, however, she must dispose of the current 'isms'. Anglicanism, Roman Catholicism, evangelical Protestantism, Liberalism and Positivism are all tried and found wanting. While it could be argued that none of these 'isms' is given a completely fair hearing, her criticisms are often on the mark. What she chooses to take as the essence of Christianity is something of a caricature; yet, as a study, not of what the theologians were saying but of popular religion, it makes arresting reading.

She believed that her contemporaries, regardless of their denominational affiliations or expressed beliefs, remained essentially untouched by religion. Faith had vanished leaving only an empty form. Religion had become merely a denominational label, the indication of a social clique.

> Opinions on religion do not *now* model life. The habits of life are stamped in strong and durable fashion. That certain individuals here and there, differ from orthodox view makes little impression on modes of life. Except in religious orders, the Roman Catholic, the Puseyite, the Evangelical, the Jew, in the higher and middle ranks of life, live much after the same fashion, though in different coteries, and refraining more or less from each other's society but their habits do not differ materially or generally according to their religious views. . . .
> If we study the varying matters of society (in our country at least), we find them little influenced by religion. That which is called civilization in manners and habits, has it sprung from religion?[6]

This indifference to truth, while found in all religions, she sees as particularly characteristic of the Church of England. The *via media* of Anglican theology had led to compromise and contradiction. On the 'abominable doctrine' of baptismal regeneration,

> the Church of England one day, some years ago, sought to look this thing fairly in the face, and to say whether God did thus condemn babies or not, answered, it was an open question. People might believe one thing or the other, as they liked, which is equivalent to saying, it did not signify. Did not signify whether God was the worst of tyrants and murderers or not![7]

To their peril Anglicans have substituted for faith the cultural conformity of institutional religion. She compares Anglicanism with an 'over-idle mother, who lets her children entirely alone, because those who made her had found the Church of Rome an overly-busy mother'.[8] Having taken the forms of religion from Roman Catholicism, it emptied them of meaning before presenting them as civil injunctions.

You may be married, that is, have a form of words pronounced over you, which makes your marriage the law of the land, and you may be buried, or the feelings of your friends gratified by having certain words read over you.[9]

Convention and indifference have replaced devotion and fervour.

Florence believed that England was, in effect, a country without a religion. People were too frightened to admit this and clung to the little faith they had.

The feeling of the Church of England is very intelligible. Many know that they are in a state of 'twilight faith'. But what can they do? If they step out of it, they step into a state of darkness. They have not admitted the principle, 'Search', and it is like stepping out of a rickety house into the blank cold darkness of unbelief.[10]

Florence Nightingale had greater respect for Roman Catholicism. Though critical of many of its doctrines, she never lost her admiration for its central purpose. 'The Roman Catholic idea is not nearly so fine as God's thought. But it is the *next* fine idea to it.'[11] 'It is serious in its attempt to organize life so as to encourage people to act out their beliefs.'[12] When as a young woman she had looked for a place and something to do, she had noted that, unlike her own Anglican Church which offered its female communicants nothing but menial or trivial jobs, the Roman Church offered women a life of responsible service. As teachers, nurses, and administrators of schools and hospitals, it sent its women all over the world.

She could not, however, accept a view of authority that put absolute power into human hands. Widening her attack, she turned to two doctrines that the Romans held in common with other Christians — special providence and original sin. Riding roughshod over some important theological subtleties, she dismisses election as a muddled and evil doctrine.

> Christianity then lays it down as an absolute truth that the scheme of God is the creation of a vast number of beings, called into existence without any will of their own, the fate of the greater number of which is to be everlasting misery, of the lesser number eternal happiness, and this after a period of 'trial' (Qy. 'trial' of what?) of the average duration of, as it was in Liverpool, seventeen years; in the healthier districts of about double that time. (The only variation in this doctrine is a greater or less preponderance given by Calvinism to the 'atonement,' by Roman Catholicism to a *second* period of uncertain duration (called Purgatory), before the everlasting happiness begins; and by other Churches to different words, called 'faith', 'works', etc., etc.)[13]

She describes the depressing effects of this doctrine. 'A poor man, dying in a workhouse, said to his nurse after having seen his clergyman: "It does seem hard to have suffered so much here, only to go to everlasting torment hereafter".' She speaks of the common belief that God 'keeps, as it were, a rod in pickle for us in the next [world]; which rod in pickle is to be averted, it really seems to be taught, by a certain number of ceremonial observances'.[14] With mounting indignation she deplores the monster God implicit in such a view. What monster would torture his enemy, if he could, forever? God would be worse than man if he did not have a scheme by which every man will be saved.

The doctrine of the Atonement is similarly incompatible with the goodness of God. Florence castigates this 'barbarous' doctrine, which she construes more after the manner of Anselm than Abelard. The assumption that the forgiveness of God, the wrathful Father, must be bought with the bloody sacrifice of a loving son, Florence found morally offensive — based upon a primitive, quid pro quo, ethic. If God is loving, forgiveness is freely given.

Her criticism of these doctrines and of the biblical material that gave rise to them, place her in the company of the liberals and biblical critics of her day. Yet even here she did not feel quite at home, criticizing the liberals for being more effective in their negative than in their positive efforts. Even her old friend Benjamin Jowett, in whose writings she found much to commend, had failed her; he had offered no religion to replace the one he had torn down.

> [His] criticism had no sympathy with nor insight into the ways of God, the highest ways of man. ... It makes a great show of enquiry and of power; but there is nothing behind, nothing within, nothing with the principle of life in it; it is all temporary, negative, unreal. ... It has stripped religion of many superstitions and has killed innumerable parasites which choked her vigour, truth and beauty but it has not led to the knowledge of God. May it rather have killed religion with the cure of superstition? Here is my parable. 'A famous French physician exclaimed when a patient died, "Il est mort gueri".'[15]

If she was disappointed with the scepticism of the liberals, she was disgusted by the overt atheism of the Positivists. Here it is difficult to see why she could not acknowledge the affinity between their ideas and hers. Was it her childhood faith, her dedication to the God of the mystics, which kept her from recognizing the latent Positivism in her own views?

Benjamin Jowett once said that Thomas Arnold had the 'peculiar danger . . . of not knowing where his ideas would take other people, and ought to take himself'.[16] This witticism could well have been coined for Florence Nightingale. Her empiricism, her love of science, her faith in logic, and her rejection of a supernatural basis for religion all put her in the positivist tradition.

Florence Nightingale stubbornly maintained against all comers, however, that there is a necessary connection between empirical fact and rational truth and that this connection originates and derives its universality from God, the 'Lawmaker'. This belief was challenged not only by Positivism but by John Stuart Mill. In thanking her for *Suggestions for Thought* he writes, 'Another point on which I cannot agree with you is the opinion that law in the sense in which we predicate it of the arrangements of nature, can only emerge from a Will.'[17] He goes on to say that he sees no need to make the connection and points to the irony of referring to the 'unchangeableness' of a will, when in our experience will is by definition liable to change.

Florence Nightingale made no response to Mill's objections. She would admit to the word 'positive' but only when it was firmly tied to its noun 'theology'.

> There are three phases of theology; the miraculous, the super-natural, and the 'positivist' theology. At first it is quite natural (in an infant state) that infants should think God works by miracles, and should see Him in miracles and not in law; then that they should see Him in special providence, which is really almost the same as the first; that is the supernatural theology, — lastly, we see him in law. But law is still theology, and the finest.[18]

Besides asserting that the Positivists were not successful in showing that the world operated without a Lawmaker, she went futher. Anticipating later critics,[19] she searched for the worm of metaphysical assumption among the roots of radical empiri-cism. She claimed that they could not simply reject the experience of others on the basis of their own God empiricism. The best they could do would be to place their experience of 'no-God' against her experience of 'God'. But to assert that their position is 'correct' and hers wrong is to make a metaphysical statement; yet, according to the Positivists, metaphysical state-ments have been ruled out of order.

> When I think of Positivists, it appears that they have not a leg to stand on. Their more than flimsy metaphysical formulae as, 'Everything is governed by law' which is true, but they never get any further — it remains a formula — as — 'We have no faculties to enable us to apprehend God' which is not only not true but is absolutely absurd — the fact being that we have *no one* more *intimately* present to (everyone of) us or more constantly present than God. And then they expect me to believe in their Dr. Congreve (of whose existence I have no proof) and *not* to believe in God. But it does not appear to me that to say 'Ever increasing evidence shows us that by the Law of Order of a Perfect Being we are all approching to per-fection, directly or indirectly' (though this is true) is at all less

[sic] of a mere metaphysical formula than what the Positivists use. Metaphysical is: *What I think.*[20]

When a critic can show that a philosophical position is defeated by its own assumptions, he has the special satisfaction of cutting it cleanly off at ground level, sparing him the need to deal with its secondary appendages.

Florence, however, did not stop with Comte's epistemology. Warming to her task, she turned to his anthropology. Rather than find affinities between his religion of 'Humanity' and her belief that 'mankind must create mankind', she emphasized the differences. In her theology mankind marched towards a vision of perfected humanity, drawn by a God of Law and Goodness. Comte's 'Collective Humanity', on the other hand, was redeemed by no such vision. How could one worship mankind in its present sorry condition? 'Angels and ministers of grace defend us! — a collection of abortions — a collection of "me's". Is this what I am to reverence? this what I am to work for?'

By Positivists it is said, the aspirations, the 'unsatisfied instincts' of man point not to the development of that particular man, to 'eternal life' for *him*, as the moralists say, but to the development of 'humanity'. This appears strictly illogical. If one human life is a disappointing fragment, humanity means a mass of disappointing fragments — a crowd of unfinished lives — an accumulation of worthless abortions. *Is* it worth while for me to work either for humanity or myself if this is so? Above all is it worth while for me to work if there be no God? or there be only such a God as this?[21]

These were her criticisms of the creeds of her day. With what did she propose to replace them?

2   The Plan of Almighty Perfection

Florence complained that people had been lamentably lax in investigating 'the character of God'. She set herself about remedying this deficiency. She was, after all, skilled in the process of evaluation, having devised the categories for the monthly report on nursing students. In addition to the

'Technical Record' there was the 'Moral Record' with sub-divisions that included 'trustworthiness', 'ward management' and 'order'. Mrs Wardroper's marks ranged from 'excellent', through 'moderate', to 'zero'. Florence Nightingale's ratings of the Almighty also ran the gamut.

She expanded her idea of the personal God with whom she had been taught to seek communion, to include the God of Law, the Creator of the universe. This God, embodying Perfection, Wisdom, and Omniscience, earns her highest grade.

The primary fact in religion seems to be the existence of an omnipotent spirit of love and wisdom — the *primary* fact, because it is the explanation of every other. ... By *omnipotence* we understand a power which effects whatever would not contradict its own nature and Will. By a *spirit* we understand a living thought, feeling, purpose, residing in a conscious being. By *love* we understand the feeling which seeks for its satisfaction the greatest degree and the best kind of well-being in other than itself. By *wisdom* we understand the thought by which this satisfaction is obtained.[22]

It was generally to the physical world that Florence Nightingale turned for evidence of God. In the process of gathering facts, grouping them, and analysing them for the general law which they revealed, she found a spiritual meaning. Patterns of predictability, the laws of science, and the symmetry of mathematics she ascribed to an immutable and perfect God, 'the primary fact' that explains all others.

These laws are 'the expression of his thoughts'. God is not the watchmaker of Deism, who removes himself from his creation. He is intimately connected to the world, assuring its stability by the invariableness of His nature. Florence felt that this emphasis upon God as Law-giver did away with several perceived errors of Christian orthodoxy; it bridged the gap between the natural and the supernatural and brought out the true meaning of prayer. It eliminated dangerous superstitions, particularly the belief in miracles. It resolved the problem of evil. It gave men and women a high purpose, charging them with the responsibility of discovering God's laws and helping others to live in accordance with them.

If God is invariable there can be no split between the natural and the supernatural world. The Calvinist who emphasizes the arbitrary power of God, denies His goodness and dependability. Her contemporary Henry Longueville Mansel is in error because he separates knowledge of the natural world from knowledge of God, emphasizing the inscrutability and mystery of God. The belief in miracles is equally damaging, based on a false view of God and giving rise to a false view of prayer. 'The whole theory of prayer is to expect a miracle.' The God of this popular faith is an arbitrary tyrant, moved by trivial and ridiculous considerations. About the 'winking madonna' of the Rimini miracle, Florence makes this acid comment.

> The picture had been there 40 years, and had remained unnoticed; the purity, holiness, and devotion said nothing to them; the beauty of virtue had no effect . . . . God, acting by a law of goodness and righteousness which *never* fails, is really more worthy of reverence than God 'winking' at us occasionally or turning water into wine or blood, or anything else.[23]

The Roman Catholic is not alone in expecting a miracle as an answer to prayer. In asking for healing, in asking to be spared the vicissitudes of wind, sea, disease, the petitioner — whether Roman Catholic or Protestant — is asking for a special providence. He often sounds as if he is trying to divert God from a course of action which He has already decided upon. God is implicitly considered to be both stupid and evil; man becomes a wheedling, hypocritical supplicant of a Being whom he really considers to be his moral inferior: a God who breaks His own laws, a God who would hurt man if His wrath were not deflected by prayer.

Florence's emphasis upon God as 'Divine Perfection, Omnipotence, and Goodness', led her to conclude that the problem of evil is illusory. All is under law; God does not permit evil. She recognized that a cursory glance at the world around her did not support this conviction. Speaking of 'the traces of a Being who made it', she says, 'If we stop at the superficial signs, the Being is something so bad as no human character can be found to equal in badness, and certainly all the beings He has made are better than Himself.'[24] If, however, we place suffering and evil in the context of progress toward spiritual perfection, if we see them as means, rather than ends, we will recognize that what appears to be evil is in fact good, part of God's purpose for man.

There was certainly as wide a gap between Job and his follower Goethe who understood that God did *not* hate the Devil, that mankind were particularly in want of him to stir them up, and the whole Evangelical and Roman Catholic and High Church twaddle upon the subject, as there is between knowing God and not knowing God. . . . When Mephistopheles says that he is part of that force which always wills the evil and always does the good, he seems to have hit the 'mystery' exactly. But then we must acknowledge that God made the Devil.

God as universal law encompasses the thief and the murderer as well as the Devil.

The pioneer is the highest calling, and God calls the highest man to it. But the thieves and murderers who are also His calling, are in some sense His pioneers! St. Vincent summoned his missionaries to the galleys to visit the Sons of God suffering for our crimes, in the person of these men who suffer for their own disorderly lives![25]

The obvious logical objection to this view of evil was made by John Stuart Mill. It could be argued that God's unchanging laws are 'good' when applied to the species, but they can and do harm individuals. Knowledge of the laws of meteorology is no protection to the person who is killed by lightning. Knowledge of the social laws linking poverty with crime is of no help to the galley slave. The problem of the suffering of the innocent still stands.

Florence avoided dealing with this particular aspect of the issue, but her treatment of the problem of suffering is not as callous or as crude as it might at first appear. If we acknowledge that suffering is part of God's plan of spiritual education we should not, therefore ignore the pain of the sufferer; we should weep for him; we should try to alleviate his sufferings. There is no contradiction between the knowledge that the ultimate solution to pauperism lies in social and economic law and the impulse to help the individual pauper. When people are hungry we should feed them and not wait to accumulate more sophisticated and complete knowledge, or dismiss their hunger as the will of God and ignore it.

3   *Revealing the Plan*

Man cannot break God's law. He may 'keep it *one way or another;* to his weal or his woe, his health or disease, his strength or his weakness — to the improvement or the deterioration of his nature, body or mind'. In order to keep the law 'to his weal' he must first find out what it is.

Florence had always loved 'to bite on a fact' and found statistics 'more enlivening than a novel'. She was, Cook said, 'a passionate statistician'. She placed these interests and abilities in service to mankind through 'sanitary science'.

> Sanitary Science is showing how we may affect the constitution of the living and of future lives. In one direction sanitary science is understood to apply to the physical nature; but each part of man's nature affects every other. Moreover, there is a sanitary science essential to each of man's faculties and function. For each there is an appropriate state and operation — in other words, a healthy state — and there is a science discoverable as to how, by what means to bring about the appropriate state.[26]

Confident that the link between the specific and the universal is supplied by God, she moved systematically through each of her concerns trying to find in the vast accumulation of facts a common denominator. To anyone who looks at her social writing — *Notes on Nursing, Notes on Hospitals, Life or Death in India* — her genius for accumulating specific facts, and abstracting them from a generalization is immediately apparent. God's laws are universal, therefore the researcher must uncover every aspect of his subject; yet the individual fact must never be lost; nor should it appear only as an illustration of a general law; in itself a fact has divine significance. In short, the reader must at every moment be made conscious of both the trees of detail and the emerging shape of the forest. Her skill in realizing this goal was recognized by her contemporaries. John McNeill described *Notes on Matters Affecting the Health, Efficiency, and Hospital Administration of the British Army* as a literary masterpiece, a 'priceless gift to the country'.

Florence Nightingale starts with the facts which she had herself observed during her term of duty in the Crimea. She describes the life of the soldier: his food, his clothing, his psychological and moral health.

> He wore, during the winter, a single pair of laced boots, which, being wet through, he was afraid to unlace, lest the heat of the tent should dry them, so that they could not be put on again. Thus, even when asked by the Regimental Surgeon, he denied that he felt numbness in his feet, lest he should be ordered to unlace his boots.

After the careful noting of specifics Florence in summary pays tribute to

> the simple courage, the enduring patience, the good sense, the strength to suffer without words, of this handful of men defending their position, like the Greeks at Thermopylae, who drew their blankets over their heads and died without a word.[27]

More and more facts are amassed: 51,000 articles of clothing were washed in the hospital at Scutari during a month, fewer than 2½ per man. The mortality rates over a period of a year were recorded. These are represented in a series of illustrations in which she superimposed circles of different colours: the red showing deaths from wounds; the blue, the preventable; the black, 'other'. From a brief study of these 'coxcombs' even the mathematically incompetent will note that the mortality rate from 'preventable' causes decreased markedly after certain sanitary reforms were introduced — more washing of clothes, provisions for latrines, and a healthier water supply.

The book is vast — over 500 pages. By giving a brief history of the health of the British Army in previous wars Florence places the Crimean War in a larger context. She divides the analysis of the medical history of the recent campaign under sub-headings concerning the organization of regimental and general hospitals; the need for sanitary officials and for a statistical department; a survey of the education, employment, and promotion of medical officers; soldiers' pay; the diet and the cooking of the Army, including recipes ('Cheap plain rice Pudding for Campaigning'); notes on how to set up an encampment; the Commissariat; washing and canteens; soldiers' wives; the construction of Army hospitals in peace and war. The last section is devoted to a summary of 'defects and suggestions' to which is affixed a series of appendices of supplementary notes, diagrams, illustrations, and correspondence. Keeping in mind the overall purpose of preventive reform, Florence guides the reader through this maze of facts and leaves him with the conviction that the 'Laws' she has uncovered are, as she said, 'an organization leading to power'. Despite the weight of its factual detail and the abstraction of its statistics, it is a blueprint for action.

Leaving her followers to carry out the reforms her Crimean investigations had suggested, she turned to other questions. She wondered whether there was a relation between architecture and mortality rates. With her knowledge of hospitals in France and Germany as a background she set herself to study the death rate in hospitals in Britain — civilian hospitals, military hospitals, maternity hospitals attached to general hospitals and those existing as self-contained units. The death rate in the barracks of the 2nd Life Guard she estimated as 10.4 per thousand; in the Knightsbridge barracks 17.5; in the civilian hospital St Pancras, however, it was only 2.2; in Kensington, 3.3.

She then looked at the floor plans of individual hospitals — the number and placement of windows and toilets, the kitchens and the provisions for the procurement of food and water. She noted that military hospitals were poorly ventilated, and the rooms were small. Civilian hospitals in contrast had been built along Palladian lines. They provided cross-ventilation and large windows. The maternity cases were often housed in separate pavilions. In the process of correlating architecture with mortality rates God's 'immutable laws' became clear. The death rate in a maternity hospital attached to a general hospital was four times higher than in one housed in a separate building. Overcrowding and lack of air killed people.

She dashed off a furious letter to the planners of Netley hospital advising them to do away with their current plans for a building.

At Netley all consideration of what would best tend to the comfort and recovery of the patients has been sacrificed to the vanity of the architect, whose sole object has been to make a building which should cut a dash when looked at from the Southampton river.[28]

While she did not succeed in stopping the construction of Netley, her views, summarized in *Notes on Hospitals* of 1859, would be taken into account in all future hospital architecture. She had the immediate satisfaction of supervising the planning and building of St Thomas's hospital, a monument to the principles of planning that she had formulated.

Confident in her method, she turned to India. She accumulated facts and projected them against a background that was as wide as the horizons of contemporary knowledge. She looked for general principles. Then she formulated a plan of reform.

By this time Florence was confined to her room. From now on all her work would depend upon what information she could accumulate through correspondence. With the help of her medical advisers Sutherland, Farr, Martin and Alexander, she wrote directly to the 200 medical stations in India. When she moved from the Burlington to Hampstead two vans were required simply to transport the Indian material. Information trickled in from Bengal, Oudh, Cawnpore, Fort William, Meerut, Rohilund Roorkee, Madras, Calcutta, Bombay. This she placed against her knowledge of European cities. 'Calcutta in 1871 was more salubrious than Manchester or Liverpool and may be considered as a sanitarium compared with Vienna, or even with Berlin, where the city canals are still fouled with sewage.'[29] The health of the British soldier she compared with that of the Indian civilian.

Her research convinced her that the British soldier in India had some problems that were peculiarly British, most particularly a fondness for drink. 'If facilities for washing were as great as those for drink our Indian army would be the cleanest body in the world.'[30] Yet their main problems were those they held in common with all Indians. They were prey not only to exotic and deadly tropical diseases but to contaminated water and food, bad drainage, and overcrowding. She urged the need for agricultural reform in the small volume *Life or Death in India with an Appendix on Life or Death by Irrigation* (1874), which was published as a means of pointing up the reforms urged in the immensely long and therefore largely unread Royal Report. Her scope has now widened to include sociology, botany, economics. Recommending enormously increased efforts in agricultural production, she tackled the complex problems of transportation costs, irrigation, taxes and land use. 'Many farmers don't care about increasing profit since it is all taken by the Zemindara and the money-lenders.' How many acres do canals irrigate? How great an increase in food production could they provide? How much savings in transportation fees? She studied the plague in Bengal. In 1857 nine miles had been laid waste by fever and whole villages became extinct. The cause was found in a screw turned by a coolie which had flooded the lowlands faster than the water could be carried off. 'If the screw turned too much brings fever, the screw turned just right brings plenty and health.' She urged dramatic action.

> Is there anything to prevent the Government ordering at once the irrigation of from 250,000 to 500,000 acres in every district of India, 20,000 or 30,000 embracing all India, and to be completed in five years, with an absolute certainty of two or three times the present interest of money in direct returns?[31]

Closer to home, she urged research into the underlying causes of poverty and crime. She suggests that, rather than 'advertise' rewards for the apprehension of individual criminals, we should apply the same sums of money towards research on the causes of criminal behaviour. On the basis of her own observations she presented two hypotheses. 'Foundling hospital is the parent of immorality'. 'Indiscriminate dole giving from the public or the private purse is the parent of pauperism.' Writing a decade after the Foster Act of 1870 requiring universal education she pointed out that nothing is known of the results of the Act. How successful are schools in instilling knowledge? What effect does education have on the moral character of the students? Is there a link between lack of education and criminality? 'What we have to do — what God gives us to do — is to find out *what* this social state is — and how to alter it.'[32]

So strongly did she feel about the importance of the study of social law that she tried to establish a Professorship in Applied Statistics at Oxford, and sought Benjamin Jowett's help. This hope was dashed when Jowett died in 1893.

By then death was a constant companion. She had long been prepared for her own end. True to her principles she specified in her will that her body was to be given 'for dissection of post-mortem examination for the purposes of medical science'. Her wishes were not observed.

9 Mankind Must Create Mankind

1 Called to be Saviours

If man is part of nature, fulfilling the laws of Divine Perfection, why then need he be 'asked' to do what he must do naturally? To this obvious question Florence Nightingale never proposed an entirely convincing answer.

Man, she said, is under law and yet he is set apart. His complex personality is dependent upon the shifting relationship of different aspects of his nature. 'Moral and intellectual man has not been studied in his development, nor has it been studied how he is influenced by the physical man which impresses its actions at each age upon him.' Set apart from the simpler organisms with their more direct cause-and-effect responses, man has a unique destiny: he is naturally endowed to play an extraordinary role in creation. Through consciously accepting this role he will become united with God 'manifest in the flesh'.

> It will not be well with us — till we are penetrated with the conception of God's government of the world — with the conception of ourselves as the means through which it is in the course of fulfilling God's thought — till we contribute our conscious will, and work with it — as His willing servants, ministers, children — not His unconscious instruments. We must go through that state while in our natural childhood; as we advance to maturity, instead of renouncing an imaginary Devil, we should seek the service of the living God.[1]

Growing past natural childhood, he assumes the birthright of the mature man, exhibiting all the signs 'limited only in degree' of all 'that we know or can know of God'. This relationship gives man a special position in the divine economy; he is a co-worker with God.

214

There will be no heaven for me nor for any one else, unless we make it — with wisdom carrying out our thoughts into realities. Good thoughts don't make a heaven, any more than they make a garden. But we say, God is to do it for us: not we. We? — what are we to do? — we are to pray, and to mean well, to take care that our hearts be right. 'God will reward a sincere wish to do right.' God will do no such thing; it is not His plan. He does not treat men like children; mankind is to create mankind. We are to learn, first what is heaven, and, secondly, how to make it. We are to ascertain what *is* right, and then how to perform it.[2]

She grew indignant with those who, like Emerson, went into raptures over 'the Feast of Law'. She was not interested in 'pure' science and to the end of her life she remained unconvinced by the germ theory of the communication of disease; she was too busy improving washing facilities and having the floors scrubbed down to look through the lens of a microscope. To preach to a man to do right and then 'send him back to the pigsty where he cannot but do wrong is nonsense. We set about improving his pigsty.'

Florence forcefully reminded her co-workers of the weight and breadth of their responsibilities. To the evangelical John Lawrence, she wrote: 'The question is no less than one of this: How to create a public health department for India; how to bring a higher civilization into India.' By accepting this responsibility, Sir John can become 'the greatest creator of mankind in modern history'.[3]

This charge extends not only over the breadth of the globe, but backwards in time. Every generation bears the accumulated errors, ignorance and sufferings of the past 'lessons' that inform the present. The murderer and the diseased are 'pioneers' because their deviation points to a law that must be understood before we can keep it 'to our weal'. Their lives will be given meaning when the lesson they impart has been understood and acted upon.

God's plan is that we should make mistakes . . .; then comes some Saviour, Christ or another, not only Saviour, but many a one, who learns for all the world *by* the consequences of those errors, and 'saves' us from them. . . . There must be Saviours from social not moral error. Most people have not learnt any lesson from life at all — suffer as they may, they learn nothing, they would alter nothing. We sometimes hear of men 'having given a colour to their age'. Now, if the colour is the right colour, those men are saviours. [4]

Confident that God has permitted only as much ignorance and suffering as is necessary for spiritual growth, the saviour bears his burden with joy. Florence cited de Tocqueville as the first philosopher who understood that determinism, the acknowledgement that human history could not have been other than it has been, does not lead to inertia. Instead, it 'stimulates us to do everything'.[5] For God has willed that we join our will to His in the 'onward, upward, heavenward' march towards Perfection.

Acceptance of this creed brought great rewards: a high purpose, the assurance that all is for the best in the best of all possible worlds, the exhilaration that comes from knowing one's work to be important.

At the same time her concept of service, a range of responsibilities in which the human reach is almost as large as that of God, made personal relationships seem rather unimportant. Human love, which Josephine Butler took for granted and Octavia Hill made the centre of her social vision, Florence Nightingale ignored. A highly emotional woman, she had learned to protect herself — and others — against the flux of her disordered passions. She spoke of love as the desire for 'the best kind of wellbeing in other than itself'. Friendships were limited by a view in which men and women were means toward the fulfilment of a Divine Plan, rather than ends in themselves. Mrs Gaskell speaks of her lack of feeling for individuals and her 'intense love for the RACE'.[6] Florence herself said that she lacked sympathy.[7] While many valued her affection, others remarked that she had no gift for friendship. They meant that she cut people off when they did not share her views; if they would not submit to her rule, she dropped them. Sidney Herbert was dear to her, but the cause of Army medical reform was dearer. Friends, family, her own health — all must be sacrificed in the forward march.

Her model, after all, was one who had renounced the joys of ordinary human companionship and chosen the solitary route of the saviour. While rejecting the Resurrection and shying away from the Christian commitment to the uniqueness of Christ as the 'only' son of God, Florence continued to use the Christian affirmation that had been part of her youth.

> Christ, indeed, came into the world to save sinners; to wash them in his blood, to deliver man from sin and its consequences; to establish the kingdom of Heaven within him; to at-one him with God — were truly Christ's mission, and that of many more upon the earth. These things will be attained and would not have been attained without Christ.[8]

With indignation she rejected the effete and otherworldly Christ of Renan. 'I am revolted by such expressions as "charmant" and "delicieux".' Likewise she charged Titian with having falsified his subject.

> Asceticism is the trifling of an enthusiast with his power, a puerile coquetting with his selfishness or his vanity, in the absence of any sufficiently great object to employ the first or to overcome the last. Or, since I am speaking to an artist and must illustrate and not define, the 'cristo della Honeta' of Titian at Dresden is an ascetic. the 'er [sic] ist vollbract' of Albrecht Durer at Nurenberg is Christ — he whom we call an example, though little we make of it. For our Church has daubed that tender, beautiful image with coarse bloody colours till it looks like the sign of a road-side inn. And another has mysticized him out of all human reach till he is the God and God is the Devil. But are we not really to do as Christ did? And when he said the 'Son of Man', did he not mean the sons of men? He was no ascetic.[9]

Her Christ, like that of Durer, lived in the world, His uniqueness as a religious leader lay in his single-hearted search for truth and in the life of self-giving that resulted from that search. He was the 'greatest religious teacher — never referring to authority not even his own, or private judgment — but always to God's truth, God's judgment, God's work'. His life, accordingly, was complete.

The Resurrection Florence dismissed as a mythological accretion; the Crucifixion, however, is the 'most important' event 'that ever was in the world', giving the divine imprimatur to a life of service. 'I do think *that Christ on the Cross is the highest expression hitherto of God*, not in the vulgar meaning of atonement — but God does hang on the Cross *every* day in every one of us.'[10]

During the early years of her friendship with Jowett he frequently brought her the Sacrament. 'I want you to feel that in the Communion you are really united not only to Christ but all of mankind especially to those whom you know and to your own family and friends.'[11] After 1865, however, Jowett's offer is rarely repeated.

For Florence Nightingale, as for Octavia Hill, self-giving is the key to spiritual growth. Like Christ, each person is entrusted with the responsibility of the working out of God's ideal for her own nature; like Christ, the 'type' for mankind, she must find a life of service that is in accord with her nature. 'This only is human happiness.'

Placed alongside this ideal, the deficiencies of English society became woefully apparent.

It has often been said — How extradinary that Jesus Christ could have arisen among the working class! But how much, much more extraordinary if He were to arise among our class. Nay, almost beyond a miracle for Him ever to come to see us. We have no time. At eight o'clock there is geography and the use of the globes; at twelve Lablache, the music master; at two o'clock, Fielding and the water-colour class. At four, Madame Michaud. At five, the German master. Could Jesus come at six? No. At half-past six? Mr. Faraday's lecture. At eight? No, the opera at eight. Why, there's no time for inspiration — it's impossible. We're too busy — we have no time for that intercourse which our Saviour found so necessary that he sat up the whole night for it having so much to do in the day.[12]

Like Octavia Hill, Florence Nightingale felt that the family was meant to be the groundwork of God's social system. It should not be a self-enclosed entity, however, but a community that gives its members the confidence that enables them to move out into the world. Most families fall far short of this ideal. Often the family prevented the development of its members, becoming 'a thumbscrew, a Procustes bed, an instrument either of torture or of deterioration'.[13]

The constriction of the upper-class family was felt most heavily by the daughters. In the 1840s, writing from the bitterness of her pent-up frustration and disappointment, she describes the self-betrayal that occurs each day in the drawing room because there is no type, no ideal by which she can determine her conduct.

A woman who accomplished one of the greatest works which has ever been accomplished, either by man or woman, mentions that she had had the plan of it three years in her head, before she did anything. Why? Because she had no type of what her intercourse should be with her own family, nor had they, and she allowed them to monopolize all her time, — the time for doing this thing to which God had called her, — and thought it was ill-natured to go away after breakfast or after dinner — When we think of the lives around us, squandered by the fancies of children who know not what they do, we cannot but see strongly the danger of having no type. For, if you were to ask seriously, 'Do you intend your life to be spent in this way?' they would say, 'Oh! no, it is only for to-day; it would be thought unkind not to give way to to-day.'

Rather than raise children to serve God and mankind, parents gratify their own selfishness: the assumption that a daughter should give up her life in obedience to her parents perverts the meaning of parenthood.

What right have a man and a woman to absorb all the powers of five daughters? The right is all the other way. If I have brought them into the world they have the right to expect that their powers shall be exercised, their lives made worth having, opportunity given them for developing all their faculties . . . . We shall think it curious, looking back in a future state, to see that we have condemned people to do nothing, and called it a duty, a self-denial, a social virtue.

Pointing out that Michelangelo and Beethoven did not achieve their goals through working at odd moments, she condemns the relegation of the serious matters of life to such haphazard chances. People 'think nothing of being in a *state of mind* to think a great thought, to do a great work. They will fritter away all their power.' Lacking a larger arena, the imperative to service turns inward.

People who have nothing to do generally take to playing the policeman over their relations; if too gentle or too indolent for this kind of action, *ennui* consumes their lives. We do the best we can to train our women to an idle, superficial life; we teach them music and drawing, languages, and *poor-peopling* — resources as they are called, and we hope that if they don't marry, they will at least be quiet.

This denial of a serious calling can lead to spiritual death or to madness. 'There is scarcely any one who cannot, in his own experience, remember some instance where some amiable person has been slowly put to death at home, aye, and at an estimable and virtuous home.'[14]

Florence's sympathies are not only with the daughter; in the family that does not live for God, but for itself, the mother is equally a captive. Confined in a tiny, enclosed world, dependent upon a society that defines a successful woman only in terms of her accomplishments as a wife and mother, she gives undue importance to the degree of sympathy between herself and her children. Yet in day-to-day dealings with her children, who may be temperamentally quite different from herself, she may give, and receive, little sympathy. She must then consider herself a failure, adding guilt to the already heavy burden of loneliness. In short, mothers and children are caught in a tangle of false expectations.

The relation between parents and children is as difficult to find as your way in a London fog. The parents take responsibilities which they cannot perform. The parents feel that they are going through a great deal for their children; the children that gratitude is exacted from them for that which does not make them happy. ... Both sides suffer equally from disappointment, and both are alike to be pitied.

On the subject of marriage Florence is equally scathing. The limitations on choice set by family and class, the artificial circumstances of courtship conspire to create unhappy unions.

Under the eyes of an always present mother and sisters (of whom even the most refined and intellectual cannot abstain from a.jest upon the subject, who think it their *duty* to be anxious, to watch every germ and bud of it) the acquaintance begins. It is fed — upon what — the gossip of art, music and pictorial, the party politics of the day, the chit-chat of society, and people marry and sometimes they don't marry, discouraged by the impossibility of knowing any more of one another than this will furnish.

In marriage, as in courtship, the energies of the man and the woman are too often spent in fulfilling trivial social expectations. Furthermore, the contract does not place equal requirements on both partners.

That man and woman have an equality of duties and rights is accepted by woman even less than by man. Behind *his* destiny woman must annihilate herself, must be only his complement. A woman dedicates herself to the vocation of her husband; she fills up and performs the subordinate parts in it, in nine cases out of ten. Some few, like Mrs. Somerville, Mrs. Chisholm, Mrs. Fry, have not done so but these are exceptions. The fact is that woman has so seldom any vocation of her own, that it does not much signify; she has none to renounce. A man gains everything by marriage; he gains a 'helpmate' but a woman does not.

Florence Nightingale includes this critique of contemporary society in her theological writings; by describing a society that had lost its sense of purpose she dramatized the contrast with the ideal.

A society that took Christ as its type and encouraged its members to work out God's purpose would provide 'a life full of steady enthusiasm walking straight to its aim, flying home, as the bird is now, against the wind — with the calmness and the confidence of one who knows the laws of God and can apply them'.[15]

This life was of course equally liberating for men and women; sensing the greater need, however, she directed her primary message towards women. She wished to 'make a better life for women'. Her great hope had been 'first to infuse the mystical religion into the forms of others' especially among women, and secondly to give them an organization for their activity in which they could be trained to be 'Handmaids of the Lord'.[16] The sense of direction instilled by mystical religion and the conviction that they had been called by God to a life of purpose, would give them the strength to cast off the restricting claims of home and family. They would then rediscover the emancipation proclaimed in the New Testament. 'Jesus Christ raised women above the conditions of mere slaves, mere ministers to the passions of the man, raised them by His sympathy, to be Ministers of God.'[17]

As 'Ministers of God' they were equal to and independent of men. The affirmation of this status transformed the woman's role in the marriage relationship. They would seek marriage, not as a commercial contract, but as 'the highest, the only true love . . . when two persons, a man and a woman, who have an attraction for one another, unite together in some true purpose for mankind and God'.[18]

The demands of service, however, took priority over the assertion of the rights of women. Florence Nightingale, like Octavia Hill, was a disappointment to the feminists who identified the emancipation of women with the procurement of the right to vote. To John Stuart Mill's overture she replied that there were causes more important than votes for women — one of them being the right of a married woman to hold property in her own name. She signed Mill's petition but the right to cast a single vote seemed a minor matter. She was concerned with the rule of Almighty God, not with that of a majority opinion that generally paid little attention to the will of God.

The call to service, rather than rights for women, was the key to a serious and happy life. In concluding her *Notes on Nursing* she offered this advice on how a woman should choose her vocation.

Keep clear of both the jargons now current everywhere — of the jargon, namely about the 'rights' of women, which urges women to do all that men do including the medical and other professions, merely because men do it and without regard to whether this *is* the best that women can do and of the jargon which urges women to do nothing men do, merely because they are women, and should be 'recalled to a sense of their duty as women' and because 'this is women's work and that is men's' and 'these are things which women should not do' which is all assertion and nothing more. . . . You do not want the effect of your good things to be, 'How wonderful for a *woman*'; nor would you be deterred from good things by hearing it said, 'Yes, but she ought not to have done this, because it is not suitable for a woman.' But you want to do the thing that is good whether it is suitable for a woman or not.

2 Having No Other Will but God's

Man's two identities, the natural and the divine, meet in the inwardness of the soul. God and man are interdependent, man realizing his nature through union with God, God using man to effect his purposes.

When Benjamin Jowett referred to Florence Nightingale as an 'Infidel' and 'Papist' he identified her unbelief with her metaphysical notions on God and law; the 'Papist' Florence Nightingale is the penitent and believer who, until the end of her life, proclaimed movement toward union with a loving, personal God as the essence of religion. She hoped that her theological work *Suggestions for Thought* and its philosophical speculations would find a sympathetic audience, but she placed a far greater value on her readings in the devotional authors. She consciously sought out the classics of the mystic tradition, borrowing books from Georgiana Moore, copying out fragments on bits of paper for her own guidance and support. She hoped to incorporate the writings of St Angela of Foligno, Jane Frances de Chantal, St Francis of Assisi, St Francis Xavier, St John of the Cross, Peter of Alcantara, St Teresa of Avila and others in an anthology to be entitled *Notes from Devotional Authors of the Middle Ages, Collected, Chosen and Freely Translated by Florence Nightingale.*

It is possible to give an account of Florence Nightingale's doctrine of God on the basis of her theological writings alone. Her views on mysticism, however, while outlined in her writings, should not be considered apart from her spiritual biography and an analysis of her early years, particularly her experience in Rome and Egypt in 1850.

The kernel of truth that Florence as a young girl extracted from the witness of the local clergy in her Anglican parish was that there is a personal, loving God who communicates His purposes to the individual. This belief she took seriously. She recognized that, if true, it offered extraordinary opportunities and responsibilities. She would dedicate her life to trying to find out what they were and to live by them. The women to whom she turned for spiritual guidance were alike in presenting the opposition between the love of God and the love of self. The goal of sanctification, the way of the mystic, was to reject self and affirm God. In this context sin is not the ignorance of God's laws described by Florence the metaphysician; it is the perversion of the will, the turning away from God toward self described by Florence the mystic.

This message brought a burden of guilt to the strong-willed and tempestuous girl. Quiet, modest, kindly Aunt Hannah Nicholson sought out God's will on every question, humbly submitting herself. The serenity she achieved was the envy of her niece. 'Your whole life seems to be love, and you always find words in your heart which, without the pretension of enlightening, yet are like a clearing up to me.'[19] Aunt Hannah provided sympathy and encouragement, yet it is unfortunate that Florence took her as a model of female spirituality. The two women were temperamentally totally unlike. The pilgrim route of Aunt Hannah could never be, and should not have been recommended as, the path for Florence Nightingale. Temperamental qualities such as an impetuous spirit, a need to confront the whole of reality, unswerving honesty, even intellectual abilities which Florence might have understood as gifts to be used in the service of God — became sins for which she reproached herself. A more sophisticated spiritual director might have helped her find a road to God that respected and made use of her unique qualities — a direction in which 'self' and 'God' are not always at war but in which 'self' is completed in union with God.

Florence's next choice as a spiritual director continued to affirm the ever-widening gap between love of self and love of God. Her already extreme sense of guilt at not being able to cast herself on the mercy of God was further exacerbated by the spirituality of Madre Santa Colomba and the Sisters of the Convent School of Trinita dei Monti. The exhortations to turn her thought to God every hour, the spiritual exercises, became judgements on her inadequacies. In 1850 she wrote in her diary:

Oh my madre, my madre. This was the time I made the retreat with you which you said was more for me than for the children — two years ago. March 3. Did not get up in the morning but God gave me the time afterwards, which I ought to have made in the morning, a solitary two hours in my own cabin, to meditate on my madre's words. March 8. My madre said to me, Can you hesitate between the God of the whole world and your little reputation?[20]

Florence Nightingale has been compared with St Paul and Joan of Arc, with those rare people whose lives are transformed by a flash of light, a voice from on high. This comparison has elements both of truth and untruth. Like those mystics, she remembered a specific experience when she felt more than a general sense of the presence of God. 'On February 7th, 1837, God spoke to me and called me to His service.' This call, however, far from dispelling all doubt and conflict, created further ambivalence.

It was years before she acted on the call. While the delay was partly caused by her family's intransigence, it arose also from her own inability to resolve the old question of the relation of self to God. How was she to know whether she was acting for the 'God of the whole world' or for her 'little reputation'? Was it possible that God was calling her to do something that was intensely pleasing to herself? She had criticized her contemporaries' selfishness and vanity, but was not her desire to 'be a saviour' equally contaminated by ambition as Parthe's love of clothes and interest in young men? Her family, even Aunt Hannah and Aunt Mai, urged her to accept her life with its limitations as decreed by God. Were they perhaps right? Was this not perhaps the ultimate, the ridiculous, the monstrous selfishness, to want to be a saviour? In her desperation she turned to other women who had managed to move out of the immediate circumstances of their social position into active service. Of Mary Baldwin, a missionary in Greece, she asked 'the history of her coming here'. Mary Baldwin replied that she experienced no extraordinary calling, no presentiment. Preparing herself to follow, she had been led step by step. Mrs Hill, another missionary friend, said that 'it was always God who made the initiative — never she — it was never her doing — always circumstances — only to do the duty which offers itself for the day was the way, she said. Let God show the way by his circumstances.'[21]

In the end that was what Florence Nightingale did. Fourteen years later she responded to the call which had set her apart in 1837 and which she could never totally purify from its taint of self-aggrandizement. The final accomplishment, the decisive step, was not dramatic. It was a response to 'circumstances'. Parthenope was going for a three-month rest at Carlsbad. Florence announced that she would spend that time at Kaiserswerth.

At Kaiserswerth she found that the conflict between love of God and love of self was resolved by work as it could never be while she was inactive. Making beds, preparing meals, following the demanding schedule of a student nurse, she forgot herself. 'This is life. Now I know what it is to live and love life. . . . I wish for no other earth, no other world than this.'

From the vantage point of middle age Florence Nightingale looked back on the mysticism of her youth with mixed feelings. While rejecting a view that considered humanity and the love of self 'evil' and mistrusting some of the psychological aspects of the 'call', she continued to regard the ideal of mysticism, the 'casting oneself on God' as her true vocation.

To the degree to which mysticism is the searching out of the laws and 'character' of God, Florence remained a mystic.

> Mystical or spiritual religion is not enough for most people without outward form, and I may say that I can never remember a time when it was not 'the question' of my life — not so much for myself as for others. For myself, the mystical or spiritual religion, as laid down by St. John's Gospel, however imperfectly I have lived up to it, was and is, enough.[22]

Florence commends the mysticism of Plato, praising the closing prayer in the *Phaedrus*, 'Give me beauty in the inward soul, and may the outward and inward man be at one', as greater than any in the Book of Common Prayer. Jesus Christ, however, is the

> first true Mystic. 'My meat is to do the will of Him that sent me and to finish His work.'
>
> What is this but putting in fervent and the most striking words the foundation of all real Mystical Religion? — which is

that for all our actions, all our words, all our thoughts, the food upon which they are to live and have their being is to be the indwelling Presence of God, the union with God, that is, with the Spirit of Goodness and Wisdom. Where shall I find God? In myself. That is the true Mystical Doctrine. But then I myself must be in a state for Him to come and dwell in me. This is the whole aim of the Mystical Life, and all Mystical Rules in all times and countries have been laid down for putting the soul into such a state.[23]

Florence felt that when more was known about the psycho-spiritual nature of man communication between God and man would be an everyday occurrence. Mysticism would become, not a series of extraordinary emotional events punctuating the long stretches of time when the ordinary and the rational seem to have the upper hand, but a permanent state.

The 'mystical' state is the essence of common sense if it be real; that is, if God be a reality. For, we *can* only, act and speak and think of Him; and what we need is to discover such laws of His as will enable us to be always acting and thinking in conscious concert of cooperation with Him. We cannot conceive that this, the very best gift we can have, can be the gift of arbitrary caprice on the part of our Almighty Father. But if we find out that He gives us 'grace', i.e., the 'mystical' state in accordance with certain laws which we can discover and use — is not that a truth and common sense?[24]

It is hardly surprising that all of the mystics she admired had worked actively in the world — St Catherine of Siena was a consummate politician; St Catherine of Genoa a medical missionary; St Teresa of Avila a great administrator.

From them Florence took her understanding of prayer. True prayer is 'not to ask what we wish of God but what God wishes of us'. Contrasting it to the self-interested prayer of the superstitious, Florence cites the prayer of the Persian mystic: 'Four things, Oh God, I have to offer thee, which thou hast not in all thy treasury; my nothingness, my sad necessity, my fatal sin and earnest penitence. Receive these gifts and take the Giver hence.'[25]

In the notebook which she kept beside her bed and which is filled with the nocturnal jottings of the insomniac, she recorded the anniversaries of her 'calls' along with the anniversaries of the deaths of close friends.

> This is the word of the Lord unto thee, London, May 7, 1867. It is thirty years since I called thee unto my service. — Embley, February 7, 1837. It is fifteen years today since I called thee to the perfection of my service (to be a saviour). Tapton, May 7, 1852. How hast thou answered? What opportunities have I not given thee since then? I entered thee at Harley Street — August 12, 1853 — Scutari, November 4, 1854 — with Sidney Herbert, July 28, 1867. I have seen his face — the crown of glory inseparably united with the crown of thorns giving forth the same light. Three times he has called me. Once to His service, February 7th, 1837; once to be a deliverer, May 7th, 1852; once to the Cross, June 8th, 1865.[26]

This record of the passionate relation between the soul and God, the desire for union with God and its ecstatic, even sexual, connotations, the acceptance of suffering as the mark of sanctity place Florence Nightingale in the tradition of the saints of the Early Church and the Roman Catholic martyrs.

In the fullest context of her faith, however, these calls have more limited importance and their validity is called to question. She did not believe that she alone had been singled out by God. This would have contradicted her faith in the God of universal law. Every human being is called to be a saviour, a servant. This call is a continuous and daily, even hourly, reality. Further more, she had reservations about the legitimacy of a rhapsodic response of a soul to a supernatural 'call'. Painfully aware of the demands of her own dominating will, she knew that the voice of self can be mistaken for the voice of God. It may seem odd that a woman who claims union of the soul with God as the fundamental premise of her life should also question the meaning of this experience — but such is the case. 'It is said that those who do not admit "authority" do not know *when* it is that God speaks, and when it is the excitement of a cup of coffee, that they cannot tell whether their vessel be pure.' She felt that what the Wesleyans believed to be the voice of God was in reality the cries of their own 'distempered spirits'. Suspicious of fasting and self-mortification, she points out that 'denying the flesh makes it cry out'.

Her purpose is not to deny the spiritual meaning of 'estatic' states but to show that they must be confirmed by other kinds of experience.

Unless a proposition can be felt by the feeling, approved by the sense of justice, conscience or whatever other faculties we perceive in man, and unless we have evidence for it from the reason, it ought not to be admitted as a truth.[27]

A true 'call' never contradicts the universal requirements of order and duty.

'Let us do instantly whatever we have to do, without even staying to finish the letter we are making', the Roman Catholic says, 'For it is the voice of God that calls'. It is the spirit of order, or punctuality, or duty, and that *is* the spirit of God. But it is *not* the thought of God that we should become like a 'dead body' surrendering up the whole being to the Superior.

While a call from God may lead to self-denial, it should not lead to self-contempt. The true mystic is no ascetic, nor does he make his own sanctification an aim. On these points Florence found herself in emphatic disagreement with Roman Catholicism.

The three things which prevent us from thinking of ourselves are, interest in the work we are doing, devotion to God, or devotion to our neighbour. And any one of these three things would prevent us from taking pleasure in praise. This would be a healthier and more real state of mind than 'loving contempt', as the Catholic has it. And this is more in accord-ance with the thought of God than to 'love contempt'. It is much easier for some of us to hate our lives than to love them. Yet it is more the thought of God (and in everything) that we should love our lives than that we should 'hate them'.[28]

Summarizing her attack on asceticism, Florence declares that its basic premise is erroneous. 'To "renounce worldly enjoyment" implies a mistake. It should *be* our enjoyment to do the world's work.' Admittedly, she found it difficult to live up to her credo: she did not love her life. Although she tried to believe that God's laws worked for the best, there were times when she cried out in protest. Her rationalization cracks under the strain of trying to contain her grief and her anger at God. After Sidney Herbert's death she writes,

> Yes, I can truly say that it is better that God should not work a miracle to save Sidney Herbert, although his death involves the misfortune, moral and physical, of 500,000 men and although it would have been but to set aside a few trifling physical laws to save him. [29]

Sure that everything that happened was in accordance with God's will, she yet rebelled against the cruelty, the suffering she saw around her. Were these in fact essential to the process of sanctification? She knew that such a question carried the implication that, had she been God, she would somehow have arranged the world differently. The root issue once again was that, divided between her love of self and her love of God, she felt continually drawn toward self. Even her work could become 'an idol, a Moloch', distracting her from confronting her own pride. Looking back on her service in the Crimea she concluded 'Oh, God! Nothing done for Thee. . . . None of it was done for God.' She compared herself with the rich young man: he would have 'done a great work like the Crimea, but would not give up all'.[30]

To Georgiana Moore, her old friend from the Crimea, now Madre Superior of the Convent of Our Lady of Mercy at Bermondsey she confesses:

> Alas, dear mother, you ask after me — I feel as if I was only quite in the infancy of serving God — I am so careful and troubled and have such a want of calmness about His work and His poor — as if they were my work and my poor instead of His. I have not as yet learned the first lesson of His service. 'Je m'en vais a Dieu; cela seul doit m'occuper', as Brother Jean d'Avilla says, meaning, of course, in serving Him I know you pray for me. *Offer* me to *Him*, that His will may be done in me and by me. I feel you know, that if I really believe what I say I believe, I should be in a 'rapture' (as St. Teresa calls it) instead of being so disquieted. And, therefore, I suppose I don't

believe what I say I believe. *I think* I seek first the Kingdom of God and His righteousness. But I am sure I don't succeed in being filled with His righteousness.[31]

Increasingly, the dialogue becomes one between two jealous deities vying for power.

November 8 – 9. Take, oh take from me ever the wish to impress — cause of my unrest.

December 12 – 13. Oh God, I do not know at 57 whether I am thy servant or even whether I wish to be thy servant. I wish to be allowed to do this irrigation, to work for myself. Oh God, how canst thou take on as Thy servant one who is bedridden and unable — oh take me as thy hired servant.

August 9 – 10. If it is possible take this cup from me (not doing India in irrigation) God — it is all *imagination* and *self love* (your agony).

December 7, '77. 7 A.M. The Voice: If I do what you want about the Indian irrigation, would you give up all your name in it? Yes, Lord, I think I would; answer before 7:30. or: Yes, Lord, I am sure I would.

December 7. '77. Perhaps when all things go wrong for me and my name it is a sign that God is fulfilling his promise that things are going right with the Indian ryot [peasant].

December 8. Oh God, how couldst thou put such a creature as me in this place? Oh God *take my place* and cast me out, act instead of me. Oh God, Mrs. Ward: no thought of thee in all my doings, no thought of what is expected of me: no prayer for her. Oh, Lord here is thy wretched enemy.

November 18. Does he know what he is about? Is he to be trusted?

August 16. Oh God, who makest the stars, sun and moon to obey thee, makest the beautiful sunrises, can nothing be done for these poor people in the India family?

'I want to help God'; how preposterous. . . . It is He who has set my work. [32]

Doggedly she continued to record her thoughts. Over the years her prayers and self-searching brought little serenity. She could never silence her own voice; yet in the dialogue she often took God's side.

Oh, my Creator, art thou leading every man to perfection? . . . Thou knowest that through these twenty horrible years I have been supported and only supported by this belief (I think I must believe it will, or I am sure I could not work) . . . I took you to S.[idney] H.[erbert], brought you back from Scutari; completed your first R.C. (Royal Commission). Raised up your work after S.H.'s death; completed your second R.C. for India; set the India work on its legs. Have I led you so wonderfully all these years and you cannot trust me now?[33]

Even if she could not fully believe, she could still work. And perhaps that showed that she did indeed believe.

3   The Eternal Becoming

For all her 'muddles', Florence Nightingale presents a prophetic vision. An early 'demythologizer', she sought to free the gospel message from its mythical and prescientific accretions. She anticipated by one hundred years the call for a 'Holy Worldliness', to use Alex Vidler's term. Like other liberals of her period she called for the development of a broadly based natural theology, that would give an appropriate place to science, logic, and the insights of the contemporary world. She too believed that man has 'come of age'; he must distinguish between neurotic and existential dependency. Faith is no justification for shirking responsibilities, for perpetuating neuroses and immaturity on the excuse of 'casting one's self on God'. Along with Bishop Robinson and many twentieth-century theologians, she believed that God is not found at the edge of human experience, but in the midst of life — in personal relationships and in the soul itself. Foreshadowing a later interest in mysticism and meditation, she advocated the systematic study of the psycho-spiritual laws that make possible communication between God and man.

For Florence Nightingale, as for Thomas Altizer, William Hamilton, and Daniel Day Williams, God appears in history as a fellow-sufferer. The spotlight has been turned away from the God of natural theology towards Luther's 'theology of the Cross'. Christ is the supreme pioneer, revealing the essence of God's nature. 'Jesus is Lord by being a servant; to be Lord and to be servant are the same. He exercises his divinity and his sovereign power from the cross.'[34] The voice is William Hamilton but the spirit is Florence Nightingale. The assurance that her own sufferings were divinely sanctioned gave her courage. 'God does hang on the Cross *every* day in every one of us.'

Nightingale rescued this belief from its tragic implications by attaching it to the 'advance towards perfection'. Suffering is not the last word. It is a means. Yet it is more than just a means. The 'advance' is in itself a form of perfection. She would not admit that Jesus Christ was without fault since she believed that 'perfection' would have denied him the possibility of growth. God is immanent. 'All is tendency, growth.' Life is a fluid process; the past is redeemed − perhaps changed − by what we make of the present; the present determined by our vision of the future. Her view, like that of Teilhard de Chardin, was that creation is being pulled toward its divine centre, all humans contributing to the evolution of a corporate humanity.

To describe a God who reconciles progress with immutability, good with evil, Florence draws on her memories of her visit to the Sistine Chapel, one of the peak experiences of her life.

> May we not conceive that God's present will is one with every stroke of the past and the future, which is and will be ever developing itself? The artist who begins upon twelve pictures to fulfil one purpose, has one will throughout, by which will they are developed into being.

Man with his finite vision perceives temporal divisions, but the reality may be quite different. 'Perhaps increased knowledge of the nature of God may reveal to us that each present mode of being is part of a development from a past without beginning, towards a future without end.'[35]

She expanded on the Christian belief in the afterlife so as to reflect these views. As a young girl she had felt the reality of an 'Invisible World'. In a letter to Hilary Bonham Carter written in 1845, she wrote:

> How one feels that the more real presence in the room is the invisible presence which hovers around the death-bed and that we are only ghosts, who have put on form for a moment, and shall put it off, almost before we have time to wind up our watch.[36]

Life after death offered, not rest, but continued growth. 'The eternal becoming is always going on.' As for herself, she would like, she said, 'above all other eternities, to work in Hell — with great fellowship in work, to save the burning bodies'.[37]

Conclusion

The biographer zealously defends the uniqueness of his subject. The historian, however, cannot ignore the opportunity to search out the common ground. Was the road taken by each of these women purely individual or were there factors of character, world-view, and social position, common to them all, that helped make possible the journey? In what sense were Josephine Butler, Octavia Hill, and Florence Nightingale 'products of their time'? Was it coincidence that these women emerged as national leaders in the same country, England, in the same period, the latter half of the nineteenth century, and that their accomplishments were accompanied by the forward impetus of the woman's movement?

Before turning to the deeper questions, one might say a word about the surface relationships of time and place. Florence Nightingale had said that one of the evils of British society was that there were no 'types' for women. She, however, found a type for herself and for others: Octavia Hill she believed was a 'saviour'.

> Why does she raise these people while other lady visitors only pauperize them? She does not remove them from their surroundings, requires the rent to be paid regularly, she herself has to work for her own bread; they see that she does not come among them as Lady Bountiful. . . . Saviours work by taking people who are not saviours and setting them to work.[1]

She scolded George Eliot for having delivered her heroine, Dorothea Brooke, into the hands of two worthless men when she could have offered her the life of an Octavia Hill.

> This author can find no better outlet for the heroine . . . than to marry an elderly sort of literary impostor, and, quick after him, his relation, a baby sort of itinerant Cluricaune (see *Irish Fairies*) or inferior Faun (see Hawthorne's matchless *Transformation*). Yet close at hand was a woman — an Idealist too — and if we

mistake not, a connection of the author's, who had managed to make her ideal very real indeed. By taking charge of blocks of buildings in poorest London, while making herself the rent-collector, she brought sympathy and education to bear from individual to individual. . . . Could not the heroine 'the sweet, sad, enthusiast', have been set to some such work as this?[2]

If Florence Nightingale found Octavia Hill a type, Octavia Hill returned the compliment. Her comment shows that Florence Nightingale was an inspiration to many daughters — and a cautionary example to their mothers.

Miss B. has been offered the Secretaryship of the Children's Hospital, but her father and mother say that no daughter ought to leave home except to be married, or to earn her own living, witness Florence Nightingale, who has returned a mere wreck. Why if there ever was an example fitted to stir up heroism, it might be hers! I wonder if her mother were asked whether she was prouder or fonder of her before her work or after? Or whether she grudged the health which she herself has sacrificed so willingly?[3]

Sociologically speaking, Josephine Butler's work with the 'undeserving' poor started where Octavia Hill's left off. The two spheres touched geographically at least once. The readers of the *Pall Mall Gazette* had been scandalized by what they read of child-selling in London and they reacted with the usual sequence of response to the revelation of an unpleasant reality: fear was quickly followed by flight. Property values plummeted on James Street, Marylebone, the street inhabited by the now notorious Armstrongs who had sold their daughter to William Stead. Octavia Hill, with her eye for a bargain, bought the houses, improved them, added some new cottages, persuaded the London County Council to change the name of the street, and moved in her people.

It could also be argued that Florence Nightingale was partly responsible for Josephine Butler's ordeal. The Contagious Diseases Acts were passed in the heat of the reforming mood that swept the country, a mood created by her Crimean revelations. All the medical men — and the few women doctors — favoured the Acts. Given Florence Nightingale's dedication to the health of the Army, she might have been expected to follow suit. She was, however, morally disgusted with the Continental system. (She also clung to the conviction that if soldiers were given tea and books they would lose interest in alcohol and sex.) She was ambivalent to Josephine Butler's overture and the Manifesto of 1869. Benjamin Jowett, no doubt remembering his own awkward encounters with Josephine Butler, wrote, 'Refer her to Army reports, say you have no time for it.' She rejected Jowett's advice. To the distress of her medical colleagues and the satisfaction of the Abolitionists, she added her signature to the Manifesto.

1   What They Were Given: Family, Class, Place, and Time

All three women were remarkable from the beginning. As children their exceptional abilities were recognized; their parents and close relatives respected their character, energy, imagination, and tenacity. As adults they displayed an impressive combination of gifts: the intellectual abilities of the writer; the charisma of the leader; the intuitive knowledge of character; and the sense of timing of the politician. These gifts were present in embryonic form in each child.

They were in fact exceptional children born to exceptional parents, their abilities differing only in degree from those of their brothers and sisters. Hannah Grey was a woman of character and good sense. Although John Grey never sought political office, his wise management of the vast estates under his care and his work in political and agricultural causes established him as a policy-maker of national scope. Caroline Hill's courage and independence, her abilities as teacher, writer, and administrator made her a strong model. James Hill ended a defeated man; yet he handed on to his children an optimism, a willingness to work for reform, a dedication to the cultural life of the community that anticipated the aspirations of The Society for the Diffusion of Beauty founded by his daughters. It is hard to make a case for Fanny Nightingale but William had his good points: he cared deeply for his family and took responsibility as a community leader. The Greys, the Hills, and even the Nightingales, expected that their sons and daughters would carry on the family tradition of active involvement in national life.

These parents supplied an education that extended and developed the innate abilities of their children. If you were born a Grey or a Hill or a Nightingale you were blessed in being spared much formal schooling. You were given time to be alone, the discipline of family living, animals, sports, a beautiful countryside, lessons in history, classics, music, and geography offered by teachers who loved both their subject and their student-daughters and sons. To a degree the education given these children unwittingly — and in the case of the Hills, deliberately — followed the principles of liberal education advocated by Froebel, Pestallozzi, and Rousseau, which were beginning to make themselves known in England. Along with Wordsworth and the Romantics, it celebrated the innocence of childhood. Based on the ideal of maintaining the unity of thought and feeling, experience and intellectual learning, introspection and action, it produced individuals of rare integrity.

What the parents expected of their sons they also expected of their daughters. John Grey hoped that all his children would, in the light of the Christian principles he had given them, play a role in shaping England's future. Having been brought up by his widowed mother, he admired women and was active in feminist causes, particularly that of education for women.

> He had indeed been so long accustomed to give his wife and daughters a share in, and to confer with them on all matters of interest and importance, political, social and professional, as well as domestic, that to him it did not appear at all strange that women should rise up to claim a higher education.[4]

His regard for women and his expectations for his daughters were complemented by Hannah with her 'moral discipline' and her stress on thoroughness. Caroline Hill, who had always worked in the world, brought up her daughters to assume that they would have the need, the duty, and the right to use their gifts. While William Nightingale could not encourage Florence to undertake a role that ran counter to society's norms, he had no doubt of her energies and abilities: he had helped to train them.

The feminism of the Greys and the Hills — and to a lesser degree the Nightingales — was unusual. The assumption of class privilege and its link with social responsibility, however, they held in common with other members of their class. As gentry, they chose to lend their support to the middle-class hegemony that ruled England. They expected to get things done; they took it for granted; they thought of themselves as the policy-makers of

England. Though aware that they lacked the power of great wealth, they felt that as moral leaders they were better equipped to govern than the aristocracy. They were not burdened by the requirements of a personal life that involved the management of lands and households the size of medieval kingdoms or distracted by the enticements of picture-buying, horse-breeding, and maintaining the wine cellar; and they were uplifted — and constrained — by a religion that stressed social responsibility as a mark of piety. Thomas Hughes's enormously popular novel *Tom Brown's Schooldays* pays tribute to their qualities, describing them as the backbone of England. While France and Italy were being torn apart by the conflict between a decadent aristocracy that lived in the past and an ignorant working class that inhabited the fantasies of a bloody future, they, the Browns of England, would keep the peace by extending their values as well as a helping hand to the class beneath them.

To a large degree history bears out Hughes's assessment of the Browns and their influence — they helped avert bloodshed; they made peaceful change possible. To take some examples from the field of inquiry of this particular study: all of the reforms described took place in England; they were all initiated by and dependent on middle-class support; in every case the Continent with its weak middle class lagged behind. Both the regulation of prostitution through the suppression of civil rights for women and the establishment of a special police force with its inevitable corruption and venality were initiated by Napoleon. If there was opposition it was muted — aristocratic women were indifferent; poor women were powerless. It was only after an Englishwoman had proved on English soil that the Continental system could be defeated that the hopes of the European middle-class reformers took root. The International Federation for the Abolition of the Governmental Regulation of Prostitution was not founded until 1876, and then only with British encouragement.

Similarly, the accomplishments of Florence Nightingale and Octavia Hill brought new hope to feminists and social reformers on the Continent; *Notes on Nursing* had a large sale; *Homes of the London Poor* was translated into German, and workers came from Holland and Sweden to study the Hill management. French society had welcomed, or at least tolerated, the flamboyance of individual women, a Madame de Stael or a George Sand, particularly when she was witty and charming. It had provided a model for the woman as a dispenser of charity, one who binds up the wounds inflicted by a cruel and male-dominated culture. In the Crimean War the French nurses with their brass-buttoned uniforms and their crisp ways contrasted favourably with Florence Nightingale's 'Mother Brickbat' and her crew of 'fat, drunken old dames'; yet in the nineteenth century it is hard to imagine a Frenchwoman arguing with medical men, soldiers — and winning.

In short, Continental society had not welcomed women as policy-makers. With the exception of the religious communities, it offered them no supportive community and minimized their efforts at reform. In Britain the atmosphere was both more stable and more accommodating: it could impede, but not prevent, the accomplishments of three determined women.

There had been other women of equal ability and gifts, placed in a circle of privilege, raised by devoted and feminist parents, confronted with a world of opportunity for service, who had never moved outside of the family circle. Such was John Grey's sister Margaretta, one of those who had contributed to his high estimate of women. Margaretta had her niece Josephine Butler's intelligence and fire; she was strong-willed and self-confident. 'She possessed great natural eloquence and wished to use it', Josephine reported. 'There is evidence in her writings of some sore and secret rebellion at times against the limitations of her woman's estate, and the hindrances to the use of powers which she felt within her.' Josephine ends her recollections with a direct quote. 'I trusted much in my youth to what might be done by argument, demonstration, and eloquent persuasion, and know now that the truth heeds none of these things.' Margaretta had come to realize that her ability would get her nowhere; 'truth' was heedless because she was living in the wrong time.

She developed a thesis to explain her impotence. Along with other feminist historians she believed that women were living in a particularly difficult era, trapped between a Golden Age — relatively speaking — of medieval Europe in which a few competent women — the Queen, the Lady of the Manor, and the Abbess — had achieved positions of ascendancy, and a new age that had not been born. This interim period of the Industrial Revolution had deprived women of work and responsibility. 'The wise and the unwise, the gifted and the imbecile, yield themselves to the impertinence of custom and limit themselves to what has been the fashion in their circle and station.'[5]

Her niece, along with Florence Nightingale and Octavia Hill, was living in the right time. The mould of social institutions that had so constrained Margaretta Grey and her generation was beginning to crack.

For us today, living in an age of rapid change, it is difficult to appreciate the traumatic psychological effect of the changes of the nineteenth century on those who lived through it; it seems that the lives of the rich and the poor were essentially what they had always been. To the servantless, a household run by thirty servants would not appear too different from a household run by eighty. Hunger and disease, whether they accompanied the rural poverty of the eighteenth-century farm tenant, or the urban poverty of the nineteenth-century slum dweller, are everywhere the same. Nevertheless, the Western world by the end of the nineteenth century had entered a new age.

The changes were revolutionary and essential. Their effect can perhaps be summarized in one simple truth — before the Industrial Revolution English people had looked at their children and grandchildren and had seen themselves: individuals who would grow up to look out over the same fields or rooftops, whose values were formed by the same religion, whose work and play, marriages, and political activities reflected the same interests. Even if they died on a battlefield halfway across the world, they died for the same Sovereign, the same Defender of the Faith, who had sent their forefathers to Crécy, Agincourt, and Jerusalem, under the banner of St George. By the end of the century this was no longer true. Judging by the changes in their own lives, they knew that the lives of their children in context, values, and the texture of daily living would be radically different from theirs. They looked at their children and saw strangers.

Technology had changed the face of England and the lives of its people. The country had moved to the city. The growing lines of division between rich and poor which observers had begun to trace in the 1860s, thinking that the angle of divergence was but a temporary phenomenon, remained unaltered. The predictions of the gloomiest prophets were coming true. By the 1880s the population of London was increasing by 80,000 people a year. Charles Booth's work in the 1890s showed that one-third of London lived in conditions of extreme poverty; General William

Booth's *In Darkest England* illustrated these statistics in a frightening manner. By 1884, according to Jane Addams, the poor in the East End had become a tourist attraction. The cumulative evidence was overwhelming; the promises of capitalism had proved to be illusory; it had brought great wealth to a few, prosperity to some, and misery to millions.

The acknowledgement of this reality destroyed the mid-century harmony on which the ideals of thrift, 'self-help', and domesticity had been built. To an observer returning from Mile End Road and the crowds who huddled around the vegetable vendors' carts, with their 'myriads of hands, empty, pathetic, nerveless, and workworn, showing white in the uncertain light of the street, and clutching forward for food which was already unfit to eat',[6] the words of John Bright, as quoted by Samuel Smiles in 1860, could only have had an ironic ring.

> There is no reason why the condition of the average workman in this country should not be a useful, honourable, respectable and a happy one. The whole body of the working classes might (with few exceptions) be as frugal, virtuous, well-informed, and well-conditioned as many individuals of the same class have already made themselves. What some men are, all without difficulty might be.[7]

The failure of capitalism and the radical change in the relation between rich and poor, country and city, affected perceptions and values. It was impossible to speak of the Englishman's home as his castle when many did not have homes. The Victorian emphasis on the family as an enclosed sanctuary had not been able to keep at bay the anarchy and hunger that threw their shadows over the warmth of the hearth. Earlier scenes of domestic interiors with their saccharine depictions of the rosy-faced wife and children, clustering around the reclining figure of the tired but happy Papa — 'Home at Last', now seemed an almost demonic mockery.

These domestic and agrarian values had become increasingly isolated; unconfirmed by the facts of the natural world, they found little support in the supernatural one. If Thomas Arnold could speak eloquently in the 1830s of the essential truths of Christianity and the fullness of the 'sea of faith', his son in the 1880s heard only its 'melancholy, long, withdrawing roar'. The scepticism that had weakened faith, substituting for many faith in science for belief in God, gradually permeated the realm of ethics.

If God had *not* created a patterned universe with matched species, each one with a given nature and a specific role to play in the Divine Plan, was it not equally likely that ethical views were also relative, products of the tumultuous 'survival of the fittest'? If the Bible was inaccurate in its account of the geology of the earth and the history of Israel, how could it be trusted in its views on the ordering of society? Was it not time perhaps for women to question a view based on the norms of an ancient, primitive, tribal, oriental, patriarchal society that defined them as 'Adam's rib'?

When times are changing, the 'haves' retreat, reaffirming a narrower version of their old values. The 'have-nots' — and the small percentage of 'haves' who choose to identify with them — move forward, opening themselves to the possibility that the changes they have endured will be positively reshaped by changes in other areas. Economic changes bring social change, perhaps not as mechanistically as the Marxists claim, but by creating the possibility of a new vision. As Canon Barnett has said, 'the need is for a poet, . . . someone who will make a vision, or give a conception of the city or society which will unite the actions of good people'.[8] Stirred by the hope of a better life, impelled by the acknowledgement that the old is not working, a few people permit themselves to dream.

By 1880 there were many women — and some men — who felt that women should no longer be considered primarily as domestic functionaries: the time had come to invite their full participation in British national life. These new feminists joined their voices to those of the old feminists, most notably the Quakers, and formed the basis for Josephine Butler's, Octavia Hill's, and Florence Nightingale's support. Without this support their accomplishments would have been impossible.

In opposition, the conservatives held with renewed tenacity to the Victorian ideal of family life and the place of women; they could not, however, deny reality forever. Their ideal was as fragile as it was rigid. The 'woman-on-the-pedestal' could not resist the pressures of events; there were problems that demanded resolution; people were on the move. 'It is time to rise out of this, and for women of principles and natural parts to find themselves something to do', wrote Margaretta Grey in the 1840s. The times had held her too tightly; she had been unable to move, but twenty years later her niece would break free.

2 *What They Made of It: Feminism and Faith*

In its impatience with the Victorian age, the twentieth century has been guilty of accepting its stereotypes at face value.

In reality the view of women was far from simple. On the surface all seemed clear: women were considered to be modest, weak, incompetent, emotional, irrational, submissive, and dependent. (Men were courageous, strong, aggressive and decisive, competent, rational, and independent.) Yet one must remember that this view of the female, and its polarity with the male, represented the male view of the ideal. Its relation to reality was not fixed; there was tension and ambiguity. Sometimes the ideal served as wish-fulfilment; sometimes it acted not merely as a disembodied hope but as a value, a role-model presented for its pragmatic power to change reality. Grandfathers pressed upon their bloomered progeny copies of Maria Edgeworth and Charlotte Yonge, taken from the family library, hoping to soften the edges of emergent womanhood. Sometimes the ideal was deliberately presented as the reality: medical men gave biological facts that would account for the instability of the female nervous system; they served up statistics on the small cranial capacity of the female. But the attempt to deny women opportunity on the basis of biology was doomed by a flawed assumption: if reality and the ideal are one and the same, the ideal becomes redundant. If women had really been docile they would not have needed to be told to be docile; had they really been stupid, there would have been no cause to steer them away from intellectual pursuits.

To find out what Victorian men really thought women were like, one should turn to the male authors. Presented with Mrs Prouty and the managing Lady Glencora, the reader was reminded of women he had known — a grandmother or a difficult great-aunt. Equally it is evident that the women characters Dickens chose to admire were not the soppy Noras or Little Nells but Betsey Trotwood, Peggotty, and Edith Dombey.

By the end of the century the wise, strong-willed older woman, who, like the Chinese grandmother, manipulates her world, who brings about the reversal in the third act and reunites the young couple, was to become a stock figure. The theme of James Barrie's 'What Every Woman Knows' is expressed by the title; yet it is incomplete if its wider meaning is not recognized. Behind every man there is a woman, a woman whose greatness includes the ability to mask her powers, thus catering to male vanity — so speaks Barrie. This theme, along with its highly insulting view of the male, was presented by a male writer for an audience that was at least half male. And they received it with delight. Perhaps Barrie knew that after the curtain was down they would turn to their women companions and confess: they had known the truth all along — they had in fact gone along with it, making the most of it. The battle between the sexes had become a kind of shadow-boxing, ending sometimes in estrangement and a deadening isolation, in other cases redeemed by affection and common sense. It was based on fantasies that no-one fully believed. Barrie's joke, then, was not told at the expense of men, or of women — it was 'what everyone knows'.

Twentieth-century critics have been equally guilty in over-simplifying the Victorian male. Here the problem is not so much that the man did not live up to the ideal as that the ideal itself was weakened by inner contradictions. The male is courageous, strong, aggressive, rational and independent — so runs the description. Yet this is only part of the picture. Man is rational, according to the Victorians — but not too intelligent. A display of intellect was often considered suspect, even effeminate. Tom Brown, everyone's hero, a bluff, loyal fellow — a man's man, was proud of being a poor scholar. As for emotionalism, this was a male as well as a female prerogative; nor was it a sign of vitiated masculinity. 'Muscular' Christians, proud of their manliness, enthusiastically heterosexual, physically demonstrative, were particularly prone to the shedding of tears. A brief survey indicates that there was no difference between the male and the female in this respect. Not only the milestones of birth, marriage, and death, but the parting of friends, the sight of a hungry child, and even the excitement of a sunset, were liable to bring on an attack. The only distinction between women's and men's tears is that a woman sheds 'tears' and a man sheds 'manly tears'.

It is hardly surprising to find that Butler, Hill, and Nightingale reflect this complexity, speaking on the one hand of the 'comple-mentary natures' of the male and female and on the other of universally human traits shared by all. Butler describes the male instinct for the planning of large and comprehensive schemes and the female gift for compassion. Hill, in justifying her opposition to votes for women, took refuge in the argument from different gifts and spheres, even though her own life rebuked her words. Nightingale advocated the complementary relation of marriage partners, though it is not clear whether the differences arose from the nature of the partners as individuals or as members of their sex.

This 'different but complementary' view they based squarely on the value they placed on woman as mother. They felt that the maternal instinct must be extended to the world at large. Butler believed that social reform is only possible when it is based on the female instinct for caring for people as individuals, an instinct that grew out of the maternal principle; Hill attributed much of her practicality, her ability to deal with the daily life of her tenants, to her maternal nature. She was conservative in the root sense of the word, 'mothering' not only individuals but plants and old buildings. Nightingale when a girl extended a protective mantle over her young cousins, particularly her 'boy Shore', and brought back a baby owl from her trip to Greece. The organization of the medical services first emerged as a problem to be resolved because her woman's nature cried out at the loss of life. 'Oh, my poor men, I am a bad mother to come home and leave you to your Crimean graves.' To 'do the Lord's work', to become a 'handmaiden of the Lord' was to extend the maternal talent for caring, nursing, and healing to the uncared for, the sick and the unloved.

They had been warned by their culture, however, even by their religion: they must confine their talent to a small sphere. Hannah More and other tract writers stressed the social obligations of women; yet they contented themselves with reinforcing the old Lady Bountiful strain of female piety with a new fervour. The extension of the maternal instinct, the love of neighbour prescribed by religion, must confine itself to small acts of kindness to individuals — 'poor peopling', as Florence Nightingale called it, emphasizing its trivial and snobbish character. If a man were injured in the local factory the Lady might send a hamper of jellies to his family, but she must not go further. To inquire about the facts of the accident, the safety regulations in the factory, to go to see the owner — all these were forbidden to her. Elizabeth Fry was welcomed as a prison visitor who read from the Bible to inmates of Newgate Prison, but her policies for reform were defeated. Woman's role was to soothe the wounds inflicted in the immediate past; she must not interfere with the present or try to influence the future.

Butler, Hill, and Nightingale drew radical conclusions from the deification of motherhood used by the culture as a way of keeping women out of the mainstream. Like Barrie, they had seen that the emphasis upon the maternal nature of women could lead in two very different directions. It had helped create a society that was based on an unequal relationship between man and woman, which relegated woman to the home and subjected her to man's rule; yet the exaggerated importance given to maternity could lead to a dramatic reversal of this arrangement. If woman is essentially and primarily a mother, she will use her nature, not only in governing the boy, but, if given the chance, in governing the man. As ruler of the tidy kingdom of hearth and home, she has learned the art of statesmanship; set free she will apply it to everything she touches. The world cries out for her services. Her beneficence will only be felt when she gives free rein to her abilities. Her acceptance of a call to serve the family of mankind will place her in a commanding position, and through it she will reassert the superiority she has lost.

The widening of woman's sphere practised by Butler, Hill, and Nightingale undercuts their statements concerning the complementary roles of men and women. Judging from their actions and deep-seated attitudes, one concludes that they found little that distinguished the male from the female in terms of gifts or appropriate spheres of action. The paternal instinct, like the maternal, is a source of affection and compassion. Josephine Butler gave full expression of appreciation to her male co-workers. She did not consider George's fatherly solicitude towards the poor and the outcast to be less profound than her own maternal concern. Octavia Hill, taking her cue from a Christianity that likened the love of God for the world to that between father and child, describes 'fatherly' concern as immediate and deep, as intense as that of a mother. Florence Nightingale felt that her men friends threw themselves into her work with a complete understanding and sympathy.

They stressed woman's maternal nature; yet they felt no need to tie their identities to a set of traits labelled 'female'. Josephine Butler at her most aggressive — stubborn, fearless, and coming up fighting — continued to think of herself as an intensely feminine woman, a view shared by her male colleagues. Octavia Hill, on the other hand, enjoyed being called 'Loke, my brother' by her sisters, and probably would not have objected to the estimate of those friends who saw an element of masculinity in her 'massiveness of character'. Florence Nightingale, particularly as she grew older, tended to shy away from any identification with the corrupt and weakened version of womanhood that she saw around her. She extolled the male and his virtues. She proudly compared her friendship with Sidney Herbert to that between two men. It was 'just like that between Sidney Herbert and Gladstone'.

Looking at the current debate, it is hard to see that much has been clarified. Some stress the differences between male and female, yang and yin, active and passive. Like the Victorians, they advocate a complementary relationship. They believe, however, that this exists not in society but within each individual, whose nature is essentially androgynous. Others, noting that maternity has been used as an excuse to confine women, advocate cutting them free from biology. They play down biological mothering, while claiming social mothering as woman's natural role. They perceive the yang principle as exploitive. They look to the maternal instinct to nurse the ravaged earth back to health.

It is hardly surprising that these issues are unresolved. Like the 'nature—nurture' controversy of which they are a part, they are irresolvable. No matter how 'liberated' we become, sexuality can never be purely 'natural'; it will always be conditioned by the imaginations and visions that have shaped our culture. Studies may provide useful insights. We can purge the language, rewrite history, study the effects of raising and lowering hormone levels, compare the behaviour of mothers and fathers in parenting infants and analyse the dynamics of men's and women's groups. But with none of these can we penetrate to 'pure' male and female nature. At birth every child is male or female in a social as well as a physical sense, an unwitting receptor of his or her society's expectations.

Here Butler, Hill, and Nightingale speak to us with great good sense. They say — first, give women and men equal opportunity. Then, forget definitions: men and women will find their identity not through mimicking attitudes and behaviour that have been labelled 'male' or 'female' but in expending their energies and talents in service to the community. Nightingale was annoyed with the focus on 'rights' only because she felt that it deflected women from a more important task — the finding of a 'type'.

'Surely woman should bring the best she has, whatever that is, to the work of God's world .' In bringing 'the best' she would find a 'type' for herself as an individual woman.

The chief contribution of these three to the women's movement thus grew out of the Christian and humanist assumptions that were the basis for their work. Their originality lay not in their social concerns but in the way they expressed those concerns. Casting off their culture's view of woman's role, they became policy-makers. Like Gladstone impelled by his High-Church sense of duty, and Shaftesbury, driven to social action by his evangelical faith, they used every means at their command. Even Octavia Hill, who professed to dislike politics, would have admitted that her lasting influence came from her work as a policy-maker. Her stress on the importance of individual influence was after all a policy, perhaps the key principle she left her workers. She worked for it with every means at her command. Like the male leaders of their era, they used persuasion, political influence, money — all the perquisites of power, the means made available by their class, position, and ability. Serving the world, engaging as deeply as possible with its needs, they achieved their own self-fulfilment and helped break new ground for the next generation of women.

In 1838 Octavia Hill's half-sister had written of her hopes that in the course of the century 'great changes' in the position of women would occur. These changes were slow in coming and each advance was accompanied by a partial defeat. Courageously many women and a few men succeeded in doing away with economic and political disabilities that afflicted women as a group — property and marriage laws, voting laws, and regulations affecting education. By placing women and their problems in a special category, however, the movement also played into the hands of those who wished to deny women full equality. The inference was drawn that while men concerned themselves with the serious and important affairs of the world, women were interested only in women. What was progress on the one hand was on the other fed back into the steadily grinding mills of prejudice.

Butler, Hill, and Nightingale showed that women could work in the world as effectively as men. The scope of their accomplishments is remarkable. Octavia Hill's views on housing and community had important implications for national policy. All of Great Britain is indebted to her for the preservation of the countryside and the national heritage. Florence Nightingale's personal concerns affected much of the globe. Josephine Butler worked on behalf of a particular group, prostitutes, but she always considered her natural constituency to be the community of mankind. 'I wish it were felt that women who were labouring especially for women are not one-sided or selfish. We care for the evils affecting women most of all because they react upon the whole of society and abstract from the common good.'[9] There cannot have been many who believed with her that by lifting the poor female she also redeemed the wealthy male. But her friends understood her. 'She alone saw the question as one.'

* * *

'The common good', 'community service' have a dull ring, evoking endless meetings in stuffy rooms. For Hill, Butler, and Nightingale, however, community service was a journey, undertaken with the eagerness of the explorer. As 'Daughters of God' they had been freed from the restrictions that caste and society had imposed upon them and set on their way.

Voyagers, they were also builders. They followed a single plan; yet each shaped it according to her individual vision. Secure in her own life, Josephine Butler took the happiness of the Christian family for granted; she attacked the social injustice that threatened it. Octavia Hill helped construct a home for the Children of God. Florence Nightingale spoke of love, yet the Kingdom that she fashioned was no home. It was a well-run sanatorium where windows are flung open to receive the cold, cleansing winds of 'Law', 'Wisdom', and 'Perfection' — with one locked room set aside to receive those few patients who would not accept its regulations.

Yet the image of the builder is somewhat misleading. Each believed that God, not she, is the builder. They were in fact not builders but demolition experts; their job was to clear away the evils, most of them of human origin, that had prevented the Kingdom from being fully realized. Once this is done, the spirit of God will again flow freely through the Kingdom, bringing life and uniting the community of mankind.

Their faith, its expression in their writings, was a map and a journal. As a map it showed the stopping places along the way. It helped distinguish an oasis from a mirage. As a journal it helped each find her own voice, while at the same time freeing her from the delusions of self-centredness, the accretions of irrelevant or false beliefs. It helped bring her to that 'clarity of existence' (Erikson) that comes from the conjunction of self-fulfilment and self-sacrifice, work and play, feeling and thought, God and the self.

In a world in which many have abandoned the struggle for unity, these lives shine with a strange and compelling light.

Notes

PREFACE

1. David Owen, *English Philanthropy, 1660-1960* (Cambridge, Mass.: Harvard University Press, Belknap Press, 1964), p. 394.
2. E. Moberly Bell, *Octavia Hill: A Biography* (London: Constable & Co., 1942), p. ix.
3. Edward Cook, *The Life of Florence Nightingale*, 2 vols. (London: Macmillan & Co., 1913), I, 185.
4. Robert Coles, *Erik H. Erikson: The Growth of His Work* (Boston: Little Brown & Co., 1970), p. 351.

INTRODUCTION

1. J.B. Priestley, *Victoria's Heyday* (New York: Harper & Row, 1972), p. 197.
2. John Stuart Mill, in Alburey Costell (ed.), *On Liberty* (New York: F. S. Crofts & Co., 1947), p. 43.
3. Samuel Smiles, *Self-Help* (Boston: Ticknor & Fields, 1861), p. 297.
4. John Ruskin, 'Unto This Last', in E. T. Cook and Alexander Wedderburn, (eds.) *Works* Library edn, 39 vols. (London: G. Allen New York: Longmans, Green & Co., 1912 – 13), XII, 81.
5. Patricia Branca suggests that the problem of 'surplus women' was hardly new and that in fact the percentage of unmarried women was lower in the nineteenth than in previous centuries (Patricia Branca, *Silent Sisterhood: Middle-Class Women in the Victorian Home,* London: Croom Helm, 1975, pp. 2-5). If she is correct, we must then attribute the importance given by Victorian society to the single woman and her problems, not to demographic change, but to rising expectations. That the fate of 'surplus women' was regarded as a problem indicates that the voice of the governess and the maiden aunt was for the first time making itself heard.
6. Isabella Beeton, *The Book of Household Management* (London: S. O. Beeton, 1861), p. 1.
7. Quoted in Owen Chadwick, *An Ecclesiastical History of England* (series). *The Victorian Church* (Part I – New York: Oxford University Press; Part II – London: Adam & Charles Black, 1970), II, 78.
8. Josephine E. Butler, *Recollections of George Butler* (Bristol: J.W. Arrowsmith, 1892), p. 141.
9. C. Edmund Maurice, ed., *Life of Octavia Hill as Told in her Letters* (London: Macmillan & Co., 1913), p. 176.
10. Cook, *Nightingale*, I, 498.
11. *Ibid.*, 484.

CHAPTER 1

1. Josephine E. Butler, *Memoir of John Grey of Dilston*, revised edn (London: Henry S. King & Co., 1874), p. 25.
2. *Ibid.*, p. 13.
3. *Ibid.*, p. 217.
4. E. Moberly Bell, *Josephine Butler: Flame of Fire* (London: Constable & Co., 1962), p. 22.
5. Butler, *Memoir*, p. 192.
6. Josephine E. Butler, *In Memoriam Harriet Meuricoffre* (London: Horace Marshall, 1901), p. 8.
7. George W. and Lucy A. Johnson, eds., *Josephine E. Butler, an Autobiographical Memoir* (London: Arrowsmith, 1909), p. 15.
8. Josephine E. Butler, *Recollections of George Butler* (Bristol: Arrowsmith, 1892), p. 209.
9. Fawcett Library MS 8.5 (76), f. 5.
10. Fawcett Library MS 8.5 (76), f. 6.
11. Glen Petrie, *A Singular Iniquity: The Campaigns of Josephine Butler* (New York: The Viking Press, 1971), p. 26, quoting Josephine Butler to Stanley E. Butler, 1893.
12. A. S. G. Butler, *Portrait of Josephine Butler* (London: Faber & Faber, 1954), p. 74.
13. Butler, *Memoir*, p. 161.
14. A. S. G. Butler, *Portrait*, p. 180; Johnson and Johnson, *Butler*, p. 15.
15. Butler, *Memoir*, p. 168.
16. Johnson and Johnson, *Butler*, p. 15.
17. In Josephine Butler's biography of George Butler, the chief source of her own later life as well as that of her husband, she includes this charming testimony to George's love of fishing: 'I have sometimes been unable to suppress a smile in some solemn meeting when he occupied a prominent place on the platform, I have caught the furtive movement of his right hand, the graceful turn from side to side of the wrist, and the far-off look in his eyes; he was fishing in his imagination!' (Butler, *Recollections*, p. 365).
18. *Ibid.*, p. 97.
19. *Ibid.*, pp. 97-8.
20. *Ibid.*, pp. 95-6.
21. *Ibid.*, p. 98.
22. In deploring the dependence of the classical curriculum on exclusively literary sources, Josephine cites an example of the prevailing ignorance of geography. 'A letter had been received from A.P. Stanley, who was travelling in Egypt. "Where is Cairo?" someone asked, turning to the map spread on the table. I put the question to an accomplished College tutor. His eye wandered hopelessly over the chart; he could not even place his hand on Egypt. I was fain to pretend that I needed to study my performance more closely, and bent down my head in order to conceal the irreverent laughter which overcame me.' (*Ibid.*, p. 88).
23. *Ibid.*, p. 153.
24. *Ibid.*, p. 183.
25. *Ibid.*, p. 184.

26. Bell, *Butler*, p. 55.
27. *Ibid.*, p. 59.
28. Elizabeth Wolstenholme (Elmy), a friend of Emily Davies, was a leader in the movement for educational, voting, and legal rights for women. She is especially remembered for her role in promoting the Married Women's Property Acts of 1870 and 1882.
29. Butler, *Recollections*, p. 219.
30. E. M. Sigsworth and T. J. Wyke, 'A Study of Victorian Prostitution', in Martha Vicinus (ed.), *Suffer and Be Still: Women in the Victorian Age* (Bloomington and London: Indiana University Press, 1973), p. 221, f. 67.
31. Bell, *Butler*, p. 105.
32. Petrie, *Singular Iniquity*, p. 115.
33. *Ibid.*, p. 149.
34. While acknowledging the contribution of Josephine Butler and her supporters, Sigsworth and Wyke in 'A Study of Victorian Prostitution' have suggested that in the end the Acts were defeated only because they proved ineffective. Since their scope was local they could be circumvented; the cost of extending them to all of Britain and of maintaining medical and police officers on a national scale would have been prohibitive, the authors maintain.

    Yet extension of the laws to the entire civil population is exactly what the Regulationists proposed. There is no indication that they feared the cost. Furthermore, they could — and did — point to the Continent where the experiment had been tried on a national scale and where its proponents attested to its effectiveness.

    There is every evidence that Parliament was moved, not by financial considerations, but by fear of losing the support of a constituency that had been aroused by the moral arguments and religious fervour of the Abolitionists.
35. Johnson and Johnson, *Butler*, p. 135.
36. A. S. G. Butler, *Portrait*, pp. 111—14.
37. *Ibid.*, pp. 117—18.
38. H. Scott Holland, *A Bundle of Memories* (London: Wells Gardner, Darton and Co., 1915), p. 288.

CHAPTER 2

1. Petrie, *Singular Iniquity*, p. 116.
2. F. W. H. Myers, Preface to *Fragments of Prose and Poetry* (1904).
3. Geoffrey Faber, *Jowett: A Portrait with Background* (Cambridge, Mass.: Harvard University Press, 1958), p. 93.
4. Holland, *Memories*, p. 288.
5. *The Storm-Bell*, January 1900.
6. Butler, *Recollections*, pp. 341-3.
7. *Ibid.*, p. 208.
8. Josephine E. Butler, *The Lady of Shunem* (London: Horace Marshall, 1894), p. 21.
9. Butler, *Recollections*, p. 348.

10. Johnson and Johnson, *Butler*, p. 241.
11. Butler, *Recollections*, pp. 62-3.
12. *Ibid.*, p. 376.
13. Bell, *Butler*, p. 206.
14. Butler, *Recollections*, p. 74.
15. *Ibid.*, pp. 64-5.
16. Johnson and Johnson, *Butler*, p. 232.
17. *Ibid.*, p. 308.
18. Butler, *Lady of Shunem*, pp. 102-3.
19. Johnson and Johnson, *Butler*, pp. 305-7.
20. Butler, *Recollections*, pp. 248-9.
21. *Ibid.*, p. 404.
22. Johnson and Johnson, *Butler*, p. 178.
23. Butler, *Recollections*, p. 99.
24. Bell, *Butler*, p. 37.
25. A. S. G. Butler, *Portrait*, pp. 175-6.
26. *Ibid.*, pp. 181-2.
27. Johnson and Johnson, *Butler*, p. 238.
28. *Ibid.*, p. 254.
29. A. S. G. Butler, *Portrait*, p. 179.
30. Butler, *Recollections*, pp. 218-19.
31. Johnson and Johnson, *Butler*, p. 283.
32. Petrie, *Singular Iniquity*, p. 206.
33. Bell, *Butler*, p. 163.
34. Johnson and Johnson, *Butler*, pp. 135-6.
35. Butler, *Woman's Work and Woman's Culture* (London: Macmillan & Co., 1869), pp. liii — liv.
36. Johnson and Johnson, *Butler*, p. 35.
37. W. T. Stead. *Josephine Butler: A Life Sketch* (London: Morgan & Scott, 1887), p. 91.
38. Butler, *Recollections*, p. 223.

CHAPTER 3

1. A. S. G. Butler, *Portrait*, p. 28.
2. Johnson and Johnson, *Butler*, pp. 178-9.
3. Butler, *Woman's Work*, p. lviii.
4. *Ibid.*, pp. lix — lx.
5. Butler, *Woman's Work*, p. xxxi.
6. *Ibid.*, p. xxxvii.
7. *Ibid.*, p. xxxix.
8. *Ibid.*, p. xxxvii.
9. *Ibid.*, p. xxxviii.
10. Josephine E. Butler, *The Constitution Violated* (Edinburgh: Edmonston & Douglas, 1871), p. 176.
11. Josephine E. Butler, *The Voice of One Crying in the Wilderness* (Paris and Neuchatel: Sandoz, 1875), p. 33.
12. Johnson and Johnson, *Butler*, p. 285.

13. *Ibid.*, p. 281.
14. Bell, *Butler*, p. 233.
15. Josephine Butler heralded the publication of Tolstoy's *Resurrection*. This account, classic in its familiarity, of the seduction and abandonment of a woman who turns to prostitution in order to feed her child, is followed by the story of the search for forgiveness and restitution, the spiritual pilgrimage, of the man who seduced her. According to Butler, Tolstoy is unique in understanding the true nature of the tragedy.
16. Johnson and Johnson, *Butler*, p. 212.
17. *Ibid.*, p. 148.
18. Butler, *Lady of Shunem*, pp. 128-9.
19. *Ibid.*, p. 132 ff.; cf. Johnson and Johnson, *Butler*, p. 227.
20. A. S. G. Butler, *Portrait*, p. 182.
21. Butler, *Recollections*, pp. 155-7.
22. *Ibid.*, p. 161.
23. For a fascinating account of the death scene in biography and its evolution see A. O. J. Cockshut, *Truth to Life: The Art of Biography in the Nineteenth Century* (New York and London: Harcourt Brace Jovanovich, 1974), pp. 41-54.
24. Butler, *Recollections*, p. 479.
25. A. S. G. Butler, *Portrait*, p. 184.
26. Josephine E. Butler, *The Hour Before the Dawn* (London: Trubner, 1876), p. 60.
27. Butler, *Recollections*, pp. 343-4.
28. Petrie, *Singular Iniquity*, p. 227.
29. Fawcett Library MS B 5 (76), f. 9.
30. Butler, *Hour Before the Dawn*, p. 108.
31. *Ibid.*, p. 106.
32. *Ibid.*, pp. 110-11.
33. Watts had wanted to include — along with Josephine Butler — Elizabeth Barrett Browning, George Eliot, and Florence Nightingale as the four most important women. Josephine Butler's portrait is the only one that was completed.
34. A. S. G. Butler, *Portrait*, pp. 106-7.

CHAPTER 4

1. C. Edmund Maurice, ed., *Life of Octavia Hill as Told in her Letters* (London: Macmillan & Co., 1913), p. 4.
2. E. Moberly Bell, *Hill*, p. 12.
3. C. Edmund Maurice, *Life*, p. 6.
4. Bell, *Hill*, p. 9.
5. C. Edmund Maurice, *Life*, p. 4.
6. *Ibid.*
7. The leaders included the Chartist tailor, Walter Cooper, John Malcolm Ludlow, Charles Kingsley, F. D. Maurice, and Thomas Hughes. It was financed by Vansittart Neale. Started after the failure of Chartism in 1848, the cooperatives were plagued by economic problems and division among the leaders. They ceased to exist in the late 1850s.

8. C. Edmund Maurice, *Life*, p. 17.
9. *Ibid.*, p. 18.
10. *Ibid.*, p. 22.
11. *Ibid.*, p. 29.
12. *Ibid.*, pp. 38-9.
13. *Ibid.*, p. 75.
14. Emily S. Maurice, ed., *Octavia Hill: Early Ideals* (London: George Allen & Unwin, 1928), p. 1.
15. *Ibid.*, p. 130.
16. Bell, *Hill*, p. 34.
17. *Ibid.*, p. 36.
18. C. Edmund Maurice, *Life*, p. 64.
19. *Ibid.*, pp. 37-8.
20. *Ibid.*, p. 92.
21. *Ibid.*, p. 96.
22. Bell, *Hill*, p. 64.
23. Octavia Hill, *Homes of the London Poor* (London: Macmillan & Co., 1875), p. 21.
24. Scott Holland gives us this anecdote. After years of readying a court for Ruskin's inspection, Octavia Hill proudly invited him 'to see the heaven that had been made out of the horror in which she had begun; the only result was to send Ruskin back home quite sick with disgust at what he had been invited to see' (Holland, *Memories*, p. 280).
25. C. Edmund Maurice, *Life*, pp. 212-13.
26. Bell, *Hill*, p. 78.
27. C. Edmund Maurice, *Life*, p. 266.
28. Henrietta Rowland Barnett, *Canon Barnett, His Life, Works and Friends* (London: John Murray, 1918), II, 28
29. Gareth Stedman Jones, *Outcast London: A Study in the Relationship between Classes in Victorian Society* (Oxford: Clarendon Press, 1971), p. 162.
30. Bell, *Hill*, p. 113.
31. C. Edmund Maurice, *Life*, p. 306.
32. *Ibid.*, pp. 321-2.
33. *Ibid.*, p. 279.
34. Bell, *Hill*, p. 148.
35. *Ibid.*, p. 221.
36. *Ibid.*, p. 154.
37. *Ibid.*, p. 223.
38. *Ibid.*, p. 232.
39. *Ibid.*, p. 235.
40. *Ibid.*, p. 240.
41. This is the number given by A. S. Wohl (A. S. Wohl, 'Octavia Hill and the Homes of the London Poor,' *Journal of British Studies* 10 (2), 107). Enid Gauldie puts the figure between five and six thousand (Enid Gauldie, *Cruel Habitations: A History of Working-Class Housing 1780-1918* (London: George Allen & Unwin, 1974), p. 218).
42. Sidney and Beatrice Webb, *English Poor Law Policy* (London, New York, Bombay and Calcutta: Longmans, Green & Co., 1910), p. 3.
43. C. Edmund Maurice, *Life*, p. 573.

CHAPTER 5

1. Owen, *English Philanthropy*, p. 387.
2. C. Edmund Maurice, *Life*, p. 8.
3. *Ibid.*, pp. 26-7.
4. *Ibid.*, p. 30.
5. Emily S. Maurice, *Ideals*, p. 129.
6. *Ibid.*, pp. 215-16.
7. *Ibid.*, p. 234.
8. C. Edmund Maurice, *Life*, p. 146.
9. Emily S. Maurice, *Ideals*, p. 237.
10. C. Edmund Maurice, *Life*, p. 497.
11. Emily S. Maurice, *Ideals*, p. 63.
12. C. Edmund Maurice, *Life*, p. 535.
13. Hill, *Homes*, p. 46.
14. C. Edmund Maurice, *Life*, p. 160.
15. *Ibid.*, p. 33.
16. *Ibid.*, p. 54.
17. *Ibid.*, p. 89.
18. Emily S. Maurice, *Ideals*, p. 214.
19. *Ibid.*, p. 111.
20. *Ibid.*, p. 59.
21. Emily S. Maurice, *Ideals*, p. 71.
22. C. Edmund Maurice, *Life*, p. 124.
23. Emily S. Maurice, *Ideals*, p. 159.
24. C. Edmund Maurice, *Life*, pp. 572-3.
25. Emily S. Maurice, *Ideals*, p. 41.
26. *Ibid.*, p. 215.
27. Enid Gauldie, *Cruel Habitations*, p. 162.
28. C. Edmund Maurice, *Life*, p. 307.
29. Bell, *Hill*, pp. 216-17.
30. Octavia Hill, 'A Word on Good Citizenship', *Fortnightly Review* (September 1876), XXVI, 321.
31. Bell, *Hill*, pp. 242-3.
32. While Octavia Hill did not provide housing for the destitute, she did take care of many who without her help would have been homeless. A. S. Wohl has helpfully placed Miss Hill's constituency in the categories of Charles Booth (*Life and Labour of the People in London*, I *Poverty*, London, 1902). The model dwelling companies were attracting Class E (regular standard wages) above the poverty line; Miss Hill reached Class C (intermittent earnings) and Class D (small regular earnings) beneath the poverty line. Booth fixed the poverty level at 21s. per week for a family. Miss Hill's rents were 4s. a week for two rooms. Categories C and D totalled over one million people, according to Booth, or 22.3 per cent of the London population, No-one, except the Salvation Army hostels and the dormitory-style boarding houses, accommodated the 'very poor' who composed 16.5 per cent of the population (Wohl, 'Homes', p. 110).
33. Ellen Chase, *Tenant Friends in Old Deptford* (London: Williams and Norgate, 1929), pp. 218-19.

34. C. Edmund Maurice, *Life*, p. 227.
35. Barnett, *Canon Barnett*, I, 227.
36. *Ibid.*, p. 29.
37. Octavia Hill, 'A Word on Good Citizenship', p. 323.
38. Bell, *Hill*, p. 43.
39. *Ibid.*, p. 270.
40. *Ibid.*, p. 271.

CHAPTER 6

1. Emily S. Maurice, *Ideals*, p. 221.
2. *Ibid.*, p. 72.
3. C. Edmund Maurice, *Life*, p. 340.
4. *Ibid.*, p. 55.
5. Emily S. Maurice, *Ideals*, p. 95.
6. C. Edmund Maurice, *Life*, pp. 513-14.
7. Emily S. Maurice, *Ideals*, p. 40.
8. *Ibid*, p. 93.
9. C. Edmund Maurice, *Life*, p. 156.
10. *Ibid.*, p. 32.
11. Bell, *Hill*, pp. 201-2.
12. Elinor Southwood Ouvry, ed., *Extracts from Octavia Hill's Letters to Fellow-Workers, 1864-1911* (London: The Adelphi Bookshop, 1933), p. 26.
13. Bell, *Hill*, pp. 193-4.
14. C. Edmund Maurice, *Life*, p. 545.
15. Emily S. Maurice, *Ideals*, p. 39.
16. Ouvry, *Extracts*, p. 50.
17. Emily S. Maurice, *Ideals*, p. 39.
18. C. Edmund Maurice, *Life*, p. 228.
19. Chase, *Tenant Friends*, p. 1.
20. *Ibid.*, p. 20.
21. *Ibid.*, p. 68.
22. *Ibid.*, p. 9.
23. *Ibid.*, p. 68.
24. Emily S. Maurice, *Ideals*, pp. 53-4.
25. C. Edmund Maurice, *Life*, p. 243.
26. *Ibid.*, p. 279.
27. *Ibid.*, p. 185.
28. Emily S. Maurice, *Ideals*, p. 69.
29. *Ibid.*, p. 59.

CHAPTER 7

1. Sir Edward Cook, *The Life of Florence Nightingale*, 2 vols. (London: Macmillan & Co., 1913), I, 12.
2. BM 45790, f. 177.

3. Cook, *Nightingale*, I, 42.
4. Florence Nightingale, *Suggestions for Thought to the Searchers after Truth among the Artizans of England*, 3 vols. (London: Eyre & Spottiswoode, 1860) II, 26-8.
5. BM 45793, f. 75.
6. Cook, *Nightingale*, I, 43.
7. BM 45794, f. 40.
8. Cook, *Nightingale*, I, 43.
9. *Ibid.*, pp. 44-5.
10. BM 45794, f. 52.
11. BM 45794, f. 40.
12. Cook, *Nightingale*, I, 83.
13. *Ibid.*, pp. 26-7.
14. *Ibid.*, p. 59.
15. BM 45790, f. 70.
16. BM 45793, f. 89.
17. BM 45846, f. 43.
18. Cecil Woodham-Smith, *Florence Nightingale 1820-1910* (New York, London, Toronto: McGraw-Hill Book Co., 1951), p. 58.
19. Frances Baroness Bunsen, *Memoirs of Baron Bunsen*, 2nd edn (London: Longmans, Green & Co., 1869), p. 115.
20. BM 45790, f. 134.
21. BM45790, ff. 141-3.
22. Cook, *Nightingale*, I, 59.
23. *Ibid.*, pp. 133-6.
24. *Ibid*, pp. 138-9.
25. *Ibid*, p. 147, quoting letter to *The Times*.
26. *Ibid.*, p. 148.
27. *Ibid.*, p. 153.
28. *Ibid.*, p. 200.
29. *Ibid.*, p. 199.
30. *Ibid.*, p. 216.
31. *Ibid.*, p. 307.
32. *Ibid.*, p. 332.
33. Nightingale, *Suggestions*, II, 65.
34. BM 45792, f. 149.
35. BM 45849.
36. Cook, *Nightingale*, I, 373.
37. *Ibid.*, p. 372.
38. *Ibid.*, p. 70.

CHAPTER 8

1. Cook, *Nightingale*, II, 487.
2. Nightingale, *Suggestions*, I, 4.
3. BM 45787, f. 14.
4. Cook, *Nightingale*, II, 220.
5. Jowett—Nightingale Correspondence, V, 26, Bailliol College Library.

6. Nightingale, *Suggestions*, III, 80.
7. *Ibid*, I, 215.
8. *Ibid*., II, 96-7.
9. *Ibid*., p. 83.
10. *Ibid*., p. 306.
11. *Ibid*., p. 312.
12. *Ibid*., p. 118.
13. *Ibid*., I, 274.
14. Florence Nightingale, 'A "Note" of Interrogation', *Fraser's Magazine*, New Series, 7 (May 1873), p. 573.
15. Florence Nightingale, 'A "Sub-Note" of Interrogation; What Will our Religion be in 1999?' *Fraser's Magazine*, New Series, 8 (July 1873), p. 23.
16. Lewis Campbell and Evelyn Abbott, eds. *Benjamin Jowlett, Life and letters* (New York: E. P. Dutton & Co., 1897), I, 285.
17. BM 45787, f. 16.
18. Nightingale, *Suggestions*, II, 155-6.
19. Willard Van Orman Quine, *From a Logical Point of View*, 2nd edn rev. (New York, Hagerstown, San Francisco, London: Harper & Row, Harper Torchbooks, 1961), especially pp. 20-46.
20. BM 45793, ff. 210-11.
21. Nightingale, 'A "Note" ', p. 573.
22. Nightingale, *Suggestions*, II, 182.
23. *Ibid*., p. 114.
24. Cook, *Nightingale*, I, 482.
25. BM 45783, f. 75; Nightingale, *Suggestions*, III, 6.
26. Nightingale, *Suggestions*, III, 55.
27. Florence Nightingale, *Notes on Matters Affecting the Health, Efficiency, and Hospital Administration of the British Army* (London: Harrison & Sons, 1858), pp. 318-19.
28. Woodham-Smith, *Nightingale*, p. 192.
29. Florence Nightingale, 'Life or Death in India'. A Paper read at the meeting of the National Association for the promotion of Social Science (Norwich, 1873), p. 58.
30. Cook, *Nightingale*, II, 27.
31. Nightingale, 'Life or Death', p. 58.
32. BM 45842, f. 59.

CHAPTER 9

1. Nightingale, *Suggestions*, III, 84.
2. *Ibid*., p. 112.
3. BM 45793, f. 210.
4. Cook, *Nightingale*, I, 485.
5. *Ibid*, p. 484.
6. Woodham-Smith, *Nightingale*, p. 81.
7. BM 45844, f. 199.
8. Nightingale, *Suggestions*, I, 49-50.
9. Cook, *Nightingale*, I, 369.

10. BM 45790, f. 313.
11. Jowett—Nightingale Correspondence, I, 48, Bailliol College Library.
12. Margaret Goldsmith, *Florence Nightingale: The Woman and the Legend* (London: Stoughton, 1937), p. 56.
13. BM 45842, f. 90.
14. Nightingale, *Suggestions*, II, 59-65.
15. *Ibid.*, 397—400.
16. Cook, *Nightingale*, II, 306.
17. Nightingale, *Suggestions*, II, 406.
18. *Ibid.*, 231
19. BM 45794, f. 28.
20. BM 45846, ff. 21-4.
21. *Ibid.*, f. 38.
22. Cook, *Nightingale*, I, 306.
23. *Ibid.*, 233.
24. BM 45841, f. 17.
25. BM 45841, f. 73.
26. BM 45844, ff. 6-7.
27. Nightingale, *Suggestions*, I, 51.
28. *Ibid.*, III, 20.
29. BM 45790, f. 218.
30. BM 45847, f. 1.
31. BM 45789, ff. 55-6.
32. BM 45847, ff. 41-87.
33. BM 45844, f. 21.
34. William Hamilton, *The New Essence of Christianity* (New York: Associated Press, 1961), p. 86.
35. Nightingale, *Suggestions*, III, 111.
36. BM 45794, f. 95.
37. BM 45844, f. 215.

CONCLUSION

1. BM 45784, f. 55.
2. Nightingale, 'A "Note"', p. 567.
3. C. Edmund Maurice, *Life*, p. 126.
4. Butler, *Memoir*, p. 290.
5. *Ibid*, p. 12.
6. Jane Addams, *Twenty Years at Hull House with Autobiographical Notes* (New York: The Macmillan Co., 1910), p. 68.
7. Smiles, *Self-Help*, p. 284.
8. Barnett, *Canon Barnett*, I, 229.
9. Butler, *Woman's Work*, p. xiii.

Bibliography

GENERAL WORKS, BIOGRAPHIES, AND ARTICLES

Barnett, Henrietta Rowland. *Canon Barnett, His Life, Work, and Friends*. London: John Murray, 1918.

Bell, E. Moberly. *Josephine Butler: Flame of Fire*. London: Constable & Co., 1962.

——*Octavia Hill: A Biography*. London: Constable & Co., 1942.

Bell, Quentin. *Victorian Artists*. Cambridge, Mass.: Harvard University Press, 1976.

Bishop, William John. *A Bio-bibliography of Florence Nightingale*. Completed by Sue Goldie. London: Dawsons of Pall Mall, for the International Council of Nursing, 1962.

Booth, Charles. *Life and Labour of the People of London*. London and New York: Macmillan & Co. 1892-97 (7 vols).

Booth, William. *In Darkest England and the Way Out*. New York: Funk & Wagnalls, 1890.

Bradley, Ian. *The Call to Seriousness: The Evangelical Impact on the Victorians*. London: Jonathan Cape, 1976.

Branca, Patricia. *Silent Sisterhood: Middle-Class Women in the Victorian Home*. London: Croom Helm, 1975.

Briggs, Asa. *The Making of Modern England 1783-1867: The Age of Improvement*. New York: Harper & Row, Harper Torchbooks, 1965.

Brose, Olive J. *Frederick Denison Maurice: Rebellious Conformist 1805-1872*. Ohio University Press, 1971.

Bunsen, Frances Baroness. *Memoirs of Baron Bunsen*. 2nd edn. London: Longmans, Green & Co., 1869.

Butler, A. S. G. *Portrait of Josephine Butler*. London: Faber & Faber, 1954.

Campbell, Lewis and Abbott, Evelyn (eds). *Benjamin Jowett, Life and Letters*. New York: E. P. Dutton & Co., 1897.

Chadwick, Owen. *An Ecclesiastical History of England* (series) *The Victorian Church*. Part I — New York: Oxford University Press, 1966; Part II — London: Adam & Charles Black, 1970.

Chase, Ellen. *Tenant Friends in Old Deptford*. London: Williams & Norgate, 1929.

Chitty, Susan. *The Beast and the Monk: A Life of Charles Kingsley*. New York: Mason Charter, 1975.

Clive, John. 'More or less Eminent Victorians: Some Trends in Recent Victorian Biography', *Victorian Studies*, 2 (1958)), 5-28.

Cockshut, A. O. J. *Anglican Attitudes: A Study of Victorian Religious Controversies*. London: Collins, 1959.

——*Truth to Life: The Art of Biography in the Nineteenth Century*. New York and London: Harcourt Brace Jovanovich, 1974.

Cook, Sir Edward. *The Life of Florence Nightingale*. 2 vols. London: Macmillan & Co., 1913.

Cope, Zachary. *Florence Nightingale and the Doctors*. London: Museum Press, 1958.

Crow, Duncan. *The Victorian Woman*. London: Allen & Unwin, 1971.

Cruse, Amy. *The Victorians and Their Reading*. Boston: Houghton Mifflin Co., n.d.

Eisley, Loren. *Darwin's Century: Evolution and the Men Who Discovered It*. Garden City, New York: Doubleday & Co., Anchor Books, 1961.

Elliot, Hugh S. R. *The Letters of John Stuart Mill*. London: Longmans, Green & Co., 1910.

Faber, Geoffrey. *Jowett: A Portrait with Background*. Cambridge, Mass.: Harvard University Press, 1958.

Fain, John Tyrce. *Ruskin and the Economists*. Nashville: Vanderbilt University Press, 1956.

Fawcett, Millicent and Turner, E. M. *Josephine Butler: Her Work and Principles and Their Meaning for the Twentieth Century*. London: Association for Moral and Social Hygiene, 1927.

Gauldie, Enid. *Cruel Habitations: A History of Working-Class Housing 1780-1918*. London: George Allen & Unwin, 1974.

Harrison, J. F. C. *The Early Victorians 1832-1851*. New York, Washington: Praeger Publications, 1971.

Hartman, Mary S. *Victorian Murderesses*. New York: Schocken Books, 1977.

——and Banner, Lois, eds. *Clio's Consciousness Raised: Perspectives on the History of Women*. New York: Harper & Row, Harper Colophon Books, 1974.

Heasman, Kathleen. *Evangelicals in Action: An Appraisal of Their Social Work in the Victorian Era*. London: Geoffrey Bles, 1962.

Hill, Caroline Southwood Smith. 'Joan of Arc', *The Nineteenth Century*, 37 (1895), 848-58.

Hill, William Thomson. *Octavia Hill: Pioneer of the National Trust and Housing Reformer*. London: Hutchinson, 1956.

Holland, Henry Scott. *A Bundle of Memories*. London: Wells Gardner, Darton & Co., 1915.

——*Memoir and Letters*. Edited by Stephen Paget. New York: E. P. Dutton & Co., 1921.

Hughes, Thomas. *Tom Brown's School-Days*. London: Macmillan & Co., 1958.

Huxley, Elspeth. *Florence Nightingale*. New York: G. P. Putnam's Sons, 1975.

Jones, Gareth Stedman. *Outcast London: A Study in the Relationship between Classes in Victorian Society*. Oxford: Clarendon Press, 1971.

MacKenzie, Norman and MacKenzie, Jeanne. *The Fabians*. New York: Simon & Schuster, 1977.

Mackerness, E. D. 'Frances Parthenope, Lady Verney', *Journal of Modern History*, 30, 131-6.

Martin, Robert Bernard. *The Dust of Combat*. London: Faber & Faber, 1959.

Maurice, F. D. *The Doctrine of Sacrifice Deduced from the Scriptures*. London: Macmillan & Co., 1893.

——*The Life of Frederick Denison Maurice, Chiefly Told in His Own Letters*. Edited by his son Frederick Maurice. 2 vols. New York: Charles Scribner's Sons, 1884.

——*Theological Essays*. London: James Clarke & Co., 1957.

Mayhew, Henry. *London Labour and the London Poor*. London: Griffin, Bohn, & Co., 1861. Dover Publications, Inc., 1968.

Neale, R. S. 'Class and Class-Consciousness in Early Nineteenth-Century England: Three Classes or Five?' *Victorian Studies*, 12 (1968), 4-32.

Newsome, David. *The Parting of Friends: A Study of the Wilberforces and Henry Manning*. London: John Murray, 1966.

Owen, David. *English Philanthropy, 1660-1960*. Cambridge, Mass.: Harvard University Press, Belknap Press, 1964.

Petrie, Glen. *A Singular Iniquity: The Campaigns of Josephine Butler*. New York: The Viking Press, 1971.

Pickering, George. *Creative Malady: Illness in the Lives and Minds of Charles Darwin, Florence Nightingale*. New York: Oxford University Press, 1974.

Priestley, J. B. *Victoria's Heyday*. New York, Evanston, San Francisco, London: Harper & Row, 1972.

Purcell, Edmund Sheridan. *Life of Cardinal Manning*. London and New York: Macmillan & Co., 1896.

Ruskin, John. *Works*. Edited by E. T. Cook and Alexander Wedderburn. Library edn, 39 vols. London: G. Allen; New York: Longmans, Green & Co., 1903-12.

Simey, M. B. *Charitable Effort in Liverpool in the Nineteenth Century*. Liverpool: Liverpool University Press, 1951.

Smiles, Samuel. *Self-Help*. Boston: Ticknor & Fields, 1861.

Stead, W. T. *Josephine Butler: A Life-Sketch*. London: Morgan & Scott, 1887.

——'Maiden Tribute of Modern Babylon', *Pall Mall Gazette*, 1885.

Taine, H. *Notes on England*. London: Strahan, 1872.

Tarn, John Nelson: *Five Per Cent Philanthropy: An Account of Housing in Urban Areas between 1840 and 1914*. London and New York: Cambridge University Press, 1974.

Tawney, R. H. *Religion and the Rise of Capitalism: A Historical Study*. Holland Memorial Lectures, 1922. New York: Harcourt Brace Jovanovich, Mentor Book, 1937.

Thompson, E. P. *William Morris: Romantic to Revolutionary*. New York: Pantheon Books, 1977.

Vicinus, Martha (ed.) *Suffer and Be Still: Women in the Victorian Age*. Bloomington and London: Indiana University Press, 1973.

——(ed.) *A Widening Sphere: Changing Roles of Victorian Women*. Bloomington: Indiana University Press, 1977.

Vidler, Alex R. *F. D. Maurice and Company: Nineteenth Century Studies*. London: SCM Press, 1966.

——(ed.) *Soundings: Essays Concerning Christian Understanding*. Cambridge: Cambridge University Press, 1962.

Watts, George Frederic. *G. F. Watts: A Nineteenth Century Phenomenon*. Chosen by John Gade. London: The Whitechapel Art Gallery, 1974.

Webb, R. K. *Modern England from the Eighteenth Century to the Present*. London: George Allen & Unwin, 1969.

Webb, Beatrice. *My Apprenticeship*. London: Longmans, Green, 1926.

Webb, Sidney and Webb, Beatrice. *English Poor Law Policy*. London, New York, Bombay, Calcutta: Longmans, Green & Co., 1910.

Weber, Max. *The Protestant Ethic and the Spirit of Capitalism.* Translated by Talcott Parsons. New York: Charles Scribner's Sons. London: George Allen & Unwin, 1950.

Wohl, A. S. 'Octavia Hill and the Homes of the London Poor', *Journal of British Studies* 10 (2), 105-31.

Woodham-Smith, Cecil. *Florence Nightingale 1820-1910.* New York, London, Toronto: McGraw-Hill Book Co., 1951.

——*The Reason Why.* New York: E. P. Dutton & Co. 1960.

Woodroofe, Kathleen. *From Charity to Social Work in England and the United States.* London: Routledge & Kegan Paul. Toronto: University of Toronto Press, 1974.

Young, A. F. and Ashton, E. T. *British Social Work in the Nineteenth Century.* London: Routledge & Kegan Paul, 1956.

Young, G. M. *Victorian England: Portrait of an Age.* London and New York: Oxford University Press, 1937.

WORKS BY JOSEPHINE BUTLER

This listing of printed works does not include the numerous pamphlets and speeches, which can be found in the Fawcett Library of the City of London Polytechnic. A complete listing is given in Glen Petrie, *A Singular Iniquity*.

Woman's Work and Woman's Culture. Introduction. London: Macmillan & Co., 1869.

Memoir of John Grey of Dilston. Revised edition. London: Henry S. King & Co., 1874.

'Catherine Booth', *Contemporary Review*, 13 (January 1870), 639-54.

'The Lovers of the Lost', *Contemporary Review*, 13 (January 1870).

The Constitution Violated. Edinburgh: Edmonston & Douglas, 1871.

The Voice of One Crying in the Wilderness. Paris and Neuchatel: Sandoz, 1875.

The Hour before the Dawn. London: Trubner, 1876.

Catharine of Siena: A Biography. 2nd edn. London: Dyer Brothers, 1879.

'The New Religious Movement in France', *Contemporary Review*, 34 (March 1879), 781-94.

The Life of Jean Frederick Oberlin. London: The Religious Tract Society, 1883.

Rebecca Jarrett. London: Morgan & Scott, 1886.

Our Christianity Tested by the Irish Question. London: Fisher Unwin, 1887.

The Dawn (quarterly). London: Burfoot, 1888—96.

Recollections of George Butler. Bristol: Arrowsmith, 1892.

The Lady of Shunem. London: Horace Marshall, 1894.

Personal Reminiscences of a Great Crusade. London: Horace Marshall, 1896.

Prophets and Prophetesses: Some Thoughts for the Present Time. Newcastle-on-Tyne: Mason, Swan, and Morgan; London: Dyer Brothers, 1898.

The Storm Bell (monthly). London: Burfoot, 1898-1900.

Native Races and the War. London: Gay & Bird, 1900.

In Memoriam Harriet Meuricoffre. London: Horace Marshall, 1901.

Josephine E. Butler: An Autobiographical Memoir. Edited by George W. and Lucy A. Johnson. London: Arrowsmith, 1909.

WORKS BY OCTAVIA HILL

It is fortunate that the letters of Octavia Hill totalling three volumes, two edited by her brother-in-law C. Edmund Maurice and the third by her sister Emily, are in print. The manuscript sources are few. According to C. Moberly Bell, Maurice destroyed the letters in his possession. Bell, while making full use of both collections, quotes from additional letters without revealing their whereabouts. A search for Octavia Hill manuscripts at the British Museum, the Fawcett Society Library, and the National Trust has been almost totally unproductive.

The following list of published materials includes some but not all of the pamphlets. William Thomson Hill's biography contains a more complete listing and in addition includes a useful, annotated bibliography of articles and books on Octavia Hill's work.

Homes of the London Poor. London: Macmillan & Co., 1875.

'A Word on Good Citizenship', *Fortnightly Review*, 26 (September 1876), 321-5.

Our Common Land and Other Short Essays. London, 1877.

The Importance of Aiding the Poor without Almsgiving. Bristol: Social Science Association, 1872.

'Open Spaces', *Sanitary Record* (May 1871).

'The Future of our Commons', *Fortnightly Review* (November 1877).

'Improvements now Practicable (Dwellings)' *The Nineteenth Century* (December 1883).

'Beauty and Poverty', *op. cit.* (December 1889).

'A Few Words to Fresh Workers', *op. cit.* (September 1889).

'More Air for London', *op. cit.* (February 1888).

'Our Dealing with the poor', *op. cit.* (August 1891).

'Trained Workers for the Poor', *op. cit.* (January 1893).

'The Open Spaces of the Future', *op. cit.* (July 1899).

Memorandum on the Report of the Royal Commission on the Poor Laws and Relief of Distress, 1909.

Life of Octavia Hill as Told in Her Letters. Edited by C. Edmund Maurice. London: Macmillan & Co., 1913.

Octavia Hill: Early Ideals. Edited by Emily S. Maurice. London: George Allen & Unwin, 1928.

Extracts from Octavia Hill's Letters to Fellow-Workers, 1864-1911. Compiled by her niece, Elinor Southwood Ouvry. London: The Adelphi Bookshop, 1933.

WORKS BY FLORENCE NIGHTINGALE

See William John Bishop *A Bio-Bibliography of Florence Nightingale* for a complete listing.

Notes on Matters Affecting the Health, Efficiency, and Hospital Administration of the British Army, Founded Chiefly on the Experience of the Late War. Presented by Request to the Secretary of State for War. Privately printed for Miss Nightingale. London: Harrison & Sons, 1858.

Notes on Hospitals. London: John W. Parker & Sons, 1859.

Suggestions for Thought to the Searchers after Truth among the Artizans of England. Privately printed for Miss Nightingale. 3 vols. London: Eyre & Spottiswoode, 1860.

Notes on Nursing: What It is, and What It Is Not. 2nd edn. London: Harrison & Sons, 1860.

Una and the Lion. Cambridge: Riverside Press, 1871.

Life or Death in India. A paper read at the meeting of the National Association for the promotion of Social Science, Norwich, 1873. With an Appendix on Life or Death by Irrigation, 1874.

'A 'Note' of Interrogation', *Fraser's Magazine*, New Series, 7 (May 1873), pp. 567-77.

'A "Sub-Note" of Interrogation; What Will our Religion be in 1999?' *Fraser's Magazine*, New Series, 8 (July 1873), pp. 25-36.

Index

Figures in **bold** type indicate that the subject is treated inclusively.

Index